SUPERDAD

A MEMOIR OF REBELLION, DRUGS AND FATHERHOOD

CHRISTOPHER SHULGAN

KEY PORTER  BOOKS

Names and some identifying characteristics have been changed.

Library and Archives Canada Cataloguing in Publication

Shulgan, Christopher
Superdad : a memoir of rebellion, drugs and fatherhood / Christopher Shulgan.

ISBN 978-1-55470-301-2

1. Shulgan, Christopher. 2. Shulgan, Christopher--Family. 3. Drug addicts–Canada–Biography. 4. Recovering addicts–Canada–Biography. 5. Cocaine abuse–Canada. 6. Fatherhood–Psychological aspects. 7. Masculinity. I. Title.

HV5805.S58A3 2010   362.29'8092   C2010-901805-2

ONTARIO ARTS COUNCIL
CONSEIL DES ARTS DE L'ONTARIO

The author acknowledges the generous support of the Canada Council for the Arts and the Ontario Arts Council.

The publisher gratefully acknowledges the support of the Canada Council for the Arts and the Ontario Arts Council for its publishing program. We acknowledge the support of the Government of Ontario through the Ontario Media Development Corporation's Ontario Book Initiative.

We acknowledge the financial support of the Government of Canada through the Book Publishing Industry Development Program (BPIDP) for our publishing activities.

Key Porter Books Limited
Six Adelaide Street East, Tenth Floor
Toronto, Ontario
Canada M5C 1H6

www.keyporter.com

Text design and electronic formatting: Marijke Friesen

Printed and bound in Canada

10 11 12 13 5 4 3 2 1

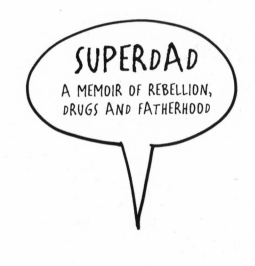

PROLOGUE

Failing your infant son isn't like failing other people. Your wife, your brother or sister, your father or mother—you fail them, they can choose to forgive you. An eighteen-month-old boy doesn't have a choice. He can't forgive his father for failing him because he doesn't know his father is failing him. He doesn't know any other father but his father. He doesn't know he could have it better. He doesn't know how bad he has it. He knows only what he has. Which makes it worse, somehow, doesn't it?

One day early in the spring of 2008, I took my son for a walk. It should have been a wonderful walk. It was the sort of April afternoon where the warmth has an urgency to it. Get outside, the warmth said. Winter's over. We obeyed those whispers. Alongside the corner grocery store my son spotted a forklift, a little propane-fuelled jitney the store owners used to move around their pallets of begonias and impatiens. Some vandal had disembowelled the driver's seat, so that the black plastic was ripped open to expose the springs and the rain-rotted foam. That was where my boy wanted to sit. His clean pants went filthy with all the hydraulic grease and the dust but I let him stay on the seat because he was transported the second his hands closed around the steering wheel. He twisted the circle left and right and stared off into the middle distance and I accompanied him with my best imitation of a diesel engine's accelerating gear shifts, revving out extended *ers* and punctuating those with tire screeches and occasionally dropping my voice to provide some impromptu broadcast analyst narration. "This newcomer, his facility with pallet transportation is remarkable," I said, imagining an Olympian contest for jitney drivers staged amid audience roars. "The crowd is on its feet, they've never seen such evasive road handling, this boy is the champion!"

All this was accompanied with lots of steering wheel spinning and gear shifting and my son was giggling and I was back into the *errrrs* at greater and greater volume and maybe that's why it took me a second to process the clattering behind me. It wasn't until I turned around that I went quiet.

"Er, sorry," I blurted.

I reached out with my hand and stopped the steering wheel's spins.

How long had the grocer been watching us? He was a black-haired, black-mustached Portuguese man. He grinned and his grin was complex. He understood he was interrupting something, the grin suggested, and excuse him for that, but he just had to deposit the ream of flattened cardboard into his recycle bin. Gravity slammed down the bin lid. The grocer wiped his hands on his jeans. He directed a nod toward my son.

"He's a good boy, no?" said the grocer.

"He's a good boy, yeah," I said.

A moment passed. The only sound was my son, behind me, kicking at the jitney gear shift.

"Miguel," the grocer said, extending a hand.

I shook it.

"Chris."

The grocer turned back toward us just before he disappeared through the rear entrance. He nodded his chin toward my boy. "You're a good daddy," he said.

Well, thanks but: how did he know? How did *anyone* know? Everyone always was sending evaluations our way. They were doing it constantly—if they weren't conveying the meaning in so many words, they did it with looks, with simpery smiles and held glances. *Good going*, these looks were saying. *Keep it up.*

Did moms get these sorts of looks? Naw. Not as much—a point Michael Chabon makes in his book of essays, *Manhood for Amateurs*. So long as a dad didn't have his kid muzzled and leashed, pretty much any father–child combination could elicit this sort of look. In Chabon's case, it makes him feel good. He accepts the compliment. It provoked a different reaction in my case, each time it happened. And it happened a lot. Maybe three came my way as we kicked the soccer ball down Dundas Street. My boy was oblivious to the sky, to earth, to automobiles and the existence of gravity, oblivious to everything, that is, but the ball. His eyes were fixed on it. He ran at it. He got up close to it and the damn thing was nearly up to his waist. Using his entire body, his whole *being* for leverage, he pushed forward with his leg and as he pushed forward he let out a grunt and his cheeks got that much more crimson and the ball went rolling away from him and the chase was on once again.

It was a cute scene, sure. Maybe that was enough to earn us the smiles. The smiles, I didn't mind. But then we stopped on the bench before Ella's Uncle, the neighbourhood coffee shop, me with momentary stewardship of the soccer ball, my boy immediately alongside, slurping up some fruit juice under his sun hat to a drum beat created by the impact of his sandalled ankles against the bench wood. Minding his own business he was, and up came one of those electric scooters and before I could cut off her arm or otherwise dissuade her, the driver got a load of me with my boy and she cupped her hand onto his cheek. "So ... *precious*," she said, and the devotion she accorded my boy was like something out of Tolkien, so that even after she split and we were ball-kicking our way toward the park I kept checking behind us, every so often, to ensure this child-obsessed scooter Gollum wasn't following behind.

In the park, so much attention was coming our way we might as well have passed the hat around to pick up some spare change. We might as well have been street performers. And the looks we got that day didn't just come from grocers and scooter Gollums. They came from bikers and joggers and baristas and cabbies. They came from horse cops and garbagemen and store clerks and Mormons. Whoever they were, they saw us and their eyes went down at the edges. Their mouths went horizontal. Their heads angled just off vertical and then this sound escaped them—"Awwww." In the interests of redundancy, sometimes they would even say it, what they were thinking: "*Cute.*"

Or variations. Their looks were *bleeding* isn't-that-nice-ness. Apparently, we were enough to make the hipsters reconsider their tilt against procreation. Apparently, we were the Platonic ideal of Father and Son. Sometimes they just watched. Sometimes they said something to a companion. And sometimes they said something to us:

"You're a lucky boy."

"What a *nice* daddy."

"You're *so* good with him."

Look: fuck off.

Because you're wrong. Every single one of you. You're wrong about me and my child.

And then, for the first time, on this lazy afternoon in April, one of them got it right. It happened while we were still in the park. We had invented a game, my boy and I. It went like this: I kicked the ball and he dribbled it back, pushing with his thighs and his knees on this soccer ball, this monster orb, until he got it to my toes and he turned, ran a few paces and when he had what he thought was enough distance he turned again and waited for me to kick him the ball. And I did.

We did it maybe ten times and his grunting was coming loud enough that I was worrying maybe I should return to Ella's to pick up some more apple juice. Where was the closest drinking fountain? Had the city turned them on yet? Should we just head back home? On like the eleventh time, he was coming my way with the ball when I crouched and leapt toward him. I got a hand behind his head and the other around his hips and pushed him so he was lying on his back. Then I was on top of him and I was rolling and he was on top of me and then again we switched as we tumbled over the grass—"Oh no!" I shouted over his giggles.

He stood on me. On my chest.

He was giggling.

He was my son.

Something behind me attracted his attention. As I twisted out from under him I saw a young woman and a big purse just a few paces away. She was dressed in that way that involves enormous sunglasses and severely tapered jeans. And she was smiling. Well, she was at first. But then her gaze went from my boy to me. And there was a moment.... She did something, her chin shrank backward. Her gaze shifted. Her mouth opened. Closed. And she was gone.

That was it.

That was more like it.

Contempt.

That's what I deserved.

THIS BE THE VERSE

This is a coming-of-age story that involves a baby, a father, and crack cocaine. Basically those are the three main characters. Putting it that way makes it look like I'm mining the experience for the shock value. It's just plain nasty to juxtapose "baby" and "crack." I know that better than anyone—I lived that juxtaposition. But I've been struggling with how to begin this weird tale of drugs and fatherhood. I've written and rewritten this story's first paragraph so many times without feeling that I ever got it right. So one night right before the drop-dead date for any more changes, I spent the whole of an evening staring at my computer screen and trying to figure out what the first sentence should say. I decided it should say what the whole story was, in one sentence. And as weird as it is, that's the sentence I came up with. The one that fits. This is a memoir about two years in my life when I had a long-overdue coming of age. One that involved a baby (mine), a father (me), and my problems with crack cocaine (fuck).

Looking back on our pre-child era I guess we made the decision to have children fairly cavalierly. The *we* being me and my wife, Natalie. I had the idea that I wanted to have kids *one* day. I wanted to wrestle with them the way my wonderful father wrestled with wonderful me. I wanted a two-year-old who spent Sunday mornings in bed alongside me, behind a spread newspaper's weekend edition. Who tagged along with me to bin-lined aisles of hardware stores as I had once tagged along with my dad. Camping and cavorting and comparing and conversing. I wanted to teach my progeny of the brilliance of Bruce Springsteen's *Nebraska*. To model each individual motion in the footwork a football lineman executed in the seconds after the snap. To teach him the semaphore-like arm motions required to turn a strip of sewn silk into the necktie's Windsor knot.

But I wanted all this the way one wants a Lamborghini, or a cottage on a lake: as something one gets at some distant point in the future. Then one day Natalie told me she had stopped taking her birth control pills. Actually, she didn't even tell me. She was talking to her sister on the phone and I overheard.

"Wait, what?" I said. "When were you going to tell me?"

"Tell you what?"

"That we're stopping using birth control."

"I did. And *we're* not stopping birth control. *I* am. Do you realize I've been taking the pill for thirteen years?"

And at this point I was thirty-one and Natalie was twenty-seven and we had some friends who had started popping out the little critters and we figured maybe we'd let biology take its course. And then it didn't. As the pill's estrogen dose faded Natalie stopped menstruating. Which was a bit weird. Then the really weird thing was that she was lactating, which is to say, her breasts were producing milk. We appreciated the fact they were so eager, but we hadn't had a kid yet, so actually that was a bit worrying, and then once Natalie saw a doctor about it, holy crap, it turned out that it was a lot worrying, this premature lactation could be caused by all these terrible things and in fact, it *was* caused by a terrible thing. Maybe a year after we began these MRI scans and specialist appointments and late-night Google research of terms like "craniopharyngioma," the various MDS decided the cause was a cyst in Natalie's pituitary gland. The cyst increased Natalie's production of a hormone called prolactin, which in turn inhibited her production of estrogen. There was some scary discussion of surgery that would have involved, oh Christ this is terrible to think about, but it would have involved getting to the pituitary gland from deep inside Natalie's nostrils. They wanted to insert the scalpels and shunt and the rest of the instruments up through Natalie's nose. Equipped with such visuals the two of us spent quite a few evenings holding each other on our bed with the lights off. And then it turned out the cyst was responding to the drugs Natalie was taking. Her cycle returned. The milk dried up. Shortly after, the doctor said, it was safe to start trying for the goal that had started this whole mess. We started trying for a baby.

Maybe it was the fact that we'd been forced to wait a while—by this time it was early summer, 2005. Or maybe we just overdid it. Both of us are fairly focused individuals. Pretty soon I discovered getting-pregnant sex isn't the worst kind of sex. I don't think. Surely there are worse kinds. Sex with animals, for example. Sex with enormously fat people. But so far as sex involving one person who really does manage to be just generally astonishingly attractive (to clarify: Natalie), and then any other person who isn't an animal or enormously fat (me), getting-pregnant sex is pretty bad. It's the notion of the goal that mucks things up, I think. Sex in my experience never has an ulterior motive. Sex is the point. *Sex* is the motive. Except when it comes to getting-pregnant sex. Then there's an ulterior motive. The end justifies the means, here, but the end also somehow sullies the means. For example, one time I found myself apologizing to Natalie for taking so long. And I thought: we've made this thing so odious I was apologizing for prolonging it. And still nothing took. This getting-pregnant thing was taking so long that Natalie decided I should go and get checked out.

"Wait, what?" I said. "Don't I get a say in this?"

"Yeah," Natalie said. "You can say yes."

I don't really have anything to say about it. I'd actually prefer not to talk about it. Did I check out okay? Yes, you inquisitive jerk. Thanks for asking. We went back to trying. At this point Natalie was using so many pregnancy tests she was buying them in bulk from the dollar store. (Seriously. You can do that.) It was December 27, 2005, when her urine passed the test. We were just home from Christmas holidays. She yelped out, "Chris!" and I raced up the stairs. She showed me the stick.

I said, "Is that good?"

"I'm not sure," she said. "It means I'm pregnant."

"Well that's good, isn't it?"

"I'm not sure," she said. "There was that wine on Christmas."

"That doesn't count, I don't think."

"Because it was Christmas?"

"No, because it's too early in the pregnancy."

"Oh you don't know what you're talking about."

"Of course I don't."

"But probably you're right. Okay then it's good."

"It is good," I said. I hugged her. "Baby, it *is* good. It's *great*."

I should have been happy. No wait—I *was* happy. There was a cupboard in my soul where all the decent parts of me lived, and this cupboard featured birdsong and fluffy kittens cavorting over the prospect of a little creature's kisses and hugs. There *was* happiness. And on top of that was relief. It was like, whew, my work here is done. It was astonishing. For the first time ever, I was relieved to be heading into a period that, compared to the one I'd just left, would feature comparatively fewer incidents of sexual intercourse.

A FEW MORE WORDS to be filed under, *Wife's Pregnancy, Shulgan's reaction to.* What's interesting about this period is that I spent comparatively little time thinking about the problem that would fuck me up later. Probably it's relevant to say that until that year, no one else among my close friends had ever had a kid. I was a magazine journalist about to mark my tenth year since graduating from university, my friends were other writers or editors, some photographers, some musicians or film types, a few bankers, a lawyer or two. During the previous decade we'd thought about kids not at all. And you know what? For the most part? Our lives were pretty great. We'd graduated just as grunge gave way to the computer-generated drum blasts of DJ culture. There were weekend-long music festivals where our strung-out selves caught just a few horizontal hours. Even during the last few years, as the culture swung back from DJs toward guitars, the all-night ethic persisted among our set. Once the bands stopped around last call the game became finding the blind pig, the cold tea, the password at the unmarked door where entrance was almost victory enough to fuel you to 5 a.m. and Friday's debauch gave way to Saturday's sleep and Sunday with the *Times*, and recovery. Back then, five movies a weekend was a not uncommon event.

And then came pregnancy. Anxiety? Sure, I had some. My biggest problem in the first few days after I found out involved a bit of angst about autonomy and inhibited freedom. My fourth decade of life on this planet was well underway and impulse gratification had become my dominant mode. Living for myself was going quite well for me, thanks. How would I fare once I switched things over toward living for other people, to wit, tiny babies? I had to get serious. Was I ready to get serious? I wondered: was I *ready* to reproduce? Well, wait. I guess I *had* reproduced. *My* work was done. But was I ready for what came *after*? At that point, that was the extent of it, my own quiet soundtrack of angst.

WHAT ABOUT YOUR DRUG PROBLEM, SHULGAN?

Oh yeah, right. That. Would you believe me if I told you that I didn't really consider it? At that point I considered my drug problem licked. It didn't really occur to me. For the most part I considered myself to be on the straight and narrow, and I figured having a kid would even out the kinks, so after the birth I'd be even straighter and narrower. That was my thinking. And then I had my first hint that perhaps things wouldn't be quite so simple. Right around this period our friends, er, Billy and Saleem, say, had a baby. Several weeks after the kid arrived they had us over for dinner. The idea was a low-key affair. Spend some time with the baby, spend some time with the couple, get out of there. Even before kids, Billy and Saleem were tilted more toward the crunchy, progressive side than Natalie and I. Billy was so progressive he never referred to Saleem as his "wife"—he referred to her as his "partner." (That threw me for a loop, the first time it happened. I was like—dude, weren't you the guy in university who went around referring to prospective girlfriends as *bitches*?) Billy was never the sort of guy to do things halfway. It was all in, or nothing. Saleem was the same. They were a good couple that way. Point is, I had some indication their baby would grow up in an all-organic cocoon. I just didn't realize how all-organic a cocoon it would turn out to be. "It's jute," Saleem said when the four of us gathered in the doorway of the new nursery, explaining the beneficial properties of the natural-fibre floor covering, primary among them being jute's inert nature—the stuff didn't "offgas." At that point I'd never heard of "offgassing." It sounded kind of nasty and I wanted to ask about it except Saleem was onto her breastfeeding pillow's raw cotton cover and then it was something about cloth diapers and the Burt's Bees soap-slash-shampoo. We saw the video-enabled infant-monitoring system, the hand-woven sleepers and the sustainably harvested basswood toys. Oh, and at some point amid all that, Billy and Saleem remembered to show us the baby. Who actually turned out to be really cool. If I had to rank the new acquisitions Billy had revealed to me over the years, I would say I was as impressed by his new daughter, if not more impressed, as I was by such earlier, purchased possessions as his Wii Fit or his high-definition projection television, which beamed football on the wall in glorious, vibrant 1080p.

This was the first time in years I'd been so close to a baby. I couldn't get over how much like a person she was—only smaller. It was neat to take bits of her face and place them on her parents to see what matched and what didn't. It was neat to hold an entire human being contained in a seven-pound sack of skin. Endless repetitive statements marvelled about the difference in scale: her fingers were so *little*. Her toes, so *tiny*. And her lips were like miniature wine-gum worms. Which I quelled the impulse to chew.

Eventually the baby talk grew stale. I dealt with the first hour; even the second was okay. But eventually the same punchline wore thin. Restated over and over, in slightly different words and phrases, that punchline was, isn't she cute. Plus, something rankled about the tone of this discourse. Lots of comments went straight from Billy to Saleem, or Saleem to Billy. This conversation amounted to our old friends giving us a slide show of a recent trip they'd made, to the new land of parenthood. They were telling us about a destination we hadn't yet explored, which was fine, except lots of their comments were things like, "We can't even begin to describe it." Or: "You'll find out." The implication being, we couldn't understand, we *wouldn't* understand, until we'd been to the land ourselves. (And bear in mind, they didn't then know Natalie was pregnant.) This started to feel a bit forced—as though Billy and Saleem were faking how much better their new status as father and mother was compared to their old status as only husband and wife. I was about to make some stupid comment intended to puncture the pretension—I had something cooking that linked the smell of the cloth diapers to "offgassing." Then there was a moment—I can't remember exactly what happened. A spilled wine glass? I looked at Saleem and I saw

the dark circles, the brittle quality to her laughter. Suddenly I
recognized her vibe. How exhausted she was, the fragile way
she carried herself—it reminded me of the way she was around
5 or 6 a.m., on those mornings I'd seen her coming down
from ecstasy.

They so badly wanted to show us how special parenthood
was. Parenthood's supposed specialness was helping them get
through this tough period. And if they needed to lord over us
their new status, if that helped them get through it, then I was
willing to let them do it, if only for the fact that tomorrow, I
could sleep in until whenever I wanted, and they could not.

My first indication I was headed for trouble happened
shortly after we'd cleared dessert. I triggered an excuse. Bad
luck, I said, but I had to split—an editor friend of mine was
having a party. I should go. Strictly for networking purposes.

"Networking," Natalie said, rolling her eyes; she'd stay to
talk more with Saleem. As I headed toward the scrabble of
shoes by the door, Billy came up behind me. "Do you mind if I
come?" he said. And something about the way he said it . . .
There was a note there. He almost ended his question with a
please. A short time later Billy and I were walking toward the
party when he suggested we stop in at the bar we were passing.
"How is it?" I asked, meaning parenthood, and this new father
regarded me for a beat too long before he said one word:
"Great." And switched the conversation back to me.

How drunk he was didn't become apparent until after we
were at the party, when I saw him sitting next to the attractive
wife of my editor-in-chief. "I was just explaining why I couldn't
sit on Billy's lap," she said as I joined them.

Billy shrugged. "The offer stands," he said, and lurched off
toward the drinks. The wife watched him go. "At first I thought

he was—what's the word?" she said. "Challenged? I thought, how nice of Shulgan, to take his friend for a night out. Then he grabbed my ass, and it became less amusing."

She shrugged off my apologies. "Don't worry about it," she said. "I get it. He's an alcoholic."

"Oh, he's not an alcoholic," I said. "He's just. . . ." Huh—what *was* his excuse? "He just had a baby," I said.

Funny—at the time, the excuse sounded lame. At the time I was too ignorant about parenting to realize the legitimacy of the excuse I'd offered. How ignorant I was, then. Kids? I didn't think of them! I hadn't thought of them! Not since—shit. When *did* I think of them?

THAT'S WHERE LIE the first origins of this mess, I think, in a rural village in the early years of the '80s, when the horrors of teen pregnancy were sprayed over the seventh and eighth graders like fake blood at a Gwar concert. Here was Belle River Public School, a brick building set amid cornfields on the southeast edge of a farming community where the typical commute was a half-hour ride in a yellow school bus. I took bus #36 mornings and nights from my lakeside village of approximately 500, called Puce, which we thought was hilarious because in French, the word meant "flea." It *was* insect-like in size, then, although today subdivisions and sprawl have turned my old village into a town. Whatever. My previous schooling had happened in the four-classroom building of Puce Public School and it's important to what comes later that my grade-seven self considered the move to Belle River to be progression. If not exactly school in the big city—Belle River's boundary marker advertised something like 9,000 in those days—then it certainly seemed like a step up. *This* public school had maybe a dozen classrooms. Another indication my pre-adolescent self now played on a bigger stage happened during a class taught once a week by the vice-principal, a stern-but-just type I'll call Mr. Villaire. In my mind he existed in opposition to the school bully, Randy something, who had a thing for trapping younger kids in the school's exit airlock then smashing them into the walls with suplexes and piledrivers and whatever other punitive wrestling holds were at that moment favoured by such WWF hotshots as the Iron Sheik and Randy Savage. As bullies go, Randy had a high standard to match, since previous tough-guy alums at the school included Tie Domi, who once convinced my kindergartener brother to part with my deluxe Swiss Army knife for a buck. Mark presented me the money as though he'd done a great thing and was crushed to see how disappointed I was. What could I do? Domi was the toughest kid in school, who, legend had it, had smashed his front teeth out on the stem of his bike handlebars, *intentionally*, so as to look more like Bobby Orr (and, as any Canadian knows, would grow up to become an enforcer for the Toronto Maple Leafs). And then there was me—set apart already because my parents were middle class in a town where middle class was the upper class, who left school once a week to attend the gifted program at another county building, who wore glasses with thick lenses that darkened in sunlight and never quite lost their tint, whose part-time job was shelving returns at the Emeryville Public Library.

In Mr. Villaire's class, I can recall being aware of the precise location of Amber and Leslie, of Fiona and Cyndy, of Zoe and Heather and Lynda. I can recall an awareness of the limited list of permissible focal points: Mr. Villaire's face, the chalkboard, the clock with its sweeping second hand. And what it was not permissible to look at: any of the girls. Any of the posters. I can recall willing myself not to blush, or, really, hold any expression at all. Because Mr. Villaire's class was what we called "Sexuality."

Most of what Mr. Villaire taught I already knew. My mother, like many other attentive, progressive parents, had read my brother and I bedtime stories that started in the seminal vesicle and ended in the birth of a tiny human creature. Our bookshelves were weighed down by the *What's Happening to My Body? Book for Boys* as well as many other volumes, many other volumes because my mother was a public health nurse whose job was to tour around showing youngsters how to roll condoms onto bananas. Which, still, I'm like, geez, what a cool job that must have been, Mom. The point: We knew our stuff.

But where my mom taught the mechanics, Mr. Villaire specialized in the mechanics' *implications*. Sex, Mr. Villaire taught, was dangerous. We saw slides of a grossness I've never seen surpassed. We learned about syphilis and chlamydia, and somehow all that Latin and Greek underlined just how truly awful were those sexually transmitted diseases. So we shouldn't have sex. Ever. But if we *were* going to have sex. If it couldn't be avoided. If such circumstances as firearms and perhaps the law removed any other option then FOR GOD'S SAKE, Mr. Villaire suggested, then FOR THE SAKE OF THE GOOD LORD ALMIGHTY, we were to use *protection*. Because if there was anything worse than a sexually transmitted disease, it was pregnancy. You get a girl pregnant? YOUR LIFE IS OVER.

That's what I learned in Mr. Villaire's class. Did he say *teen* pregnancy? I don't recall that he did. It doesn't matter. What stuck was the equation: Pregnancy. Equals. Death. What I took from those interminable agonizing hours among the penis posters and vaginal cross-sections was the moral: that getting a girl pregnant equalled not the natural conclusion of a phase of life, but the irrevocable end of life itself.

THESE CLASSES DIDN'T really occur to me much in the weeks after Natalie peed positive. But the after-effects lingered. The attitudes persisted. Their components set the stage for this mess. We passed the point where it became permissible to tell people the news, and there was something in the way they reacted that troubled me. "Congratulations," they said, and then there was an assessment similar to a first impression. *Not* a first impression, of course. The people I was telling were people I knew. They were assessing me not as a human being, now, but as a human type: a parent. In their heads they were auditioning me for parenthood. I've done this for other people. I know it happens. You look at the guy and you imagine how he'll perform with a baby in his arms and after that it's like he's become more fatherlike, more paternal, simply *because* you've performed this thought exercise. Zap—POW. He's going to be a father! And as a going-to-be-a-father I'm not sure I was very good.

During those early months of Natalie's pregnancy, before she'd even started showing, I walked around with a feeling similar to what I felt in the moments after I'd swallowed some acid. Or an ecstasy pill. Or a mouthful of mushrooms. Before the drugs took effect. Things were going to change. I could feel it. How, what, where, why—these and other details weren't clear yet. I didn't know where I was headed. And that fact freaked me out.

Some people reacted to the news of an impending baby with excitement and resolution. The news fills some deep-seated chasm in the soul and future mom and dad are able now to progress through life in a perpetual state of tranquility. Well, good for them. In my case, the opposite happened. I felt like a traitor, and every so often I had a bad case of traitor's remorse. Obsessing me was this short story I'd read years before, the title of which I couldn't remember, involving the stalking of a family man by a former best friend. The family man has the usual accoutrements, the wife, the kids, the house, the lawn. And the best friend is stalking him because years before, perhaps over a camp fire, certainly under the influence of drugs and drink, the friends had made a promise to one another: Please, if I ever become one of *them: Kill me.* And the best friend is about to take the family man at his word.

That spring, as I walked around the city, I half expected some childless old friend to pop up from behind a nearby shrub, or a streetcar shelter, rifle butt cocked to shoulder, single eye peering through a long-distance scope that placed a red dot on my chest, just left of centre. I'd had conversations like the one recounted in the short story. What culturally informed, trend-literate geek hadn't? As an intern at the daily newspaper where I'd landed as a features reporter shortly after grad school, I can remember proclaiming to one of the investigative reporters, amid a conversation about the limited lifespan of cultural literacy, how I'd *always* be cool. (Hey, it makes me cringe, too.) Late-night conversations with gay friends grew intense, back then, on the topic of parenthood. My friend James and I denigrated what we perceived as the bovine timidity and crawl toward irrelevance of a mutual friend who'd had kids early. "We've lost him," we decided. And: "We'll never become like that." How banal, a life where one traded music, movies, and books for diapers, buggies, and creativity-encouraging playthings. How dull, we sneered. How cliché. And the suburbs? Might as well have been one of Dante's circles.

A while back, an Internet video made the rounds. The video shows footage from a ceiling-mounted security cam, and it depicts a series of office cubicles, unremarkable but for the dog lounging in the midst of the frame. Seconds into the video the canine jumps up and runs about the office, all barks and bared teeth. You wonder: What the hell is making this dog freak out? And then the frame shakes, the foamboard partitions tip and then fall, a light shatters, and things go dark. The cause is an earthquake, the occurrence of which explains the dog's behaviour: The pooch predicted it. The pooch went crazy because it knew how crazy things were going to get. And that spring, a part of me was acting a whole lot like that dog.

Basically, every time I thought about my impending fatherhood, I wanted to go out and get *wasted*. To drink my face off, and gobble drugs by the pound. At the time, little recognition existed of the danger this situation represented. Recall that drug problem I mentioned? Recall I thought it solved? Well, I considered it *so* solved that having a few beers was fine. Also fine was having a lot of beers. My drug problem was so long in the past that on the fourth night after I learned we were going to have a baby, on an evening out that fell on New Year's Eve, at a party where the stuff was around, I thought it was okay for cocaine to get me to 6 a.m. on that holiday of fresh beginnings and renewal, New Year's Day. Well, cocaine was supposed to be off limits. That was the deal. That was the agreement between Natalie and me. But I chalked up that New Year's as a one-time thing. Yeah, I wasn't too worried about it. It was a slip-up, no big deal, the last three years had been mostly drug-free but for the odd accident and this time was no different. Right? I told myself the same thing after another slip-up happened. Although even to me that one sounded hollow. Even I recognized trouble in the aftermath of wasted me going out to the old stomping grounds and finding the one poison I couldn't control.

YOU KNOW THOSE LITTLE vials of ginseng they sell all over the place? They're usually up by the cash register, alongside the lottery tickets and maybe a display or two for wine gums or gummi bears. I'm not talking about the ginseng vials with the green labels—the glass they're made of is too thin, and their tops are a little too wide. You want the ones with the orange labels, with the Mandarin characters inscribed on them. You can find them at corner stores in any economically depressed area. For example, in Toronto, you can find them in the corner store next to the halal stand in the little retail complex at Dundas and Sherbourne. Or the grocery on the north side of Queen, just west of Bathurst, across from the Pizza Pizza. The vials are like 99 cents, about.

The first thing you do is pick up one of those. Actually, buy two or three. And buy a lighter while you're at it. Spend some money on the lighter. Make sure it can give you a long, sustained flame. Once you're out of the store, get one of the vials and tear off the little foil cap and pull out the plastic stopper and get rid of the ginseng syrup inside. Just pour it out. I've never actually drunk one, myself, but go ahead if you want to. Although it doesn't really have any purpose. It's not like you're going to need anything to pep you up. Not anytime soon, anyway.

Now go outside and find a clear bit of pavement. Scrape the bottom of the vial against the cement. Keep at it. Little circles work best. Watch that you're not holding the vial too tight—the glass is pretty fragile. The thing could break in your fingers. At the same time, try to press hard against the pavement, and keep at it—do like twenty little circles. Now that you've scored the vial's bottom, find any sturdy object with a pointed end. A key works pretty well but the best thing to use is some sort of ballpoint pen. Bear in mind this is the tricky part. This is why you bought several of these vials, so if you break the first one you can try again. What you do is, jam the ballpoint through the bottom of the vial. If you've scored the bottom properly you should have a neat empty circle where the glass bottom used to be. Good job. You're halfway there.

Next is the screening. Some people are partial to scouring pads. And those'll do in a pinch, but those fuckers are remarkably strong. It's tough to pinch off the right amount. If you don't have scissors—and who just carries scissors around?— then the wirey steel can really tear up your fingers when you try to separate one clump from the main bunch. Naw, the best thing to use for the screening is the woven metal wire jacket that surrounds television cable cord. You bite open the black plastic protective layer of the cable and there it is, a woven sleeve of interlocking wire thread that you can use your teeth to bite through if you don't have a sharp edge to cut it with. Get enough of it that you can roll up the woven stuff into a loose mass the approximate width and shape of a new pencil eraser. Separate a single wire thread from the main bunch and use that to hold the wire bunch in the air. With your other hand flick on the lighter and use it to burn off the screening's chrome surface; word is, that shit can really mess up your lungs.

Once all the shiny stuff's burnt off, stuff the wire bundle into the narrow opening at the top of the vial. Do it so that there's extra material on both ends of the opening. Then use the back end of the ballpoint pen to get inside the vial and smush the screening up against the vial's interior top. Do the same thing with your thumb at the top end. Maybe take a minute to admire your handiwork. You've just made a crack pipe.

IT WAS LIKE, fuck. Yeah, officially I'd been off the stuff for three years. And I was still off the stuff. I was. Nothing had changed! Did it even count? Did it count if it happened when you were drunk? Did it count if it happened on the evening of April 1—April Fool's Day? Did it count if you felt pretty much the same the next morning? If the only evidence that existed was your memory—and even that was a bit hazy? These sorts of questions still percolated through me the following Tuesday as Natalie and I showered and dressed before the appointment for our eighteen-week ultrasound.

Residual guilt aside, I was looking forward to the appointment. What would the baby look like? How would his heartbeat sound? As a labour-and-delivery nurse Natalie had lots of experience with ultrasounds, and she spoke of the procedures as though they were a kind of secular communion; contact with an alternate version of oneself. Then there was the possibility about discovering the—well, gender. Er, the sex. Which sounds weird, doesn't it, when applied to a baby. Some people opted to put off learning the sex until the birth. Not me. I craved that information, which Natalie pointed out may not come today; the ultrasound tech might not be able to see those bits. I craved that information even though it meant relatively little. Would this creature like sports or dolls, prefer blue to pink, wear black skates or white? Really, the presence or absence of a penis had little bearing on such dichotomies. I knew all this. And yet I craved the knowledge anyway. If it only meant the precise method of urine dispersal, whether it would be possible to teach the child how to write one's name in the snow— amid all my questions and anxieties, amid the cloud of unease I had not yet acknowledged existed—at least this represented one question answered.

And then, as we walked toward the stop for the streetcar that would take us to the ultrasound appointment, it occurred me to ask, "So where is this happening, anyway?"

"Down around Queen and Church. You know, that medical building? Across from the hospital?"

"The hospital" being St. Mike's, where Natalie worked. St. Mike's also happened to market itself as "Toronto's urban angel" because it was in a pretty rough area. Worry gave my digestive tract a good squeeze. I didn't say much—maybe I affected a tone of faux joviality, maybe I said something like, back to the old neighbourhood, eh? Because it was—before we moved to the new place, we'd passed five years living around the hospital where Natalie worked.

And then I went silent. We sat in the streetcar's rear, me on the aisle, just another professional couple on their way to any old appointment. Without discussing it, both of us had dressed up for the event. Natalie wore a brown shirt-dress she'd ironed before the appointment. She'd *ironed*. In our house, the iron and its rickety partner, the ironing board, lived deep in the fearsome cavern of the junk closet under the main-floor stairs. The iron was in there deeper than the vacuum, deeper than the cleaning supplies and the gift-wrapping stuff. Retrieving the iron required a flashlight, as well as dexterity and patience. If Natalie had ironed, then this was an occasion. And me, I wore a dress shirt and jeans, my usual uniform, complemented by the blazer I wore only for business meetings, and lace-up Cole Haan shoes I reserved for the same purpose. Who were we trying to impress? The ultrasound techs? Naw. Of course it was the baby. As though the same ultrasound frequencies that showed us our hazy portrait also returned an image in the other direction. We wanted to reassure our creature: Hey, baby, we're okay. I did not, however, feel okay. Oblivious to my state, Natalie was turning to me every five seconds or so and presenting me with all sorts of hypothetical dilemmas. What if it was a boy? How would I feel if it was a boy?

"Happy, I'd feel happy."

And if it was a girl?

"Happy. I'd feel the same."

Natalie was a font of potential names. She spouted plans and paint colours. And meanwhile I was there, next to her, physically, sure, physically I was definitely there.

And here was the extent of the conversation I could manage:

"Why'd we have to get it done in this sketchy neighbourhood?" I asked. "Wasn't there one around the house?"

Natalie stopped her monologue of *what if's* and *if only's*. "Maybe," she said. "I didn't think of that. It's just, this is the one on the ultrasound requisition."

Fine. Great.

We stepped off the streetcar about a block before the clinic's office building. As soon as we were on the pavement I was scanning the sidewalk, the street, the opposite side of the road, where the hospital was. Considering the occasion, I should have been noticing sunlight glinting through young leaves or hailing the return of migratory waterfowl. Or some such cheerful things. I mean, this *was* the week of spring's arrival. The air had that scent of wet fertility. It was the week when women first started going outside with bare legs. Maybe I could have been observing how appropriate it was for us to be heading to the ultrasound appointment at this particular point in time. Maybe I should have been sprinkling my conversation with terms like the rites of spring. But I wasn't talking. Instead I was looking all over the place. Across the street was the hospital, and next to that was a big church: Metropolitan United. The church yard featured a cluster of trees, and under those, some stone chess tables that were always surrounded by various disreputable-looking characters. That's what was drawing my attention: The two dozen loiterers doing their thing in the church yard. Some were on bikes. Some were sleeping on the grass around the tables. And, I was relieved to discover, none of them took any notice of me.

Good. Natalie and I crossed with a traffic light to the block where the clinic was. And then we approached what was, at this time of day, probably the most dangerous spot, as far as I was concerned. It was at the corner of the clinic's office building. It was a spot where a set of metal bars separated a ventilation grate from the street. For whatever reason, the railings usually supported a couple of people similar to the churchyard set. They stood at the railing, leaning and watching and just generally looking shifty and furtive. But I was lucky. Only one was there as we passed. He wore a greasy trench coat despite the temperature. He wasn't one of the ones I knew.

Again, good. I stepped ahead of Natalie to help with the door and stopped short when the door slid open, smoothly, automatically. Once we were past that threshold I stopped scanning the faces of the people around me. The elevator was crowded. The waiting room had the usual dead magazines and uncomfortable chairs, plus an old TV showing the local all-news channel.

"Could you sit down?" Natalie said. "You're making me nervous."

What a lot of shapes and sizes pregnant couples could come in. Two others waited with us, plus a solo woman and her child. The other couples' presence made me feel like a cliché: One more couple hoping to get a glimpse of their baby. I tried and failed to read a doctor's magazine. I monitored the others for signs of how they were feeling. I saw a lot of physical contact. Some handholding. Some thigh pats. Every so often one of them would look at their counterpart and smile.

The attendant called Natalie's name. I stood up to go with her until the attendant held up a hand—I was to stay in the waiting room for the first part, apparently. Thumb-twiddling and other time-passing methods ensued. Remember that solo woman I mentioned? She was Muslim, I think. At least, she wore a hijab-style of dress. Her child was a dark-haired boy around two or three, who stood a couple inches from the waiting room's television, randomly pressing buttons on the console. His mother asked him to quit it with the button-pushing. She asked him again. After maybe the fifth request she heaved herself up to a standing position, went over to him and yanked the squirming kid away from the TV, back to the seat, where she set him on the little bit of her lap that her pregnant belly didn't already take up. The kid wailed. She *had* really yanked him. I snuck a look around. No one else seemed bothered. I think they were trying to ignore it. The only guy who seemed to have noticed anything had traded his fixed smile for a fixed frown. It looked like he was thinking the same thing I was: this is what we're in for.

THIS BIG BLONDE woman came into the waiting room and said, "Chris?" I stood up. She led me down a hallway past a lot of curtained enclosures. Toward the end of the hallway she held open one of the curtains. I went in to see Natalie reclined on something halfway between an operating table and a La-Z-Boy. I went to sit in the chair next to her.

The ultrasound tech made this sound, like "Tsk." In Russian-accented English she told me the chair I was in was *her* chair, and please would I sit on *this*, this being a wheeled stool that almost skittered out from under me as I lowered myself onto it. With the flourish of a show-off bartender the tech produced a squeeze bottle of lubricant and aimed a blue-tinged jet of translucent goop at the approximate position of Natalie's navel. Soon we heard a hushed drum beat.

"That's the heart," Natalie said in a hushed voice.

I tried to think what to do.

My eyebrows went up.

"Wow," I said.

But Natalie's attention was still on the screen, this monochrome monitor where ghostly squiggles appeared and faded with remarkable rapidity.

"There's the arm," the tech said.

"Awwww," Natalie said.

She looked at me.

"Awwww," I said.

The tech did something with her keyboard and mouse and suddenly a line was on the screen, next to the arm. Muttering to herself, the tech keyed in a number—a measurement? Then it was on to the next anatomical feature. We went through this routine several times. And then:

"That's the head," the tech said.

"Awww," Natalie said. Then she looked at me.

"Ooooh," I said.

Silence in the room. Wait a second. It *did* look like a head. And there in profile were the lips, and the nose. I tried to see myself in the profile. I tried to see anybody in the profile. But that profile didn't look human. With its oversized cranium, the baby looked like one of those futuristic, super-intelligent extra-terrestrials from '60s science-fiction TV shows, the ones always coming back to the present to warn mankind to cease its profligate ways.

The tech said a number and keyed it into the computer program. "Perfect," she said. "He's all perfect."

Natalie squeezed my hand. "That's our baby," she said. Her voice was soft. Her eyes were moist. I returned her hand-squeeze and tried to look affected.

"He?" I asked. Had I missed something? I cleared my throat. "He's a boy?"

I seemed to have asked whether the sky was blue.

"You didn't see the penis?" the tech asked. She fiddled with the monitor and replaced my baby's head with one of the more galactic-looking images. Her mouse cursor hovered around something like the Horsehead Nebula. "There," she said. "That's the penis. It's a good size." She looked at Natalie and smiled. "The girls will like him."

Three minutes later we were alone in a descending elevator. Natalie clutched a sheaf of Polaroid-sized black-and-white printouts; ultrasound images. "I think he looks like me," she said, then angled it my way.

I tried to look appraising.

"Like you?" I said. "He doesn't even look *human*."

Her mouth twisted. "What's your *problem*?"

I should have been excited. But my mind was on other things. Namely: Vince. My mind was on Vince, who I spotted immediately as we stepped out onto the sidewalk. He was on our side of the street. Shambling toward us. My intestines, my bowels, my entire abdomen reacted: everything shrank.

Vince was maybe fifty years old but he looked older. Terrible posture hunched his five foot eight down to five foot five or so. He looked like he hadn't changed his clothing in two weeks. His T-shirt stretched across a belly that bore some resemblance to Natalie's growing orb. And above all this, a loose mass of black and white hair—wild curls on top, bristles obscuring his cheeks. Filthy, he was. He *surpassed* filthy. Drips of food grease, stale sauce and skin oil, grass stains and old blood, the grime spread from a stain to a blotch to a coating that sat on the fibres of his clothing the way Teflon protected my own Brooks Brothers non-iron dress shirts. Somehow, Vince managed a louche air. There were people who spent hundreds of dollars to pull off what Vince managed with obliviousness and apathy.

It was getting toward five o'clock. Most of the commuters walked toward the subway, which meant walking west, toward Yonge Street. Natalie and I were swimming with this afternoon tide. Vince wasn't. He was heading toward us, against the current. It was slowing him down, so that for all his dodging and feinting to get through he was pretty much staying in one position, like a navigation buoy getting bashed around by a river current. It didn't seem to bother him. He seemed to be concentrating on something besides progress. You could tell when you looked into his eyes. They were dark and opened wide and flicking from face to approaching face.

Customers. That's what Vince sought. Customers seeking to buy drugs. Vince wasn't a dealer. He was too messed up for that. I guess you'd call him a broker. Plenty of people like Vince paced the sidewalk around St. Mike's, walking along Queen Street East, from the park bench at Bond and Queen to the light at Church Street, and then back. Vince had been around for years. He'd been a fixture during my first go-round and then once I was off the stuff I'd see him around and shake his gnarled hand, wish him well. Sometimes you'd find Vince over in the churchyard, across the street. Sometimes you found him leaning against the railing by the bike racks. Wherever you found him, you went up to him and you asked, "Food?"—the downtown slang term for crack—and Vince would nod. He might say, "You got a quarter?" Disregarding the taxis and the other automobiles he'd cross Queen to the pay phone like a jaywalking Frogger.

The previous Saturday night, it had taken ten minutes for the appropriate car to show up. The only break in the silence came when Vince had asked me for a cigarette.

"Naw," I said. "Don't smoke."

Vince looked at me.

"Cigarettes. I don't smoke cigarettes."

A couple of minutes later he nodded at a passenger in a passing car. Into his palm I slipped him two $20 bills folded into a tight square. He disappeared around the corner. A minute or two later he reappeared with the few rocks of crack cocaine he'd just bought for me. I tipped him with a chunk I pinched off with a thumbnail. "That's it?" he asked. I could have given him the whole of what he'd bought for me, and he would have reacted the same way.

Now Vince was going to do what I feared since we'd left on this excursion, when I realized that Natalie had made our ultrasound appointment at a clinic located on the exact block where I went to buy drugs.

Vince was going to recognize me. And even if I walked past, even if I tried to ignore him, Natalie would notice, and Natalie would realize I wasn't as clean as I professed to be, that the crack habit I'd supposedly dealt with three years before actually wasn't so successfully dealt with. Her realization would ruin her reverie and this special moment and Christ, not just this special moment, it was going to ruin our marriage, there was no way she was going to raise a child with a guy still struggling with a crack habit. The ultrasound images of our apparent son were still in Natalie's hand. They depicted a boy just steps away from being born to divorced parents.

As I approached Vince I should have stared at the ground. Turned my face away. Averted my eyes, at least! But even with my fucking marriage at stake I couldn't resist a glance over at him to see how his eyes flicked at Natalie, at her styled hair and her understated makeup and her shirtdress belted over her slightly-protruding belly, and how Vince devoted not even a look at her apparently upstanding husband, not even a flicker of interest at me successfully impersonating a devoted father-to-be. For the moment, my marriage was saved.

-2-

THE GHOST WRITER

Yeah, if drugs didn't mess things up, everything else was going smashingly. Career, for example. My summer began with a fascinating research trip through the backwoods of Maine to investigate the final hours of a seemingly stable Canadian boy who, that Easter weekend, had paged through the state's publicly accessible online database of sex offenders, then stole a couple of his father's guns and went hunting for pedophiles. He killed two people before police caught up with him outside of Boston and he turned the gun on himself. The subtext of the magazine story I was cooking up investigated whether a human being's moral worth existed on a deeper level than the actions he conducted. It asked the question, was it possible for a good man to do evil things? Clearly I had a stake invested in the answer. Particularly since, during that research trip, I had detoured on my way to Maine from Cape Breton, Nova Scotia, where the boy was from, to a particularly seedy neighbourhood in Halifax, where I bought and smoked about a hundred bucks worth of crack cocaine.

The weekend after I returned from that research trip, a special issue of the magazine I worked for landed on newsstands across the country. The issue's big feature was a story I had written about a peacekeeper who had been murdered in Haiti. There had been a stir when it happened because the peacekeeper had been a much-respected Mountie, a member of the Royal Canadian Mounted Police's organized crimefighting detachment who was a hero for his record fighting against the Montreal mafia. The official story from the United Nations' Haiti office had blamed the man's death on bad luck; he had been in the wrong place at the wrong time, was the implication. But information I turned up during a research trip to Port-au-Prince contradicted the official account. Through sheer luck I'd happened upon a cache of photographs that had been taken at the scene of the man's death. And it turned out that tangled chains of command and bureaucratic squabbling had contributed to the man's death. In fact, the Mountie had bled to death on the side of a Haitian road, just a couple hundred metres from a hospital. *The National* picked up the story and *The Globe and Mail* provided it with several days of prominent coverage. Suddenly, literary agents were calling and emailing asking whether I wanted to write books. I began a series of lunch meetings that saw me pitching ideas to book editors. Better yet, Canada's National Magazine Awards were happening the exact week the story hit. The awards were handed out at a formal affair. It was far too early for my Haiti story to be nominated. But some of the people I considered idols told me

I was an absolute lock to win an award next year. (And I did—a Gold in the category of Politics and Public Interest.)

Things were going so well that I was a bit confused by something that happened the day after the awards fete, when I saw an ex-girlfriend at a friend's wedding. As everyone was heading from the ceremony to the reception, she looked at me and she mouthed something: "Congratulations." I wasn't sure what was causing her to congratulate me. Was it the story? The attention for the story? Had she seen me on television? The fact that my book industry lunches were going so well? Had she somehow heard a short film I'd written several months before was to be submitted to the Toronto International Film Festival by the National Film Board? But no, what an idiot I was, the ex-girlfriend was pointing at something. She was pointing at Natalie. At Natalie's belly. She was congratulating me on my unborn son.

Oh, yeah, right: My unborn son.

Well, if you boxed out what I got up to on the weekends, as I did, then things here seemed okay, too, at this point.

One Sunday afternoon that June, I was watching a World Cup pool game—France versus Korea, I think—when Natalie came into the family room with a gift-wrapped package. "What's that?" I asked in response to her smile. I opened the package. It was a book, a children's picture book. An old favourite: *Where The Wild Things Are*, by Maurice Sendak.

"It's Father's Day," Natalie said. "It's your first Father's Day present."

I was a bit floored, really. Several different reactions battled for supremacy. Natalie was so thoughtful. I mean, I'd called my dad, earlier, but I'd never thought of this holiday as being for *me*. I'd gained a holiday. That was kind of nice. And then the realness of this pregnancy hit me in a way it hadn't before. Holy fuck. I was going to be a father.

I clicked off the TV. Natalie settled herself and her pregnant belly into the couch, so that her legs were on my lap. If I leaned over and held the book just so, it was like I had the baby on my lap. From that position I read the story of Max, whose misbehaviour gets him sent to his room without dinner. This was before the Spike Jonze movie. It had been decades, then, since I'd flipped through the tale of Max's voyage to a monster-filled island, and the rumpuses that ensue. We read of the way Max missed home, and, after a sailboat ride of many months, returned on the same evening he left to discover his still-warm dinner. Sheesh, I thought to myself. I hoped my own trips among the wild things ended similarly well.

IN MID-JUNE, the men's magazine where I was a writer-at-large threw a party to mark summer's start. It happened at a downtown club. I decided to drive to the party in a car we'd rented for a weekend of shopping for baby stuff in the suburbs. The plan was to just pop in for a drink or two and then get out of there, make it an early night, I had too much work to do. No such luck. The party was sponsored by a vodka distributor, and besides that the Haiti story was earning me drinks from fellow editors and writers and well into the evening I found myself talking on the secluded patio with the magazine's editor, the two of us dapper in our suit jackets and our open-collared dress shirts and this woman came up to us, a black-haired looker whose mere presence was enough to stop us mid-sentence. The editor and I angled away from one another, so that our little conversation area now included the newcomer. With just a couple of words she made it clear she was at the party in a professional capacity, she was looking for clients and she hoped we'd consider her. She gave the editor a card and was gone by the time he glanced down at it. "There's your next award-winner, Shulgan," the editor grinned. I looked at the card. It was for an escort service. Minutes later we had mapped out a feature package about the city's high-class prostitution ring. Maybe it could be a first-person thing—an "as told to" arrangement by the head hooker. And then I realized: I didn't have time to do the story. Unusually for a freelance writer, I realized I had so much work it would be several months before I could consider taking on anything new.

When I left the party I went to my car, parked on a one-way street pointed east, away from my house. Toward Vince. When had I known I would end this night with crack? Since Natalie'd become pregnant, I was drinking more, and punctuating the serious drunks with cocaine or crack, and the thought had occurred, was I doing the drugs because I was getting so drunk, or was I getting so drunk to provide myself the excuse to do the drugs? Hello, crack. How you doing? How I've missed you. Now it was like Mary Karr's line about always moving away from or toward a serious drunk. Crack was around again. If I was honest with myself, I knew I was headed toward Vince the moment I opened this party's invitation email. If I went out, I'd do it, I knew that. I didn't spend a lot of time thinking about consequences during the ten-minute ride. I was more concerned with keeping the wheels between the dotted white lines. Stopped at a red light, a shiver climbed my spine and escaped through each limb. Excitement, or some manifestation of addiction? Excitement. Because I wasn't addicted. This stuff was a hobby. I could go weeks without it, same as I could a drink.

A block west of Church on Queen, I looked for Vince under the street lights. This was the part I loved. Well, I loved all of it. And getting the stuff was an important component of the overall thrill. A glance from the church park bench to the railing told me he wasn't around. Perhaps he was off with someone else. The thought provoked a jealous stab. Huh: was I really growing possessive of my drug dealer? Now came the challenge. Getting the stuff would require exercising the full range of the skills I'd developed over the previous five years during my on-and-off career as a crack consumer.

FINDING SOMEONE who says they'll sell you some crack is easy. I don't know how they do it in towns where sprawl has sucked out the street life. I don't know how they do it in the suburbs. Scoring crack in Toronto is a pedestrian's game. Find the right area and everybody there wants to give it to you. The distributors might as well be street furniture. They're vertical by the lamp posts and the garbage receptacles. They're tough to categorize, as a type. They don't share much besides crack. Skin colour, age, sex, cultural ties, whether they listen to hip-hop or death metal—these are variables that shift. No, rather than puffy outerwear or pegged jeans, you're just looking for people who know people. The hardest part is finding the right stretch of road; once you've done that they'll come to you. Most times, white well-groomed me wanders among the wall-leaners and post-pushers and pocket-diggers and it's only moments before someone greets me with a nod or a smile. Not so unusual in a small town, perhaps, but a clear violation of the conventions that dictate urban behaviour in North American cities. It's at this point that experience proves useful: the trick is choosing someone depraved enough to act as a broker in a crack deal but not so depraved as to "vic" you. Vic being the catch-all term to describe stealing your money, yes, as well as giving you a smaller share of the stuff than your money would otherwise warrant. "Don't vic me," I might say, as I hand over the money. "Am I getting vicced?" as I accept the handful of rocks. Most times I am—the question is, how much? A crack deal is slanted toward the seller. What are you going to do if they vic you? Around here crack comes twisted into little cellophane bubbles. The off-white fragments, just smaller than your littlest fingernail, resemble pebbles or candle wax chunks, both of which can be sold to you as counterfeit product. Once the exchange happens, will you stand on the street, untwist the cellophane, taste it for the telltale coke numbing? Maybe you do this on the evening's first rock. But not if you're drunk, as I always am, and certainly not if you've already smoked your first batch and paranoia blooms police cars around every corner. No, dude— usually, the deal happens and you speedwalk away. One option: insist you won't pay until the product is verified potent. Well, sure. But in general these are street deals. Because in subsequent days, amid the hangover's self-hatred, I tend to throw away whatever phone numbers I get from dealers eager to snare me as a customer. Street deals mean I'm dealing with a broker and he or she needs to pay the source, so this is an upfront deal, Tex. Find someone who's sacrificed themselves entirely to crack and they'll just take your rolled-up $20 and disappear. To buy crack. The trick is to find someone only slightly farther into the crack economy than you are. They've spent all their money. That's why they're looking for you. And then dangle future deals as an incentive not to vic you. If I am sober enough to talk when I'm trying to get the crack, which is maybe half the time, then I try to make reference to the (fictional) guys back at the (fictional) party, the guys who want to just try the stuff, the guys who will send me back in an hour with more money, in search of a bigger deal. Screen out the street people with carnivorous eyes. Screen out the android jitters and the vicegrip jaws. You see any of that, you run. Like, *literally* run. You won't get rid of them otherwise. You're in better shape than they are. (You're in bad shape, sure, but trust me: they're in worse.) "Hey," he smiles, and you say, "hey" and wait for the request—"You looking?" And that's how long you have to decide. Are you going to do business with this person? Back in the day, back the first time the stuff was a serious problem, I declined about 50% of the approaches. From the second you indicate what you seek, they have ownership of you. You're their bitch. "He's mine," they'll hiss at the other zombies who approach you, before they take your money, before they disappear to the walk-ups at Queen and Sherbourne or inside the high-rise south of Mutual and Shuter or in the subsidized housing off Jarvis. Why are they so territorial? Your money represents rocks for them, too: Because they vic you. They take your $20 and you get only $15 worth of crack. I don't think of that as an out-and-out vic. It's a commission. A tip.

I misjudge all the time. It's the nature of the scene. Crack's economy is one of changed minds and consuming impulses. Of course I misjudge. And they fuck me for it. There was the time I asked for a twenty and she asked me for the money, right off, and I saw how high she was, there was no way she was together enough to live up to her end of the deal. I said, you know what? I just remembered, I forgot something, I have to go. And she snatched my eyeglasses from my face. Just like that. She held the glasses up in front of me as though she would snap them in two. "Gimme the $20," she hissed. I was stunned. Her speed was remarkable. I could see, I couldn't. It was brilliant, what she had done. Few other threats could have rendered so powerless near-sighted, astigmatic me. Here was the greed and desperation crack could drive a person to. Here was an act that displayed how different she and I were, how I was a tourist in the land of crack where she was a denizen, and I had the tourist's set of vulnerabilities. Wordlessly, I handed over the bill. She threw my glasses to the ground and fled, to buy for herself the rock I had wanted her to buy for me.

It's puzzling. I can stand up for myself. I can and do fight. I can win. My first fight was the same year as my first drunk. I was 13. It was our first Halloween in the city, a half hour after dusk turned to night. My friend Stephanie and I were leading our brothers homeward after a successful stint with the doorbell requests when a clutch of boys my age intercepted us in the middle of the street. One wrestled my brother's bag of candy from his grasp. I got hold of the would-be larcenist. I punched. I kicked and got the kid to the ground and somehow an adult intervened and separated us and returned my brother's candy to him. That was the first fight; its recollection later that night had me sobbing in my father's arms. He was bewildered. "What's wrong, boyo?" he said. "Didn't you *win*?" Yeah, but Pop: I wanted to *kill* the guy. It was astonishing. Where did this come from, this blackness inside me, this power, this violence? I've been in dozens of fights since then and I still don't know. I've kicked ass and I've had my ass kicked and I've learned I can take a punch in the head. It's the *kicks* in the head that get you: they knock you out. That's how I got the concussion. That's what happened to my nose.

It's different in the land of crack. Here, I'm a coward.
Something about it paralyzes me. Take the attempted purchase
that happened during my first round of problems with the
stuff. He was a black kid about my height whose smile envel-
oped him in the spirit of bonhomie. In fact, readers, his well-
fed frame and eye twinkle gave him a vibe similar to that of *the*
Bonhomme, the sentient snowman mascot of Quebec City's
Winter Carnival. It was my second purchase of the afternoon.
Maybe that's why I didn't see it at first. I can't remember who
approached whom. But I caught the desperation in the way he
said, "How much you have to spend?" Some bugged-out hunger that suggested certain vic. I don't remember even the exact
phrasing. What I do remember is the pressing nature of the
need to escape. I made up an excuse. Despite my bill-crammed
pockets I invented a need to visit an ATM. Stay here, I said. I'll
return in ten minutes. But as I walked along Queen he followed
me. Bear in mind this was some years ago. Now, gentrification
has spread past Sherbourne, but back then along Queen, the
border between crack city and city city was Church Street.
There was a moment I thought he wouldn't pass the border.
To discourage him, I stopped and muttered something. I didn't
want it. I changed my mind. He shook his head. "You said $20,"
he said. Almost to himself. Then he looked at me. "You owe
me $20."

Come on, he said. He kept saying it. Come *on*. Sprint, I
should have. But something prevented me from breaking into
a run. Friends toiled high in these towers. And Bonhomme
looked like he could keep up with me. Maybe I could have
punched him, and hurt him badly enough to keep him down.
But a punch or more would have drawn too much attention in
this gentrifying scene.

An excuse about my choice of bank split my lips—I needed a Toronto-Dominion ATM, I said, and we headed into downtown Toronto's vast mall with its escalators and crowds. The Eaton Centre is so long it spans the distance between two subway stations. Would he follow me in? He did. The motherfucker did. The lines for the bank's ATMs close to me were full and I muttered something about the next-closest kiosks, then at the mall's north end. A strange stasis afflicted me in that commercial canyon. Perfume advertising beamed white teeth and sensual health over the good consumers. They pushed strollers. They toted shopping bags. These were my people. Why didn't I lead my black Bonhomme to a security desk? Run, you idiot! But someone might see the resultant flight or fight, Natalie's friends or mine, and the sketch I'd taken such care to keep clear of would smear over me. Sure, I could have just given him the bill. But something prevented that, too. And so I wandered north with my shadow. I passed escalators and contemplated scaling them. I passed elevators and thought about fleeing through their closing doors. I progressed with an awareness of Bonhomme a step or two behind and slightly to the right of me. He announced his presence, too: *Come on*, he hissed. *Let's go.* At times, the crowds in the mall meant we progressed in single file.

It occurs to me now the paralyzing discomfort I felt in those moments stemmed not from fear but shame. Here was a picture of me with my crack habit, my secret vice, and the radical steps required to separate me from broker Bonhomme would threaten this façade I'd cultivated, the allure of the secret life would dissolve and just become my life, with all its weirdness exposed. Here was a situation that made plain my hypocrisy. I did it for the thrill, I did it for the danger, but a situation that threatened to expose these buys and what came after could render me a coward. Here was me, and here in the form of Bonhomme was evidence of my slumming and the mall's fluorescent illumination washed the glamour from the rebellion. All it made me feel was shame.

I had an idea. It's a quirk of this mall that it's set into a shallow hill, the result of the city's easy southern lakeward tilt. What's the ground level at the south end goes underground by the mall's opposite end, three blocks to the north. My hands found the required coins in my pocket. "Just over here," I said, and led Bonhomme through the double doors that formed an annex between mall and subway station. It took only seconds to arrive at the ticket booth and by the time I did I had the coins ready. They clinked hollowly into the attendant's receptacle. The turnstile felt greasy and cold, as it always did. Several steps past the entrance I chanced a look back to verify Bonhomme stayed on the barrier's opposite side. As I'd expected, he didn't have the money required for subway fare. A train filled Dundas Station's sleeve of acid yellow while I held Bonhomme's gaze. Around me the platform filled with the middle classes. I shrugged, as though to say, nothing personal. The expression he threw back my way had a power to it; contempt like that I've felt only once since—from the girl in the park while I played with my boy. This contempt was founded on an accusation of hypocrisy. Later I'd think of this look when I happened to hear Jarvis Cocker's character sketch of upper-class slumming, Common People: "You'll never understand," he sings. "You'll never get it right . . . You'll never watch your life slide out of you." Here were those lines summed up in a single expression. Tourist, Bonhomme accused. Hypocrite. I wanted it both ways, I was having it both ways, and as I melted into the middle classes the addict who tailed me for ten city blocks threw his resentment my way, his accusation, his loathing, that I, unlike him, could so easily melt into a milieu where my drug use did not exist.

ON THIS EVENING in June, I walked east along Queen Street into crack's blocks watching the eyes of the people headed the other way. A block west of Jarvis I encountered the correct kind of returned gaze, the mutual nod.

"How you doing?" he said.

"Could be good," I said. "You got a $20?"

"Are you police?"

"Do I look like police?"

The dude stepped back.

"Yeah."

We both looked at what I was wearing: my suit jacket and the open-necked dress shirt.

This was a not-unexpected retort. My broad shoulders and the fact, at that point, that I wore my thinning hair in a close-cropped buzz cut, did give me an air of enforcement. In these situations I used a kind of inverse argument—that I looked too much like a cop to be a cop. "What kind of a cop would go to a crack bust wearing *this*?" I said. "I'm not police."

He shrugged. A denial seemed to be all he needed. There was, apparently, a rumour of some ontological requirement. A cop couldn't deny being a cop. If he did, the bust was invalid. (I don't know whether this is true.)

The broker said, "Whatever you say . . . Wait here. No, wait at the park bench."

By this time I was across from Moss Park.

"Okay," I said, working on a feeling here. He seemed straight up. Once I'd found someone like him I wanted to get all the product I needed for the night. In effect, I doubled down my bet. "Hey!"

"What?"

"Make it a $40. No: A $60."

He returned five minutes later. We entered what constituted the trickiest aspect of the deal. The handoff. If the stuff was real the sight of the transfer from palm to palm amounted to the illicit transaction's most clearly visible component. On the border of Moss Park, at 2 a.m., what other transaction might be happening but something illicit? Back in the day I'd encountered dozens of methods that masked the exchange's nature. There was the time in the smoking section at a nearby coffee shop, no longer there, where I handed money under the fibreglass table then asked where the other end was, and the female dealer told me the surprising answer: somehow, some sleight of hand managed to put it already under the bottom of my coffee cup. Another method started with the storage of the rocks in the mouth. The garbled enunciation employed by my interlocutor was explained when he spat out two or three cellophane baggies into his palm and handed over the drugs in a sarcophagus of salivated plastic.

This time it was nothing so elegant or sophisticated. Dude just left them on the park bench. I scooped up the bits and walked back to the car feeling cop eyes in every street-facing window. I didn't examine what I'd bought until I'd made it safe to my car. Three pebbles, two in cellophane packages, the single unwrapped stone substantially smaller compared to its compatriots. Proof of a low-level vic allayed some anxiety. That the broker had bothered to unwrap the third rock, to nick what he considered his commission, suggested the stuff was not wax, not pebble, but actual cocaine in rock form.

I was minutes from home when I noticed the police car behind me. No problem. Stay cool, that's all I had to do. Drive well. A minute later, his lights flashed and there was a blast of that high-intensity horn that cops have—the one that sounds more like a buzzer. I pulled over. Maybe he had been summoned somewhere. Maybe he just wanted me out of his way. Nope. He pulled in behind me.

The worst case involved me jailed for the evening on some possession-related charge. Perhaps I'd lose my licence. Natalie would have to bail me out. Anxiety mixed with unexpected relief. Maybe this was a good thing. Maybe this was the end. I retrieved my licence from my pocket and the ownership from the sleeve on the sun visor. Too late I realized the drugs were exposed in the cupholder that lived between the bucket seats. The sideview mirror provided an image of cop exiting car, then expanding cop. He stood in that position police used, a little behind my left shoulder. I twisted and received a face full of light for my trouble. His flashlight. He asked for the paperwork. "Do you know why I pulled you over?"

"No sir."

"You went through the red light at Queen."

I winced. "I was too busy watching you behind me, I guess."

When he returned to his car, I moved the drugs from cupholder to the carpet underneath my seat. Maybe I'd go to rehab. Maybe Natalie would stay with me. Maybe this was a good thing.

"What were you doing tonight?"

This was maybe five minutes later, after he'd spent some time in his car. Again I had to twist to look up at him. No flashlight, this time.

"I was at a work party," I said.

He asked what I did for a living and I said journalist, that I wrote feature articles for a men's magazine.

"Did you have anything to drink at your party?"

"Yes, sir."

"How much did you have to do drink?"

Again, I did that twist.

"Probably a little too much."

"Where was the party?"

I named the club, just a couple of blocks away. For a second or two we just looked at each other. He looked again at my licence. He said, "You're pretty close to home." He looked away, in the general direction my house was. Looking back at me now, he said, "You have a clean record. And a drunk driving charge would have some serious consequences." He held up a yellow leaflet. "Here's a ticket for running the light," he said, and already my hands were loosening on the steering wheel. He said, "I'm going to let you off with a warning. Be careful the rest of the way home. I hope you learned a lesson today."

I accepted the piece of paper like he was handing over a winning lottery ticket. I thanked him repeatedly. I thanked him so much I realized I was overdoing it and then turned to avowals of the transformative nature of this encounter: "I *have* learned a lesson today," I said.

Liar. With the care of a neurosurgeon I drove the five blocks home. I carefully parked the car in the lot across the street from my house, just like I carefully extricated the three pieces of crack from underneath the seat, just like I carefully constructed the pipe from materials I bought at a nearby corner store. And then I set off on what I usually did when I smoked crack. I went on a walking tour of the neighbourhood.

MAYBE AN HOUR later I was in a situation that must have looked pretty weird, at five o'clock in the morning. Hell, at any time: I was down on the pavement on my hands and knees peering through the iron grill of a sewer drain. I was considering something. I was having a moment.

Crack is different from powdered cocaine. It isn't like the old recipe. Think of the old recipe like a Sunday drive that follows a route over a hill. You go up, you go down. It's kind of gentle. It's slow. It's sort of nice, really. And then think of the new coke, think of crack, like one of those bungee-things they have at carnivals or street fairs—you know, that thing where they strap you in and winch up the bungee cords and then you're catapulted straight up and then dropped into a free fall and then repeat. That's how crack is compared to cocaine.

What makes crack so different is this moment that happens at the ride's apex. You're at the top and you're looking down and you think to yourself: I don't want to go down. I want to stay up. And the thing with crack is, you can. You can stay up. You just smoke more of the stuff.

Oh, there's that nasty moment when you run out. You look down, you're aware the drop is next. Worse: you're aware that the drop is going to be horrible. You're going to feel guilty and sad and angry at yourself. You're going to feel like you're letting down everybody who ever believed in you. Which is right. Which you are.

And a brilliant thought occurs to you: *more*.

Way back when, when I first started smoking crack, the *more* moment was pretty easy to get through. I just reasoned it out: oh, tomorrow morning you have things to do. For example, on this night, I was due in a few hours to go with Natalie to look for linens for our baby's crib.

Each time I did crack, however, the less such commitments mattered. Confronted with my last piece of crack, more and more frequently I found myself dashing across town to Moss Park to find one of the dealers—consequences be damned. Usually I hopped into a cab. Sometimes I took my bike. Some evenings, there were two or three trips back to Moss Park. And sometimes, there were more than that.

To stave off these return trips to the dealer I developed a set of tactics to discourage myself from making these return trips. The simplest tactic involved not smoking the crack until I had a lot of distance between me and Moss Park. Another made use of one of crack cocaine's attributes, that the really great part of the high doesn't hit you until you exhale. It's kind of a weird thing, actually. You get the bit melted onto the pipe mesh, you get your lighter ready and there's that eponymous snapping as you simultaneously burn and inhale—and then, so long as you keep that breath in, the best part of the rush doesn't hit you. So you're perched on something of a precipice. Technically, you still have more to do, so you don't actually want more, yet. Because you have more. You have more inside you.

At that moment, what I had begun doing, when I had inhaled the last of my crack but not yet exhaled, while I still technically had another toke to do: I got rid of my tools. I disposed of the crack pipe and my lighter. If I was in, say, a hotel room, I flushed the things down the toilet. And if I was outside, as I was tonight, then sometimes I stepped on my little ginseng vial of a crack pipe. Tonight, I dropped the pipe and the lighter down the sewer drain.

I kept walking. I exhaled. There was the lift. It was nowhere near the ascent from the night's first toke, but it was a lift nonetheless. It came simultaneously with the desire to do more of the drug. I resisted for maybe twenty-five paces.

Then I turned back.

I ended up on my hands and knees looking through the sewer grate. I thought I could see the thing, the way the vial glinted as it caught the streetlight's halogen glow. I looked around for a stick. If I had had some gum, I could try to fish the vial out of the sewer by sticking the sticky stuff on a branch end. I started heading toward the convenience store to buy the stickiest bubble gum I could find. Then, somewhere between the sewer grate and the convenience store, the moment passed. I did what I should have done hours before. I did what was getting harder to do, each time I did this stuff. I did what I worried, one day, I wouldn't be able to do: I went home.

Before I headed to bed I stopped in the kitchen. I took a beer out of the fridge and knocked it back. Then I got out the bottle of vodka. I filled a shot glass, downed it, filled the shot glass again. Booze helped ease the comedown.

It was around half past five when I slipped into bed beside Natalie.

"How you doing, baby?" she whispered.

"Fine," I answered, speaking softly. "I'm doing fine."

-3-

THE ANTI-DEATH LEAGUE

The next day, Natalie and I headed out on an excursion. A season of baby showers approached and Natalie and I were to prepare for it by traversing the vast plains of asphalt in the suburbs to select such articles as crib sheets and infant swings. "Can you drive?" I asked as we walked to the car.

Natalie stopped. "I'm not sure I can."

Last night kept rising up my throat. The first thing I became aware of that morning had been the desire to throw up, and the second thing I did was satisfy that desire. What I hadn't noticed was that Natalie had spent a lot of time in the bathroom too. Now that I was looking at her, I realized she looked as rough as I did.

"Some pair," I said.

She grinned.

I kept the keys. I put my arm around her. There was a tricky moment when we got to the car, when I saw resting in the centre cupholders the yellow traffic ticket from the previous night's encounter. I jammed the thing into my pocket before Natalie noticed it. We stopped at Starbucks, where a Red Eye helped me get to the suburbs. Somewhere among the linen displays and pillow-sizing charts Natalie's morning sickness passed. She constructed tableaux and vistas from the fitted sheets and crib-sized comforters. In an effort to end the suspense I'll disclose that we chose sheet patterns in several different shades of teal. "What about teal for the walls?" Natalie asked.

"Oh Christ," I said.

"What?"

"We're supposed to paint this weekend, too, huh?"

Natalie looked at me. I looked at the ground. I said, "No, I mean, I'm looking forward to it—"

She said, "I wish you were excited."

"It's just, there's so much to do."

She shrugged. "Just help me get this stuff into the cart."

Oh, there were a lot of moments like these.

Most of the time I fooled myself into thinking I was compartmentalizing my little nocturnal adventures. It wasn't just Natalie I was fooling. None of my friends knew I was back at the stuff. Nor did my brother or sister. I never did crack with anybody else. The only time I did it was when I was already wasted. It had hold of me from 2 a.m. to 5 a.m. All the harm it caused was a couple of hours of lost sleep. Oh yeah, minimization was happening a lot that summer. I convinced myself what I told Natalie actually was true: I was fine.

That summer, Natalie and I spent a weekend at a friend's farmhouse in the rural hills of Eastern Ontario. We slept in a tent, and woke in the middle of the night to a thunderstorm so violent you could see the lightning strobes even when you kept your eyes closed. We were on an air mattress, inside a mound of sleeping bags and comforters, and amid all that down and synthetic fill I snuggled against Natalie's back feeling warm and safe in spite of and partially because of the violent weather outside. I flashed back to the period nine years earlier, in December 1997, when we'd first met, and I evaluated how the old me might have perceived me now and decided, at that precise moment, that old me would have approved. I squeezed Natalie.

"Isn't this an adventure?" I said to my semi-conscious wife. "Isn't this *exactly* the way you would have hoped things would be going, when we met? Baby," I said, "there's nobody else I'd rather be living my life with. Besides you." She gave me a squeeze. I took it to mean she agreed. I mean if you ignored the fact I was secretly smoking crack, and stuffing my face with whatever else I could get my hands on, and if you ignored the fact that pregnant Natalie might have divorced me if she found out about the drugs, then my marriage was going *great*.

Oh come now, you're saying. Surely Natalie must have realized. Well, she did and she didn't. At this point, we certainly never talked about it. And bear in mind there was a huge amount to talk about. Both of us were working full time, and on top of that both of us were preparing for the baby. Every spare moment Natalie was on the couch with her laptop as she compiled the registry for her baby showers. She became expert in the frequency interference issues of certain baby monitors, and the biomechanical advantages for particular configurations of wraps, which, I discovered, were sleeves of fabric that parents used to make it easier for them to carry their babies. Meanwhile, I raced to finish renovating our bathroom before the baby arrived. The renovations were meant to rectify this problem our house had: We didn't have a sink in our bathroom. Instead the sink was in an adjacent bedroom. Don't ask me why. I remain puzzled whether the previous occupants of the house ever washed their hands.

But Natalie knew. Oh, Natalie knew. There were times I'd be nudged out of sleep by her ankle, or her elbow, or her just coming over to my side of the bed and getting me into a full-body embrace. I'd get my arms around her and stroke her hair.

"Hi, baby," I'd say. "What's up?"

Sometimes she would say, "Nightmares." Or sometimes she was a little more descriptive: "I had a crack dream," she might say. Or: "I dreamt you were using crack again."

"Oh baby," I would say. Or I didn't say anything. I just stroked her hair. I squeezed her slender frame against mine, and promised myself never again to do crack, or any drugs. I berated myself for ever trying them in the first place. Why would I do something that introduced these sorts of worries into our marriage? My wife was wonderful. I wanted to protect her. I wanted to save her from everything. Including me.

MY DRUG USE WAS corrupting my life's single great love affair. Drugs were just about the only thing that could ever cause Natalie to divorce me. From the moment we met, our relationship worked because of a quality I was now busy undermining. We met in 1997 amid the holiday bacchanal that happened after exams end in our southwestern Ontario city of Windsor. It was an annual thing, this December drunk, and it happened each year for a certain alternative type. The hometown gathered its university-age diaspora back to its bosom and all the kids who'd decamped to wherever else, to the States, to Canada's urban triumvirate of Montreal, Toronto, or Vancouver, gathered in a battered second-storey nightclub called the Loop, a warehouse attic of scarred billiards tables and a bandstand where the dance floor hosted local indie bands and British invasion nights and whatever else the alternative crowd was into that season.

Maybe it was 11 p.m. This was a more innocent time, so beer was pretty much the only substance I abused with any regularity at that point, and abuse was happening. I was twenty-four and had just finished my Master's in Journalism at Northwestern University in Evanston, Illinois. I had a job waiting for me at a newspaper in Bend, Oregon, where I planned to work my ass off and spend the rest of the time snowboarding at Mt. Bachelor. I was waiting for my U.S. work visa to arrive and looking forward to the brilliant future destiny was certain to bring me. And I was talking to one of the city's bright lights, a friend just back from Indiana, where he was a senior at Notre Dame. This was the kind of night it was—a town reunion for what amounted to the intelligentsia youth in my small southwestern Ontario city. Drinkers gathered around the bar like iron filings to a magnet. That crowd scene made it difficult to get beer. "Hey, I need another pint," I said to my friend. "We should get somebody to stand in line for us . . . Hey," I said, turning to the nearest person in the crowd. "How about I pay you five bucks to go and get us a beer?"

Ooh, it makes me cringe, this bit, the frat-boy assumption another would be willing to do what I wasn't. Christ. I got my comeuppance, however.

"Fuck you," the deal's target responded.

Her tone suggested I was being an asshole. I considered the situation. Hey, I realized, I *was* being an asshole. Simultaneous to that realization was the base understanding that it was a girl I was pitching, quite an attractive girl, tall and slim with green eyes that met mine, with long legs sleeved in worn jeans, with Doc Marten boots, with freckles accentuating her cheek bones and butterscotch hair, a butterscotch bob. And those green eyes, Christ, those green eyes ready to give me back just what I was giving her.

"What if I bought *you* a beer?" I managed, and she shrugged. Remarkably she was still there when I returned bearing the Loop's pint mugs. We retired to a table off by itself. Making small talk is not a skill I possess. It's the clichéd nature of those first couple of lines that kills me. If I was editing small talk I'd slash it out from the text. What information does it convey? Cut it! What did we discuss? Names, clearly, and backgrounds. Natalie was four years younger than me; she was in the second year of a psychology degree at the University of Windsor. It turned out I knew a guy she'd dated; it turned out her sister was the year behind mine at Queen's. Natalie resided just a friend removed from me for all these years and later, how bitter those undiscovered eons seemed—when we were separated only by an introduction. Somehow the topic of Natalie's vegetarianism came up. I asked, what kind of a vegetarian? Did she eat fish? Nope. Milk? Eggs? Nope and nope.

"Why are you so curious?" Natalie wanted to know.

"Maybe I want to make you dinner. Maybe I'm just curious."

"It's of crucial importance to you to determine what kind of vegetarian I am."

"Right."

"An ethical one—I don't think it's right to eat animals."

"How noble," I said. "What about your boots? The Docs?"

She flushed—the freckles on her pale skin bloomed and spread. Yes, they were leather, as a matter of fact.

"That's what kind of vegetarian you are," I said. "The hypocritical kind."

Here was an act that formed the inverse of what she'd done to me, moments before. Fuck you, she'd said. And I responded by puncturing her vegetarian pretension. Which didn't seem to bother her. She just shrugged.

Did she have a boyfriend? No, she said. But she hesitated. She explained. She'd just broken up with someone and more lately had been getting together with an ex-boyfriend but . . .

"What?" I said, hanging on the possibility there still remained an opening for me.

"He's living with this girl."

"He's cheating on her? With you?"

This seems unduly harsh, now. Perhaps I was trying to paint the ex as a cheater? To stain him so that I seemed sinless by comparison?

"Not exactly," Natalie said, touching the rim of her pint glass. "I'm kind of seeing her, too."

It seems out of character, now, this level of disclosure. Natalie is one of the more guarded individuals I know. She doesn't just let anybody in. But from our first exchange I was in, and in completely.

A painting hung on a nearby wall, a canvas that depicted an aged couple on a couch, the man's European whiskers silvered with experience, the woman's dress frayed and flat with age. The canvas conveyed the shared years between the artwork's subjects and I promised then something similar would exist between Natalie and me. We didn't go home together that night, although the option was there—my parents were off on a skiing holiday that included my younger sister; my brother and I had the homestead to ourselves. We made plans; I would call her the next afternoon. And in violation of dating convention, I did.

Oh man, it was exciting. The frisson of those months and early years and the sense we were doing something new. Our first date happened at my place. My dog, a golden retriever, on first introduction, leapt vertical to put her paws on Natalie's shoulders. Post-haste, I pushed down those enthusiastic forelimbs, but not too hard—I understood what my dog was feeling. I felt the same way.

Subsequent dates revealed Natalie lived with her brother and sister in a well-maintained three-bedroom home. They were pretty well set up. She and her sister drove matching new Ford Explorers. Their television was bigger than my family's television, plus they had a surround-sound system back when that was unusual. And yet there was this air of tragedy around them. I learned that Natalie's dad worked for the family business, an auto-industry supplier. He lived with Natalie's younger brother in Barbados, where he ran the company's international sales arm. And Natalie's mother was set up in another house, maybe ten minutes away from the kids. Except the kids didn't really talk to their mom.

This was subtext, in those early weeks. This was background that had little relevance to what was happening between Natalie and me. Every day felt special. Every day could have been our last together—I expected my work visa to arrive soon, and once it did, I was off to Oregon. So we spent every second together we could, and then, as it became apparent that America's immigration system didn't work as quickly as I expected, as the weeks became a month, and then two, we decided things were too special to end. Natalie would take a break from her university studies. She'd make the trip with me, to Oregon.

Our way would be different from our parents', or anyone else's. We decided this during long afternoons we spent together in Natalie's bedroom. Once my work visa finally came through, we decided this in the single long conversation that spanned our cross-continental car journey. Neither one of us are exactly the marrying type, but a few months later a border snarl meant Natalie was stuck in Canada for the foreseeable future, and I was stuck in Oregon. The snarl happened on July 3, 1998, and just to flip things around, to invert this unfortunate turn, we decided we'd get married exactly a year later. We'd get married, and our marriage would be different, too.

Fuck you, she'd said. Seconds later I was pointing out the flaws in her vegetarianism. Minutes later we explored her threesome; minutes after that I was proposing we'd be together, forever. Why did such extreme trust establish itself so early? Perhaps we recognized our personalities fit? Perhaps we were simply attracted to each other? No, not just that. What cemented this bond was honesty. We established our bond with the first words we spoke to one another. This forthrightness became the relationship's gravitational force. Ours would be a marriage defined by honesty. Our marriage wouldn't let the lies seep in and corrupt what kept it special. Jealousy, secrets, the sad little mistruths that sprung up between the principals in relationships—these we would avoid. Life was going to be an adventure—one we experienced side by side supporting one another with our strengths rather than pulling one another down with our weaknesses.

Many partners vow their marriages will be different, and manage it—what marriage is the same as anyone else's? Few are foolhardy enough to believe they can manage a vow of absolute honesty. But on almost all things, this policy of absolute honesty has worked. We remain in love. And we *are* honest with each other. We have been straight on all things. Except crack. And when I engage in our relationship's founding precept, truth, I can admit what it is that's allowed me to get away with this. You ask me? It was Natalie's mother who prompted Natalie to ignore the signs. Remember how Natalie was estranged from her mom? Well, Natalie's mother had a history with drugs. Which drug didn't matter. She'd had trouble with many of them, including crack. The awfulness that happened during Natalie's adolescence was all the more tragic because her mother was healthy through much of her daughter's first decade. Yeah, Natalie recalled happy memories, backyard slip-and-slide sessions, riotous birthday parties, and umpteen mother–daughter baking sessions—until drugs destroyed the maternal instinct so severely that many years later, Natalie's oldest sister, Jess, assumed custody of a child their mother had had long after the divorce from Natalie's father. Now, if Natalie ever spoke of her mother, she spoke of her in the past tense, as though she was a spectre—the ghost mom whose drug-free years would haunt the daughter for decades to come.

LIKE MANY MIDDLE-CLASS youths who grew up in an environment where drugs were demonized, I had a free-floating curiosity about pharmaceuticals of all flavours. Somewhere along the way I got the idea that one progressed farther along the continuum of sophistication with each additional drug type one consumed. I sampled marijuana and hash, LSD and ecstasy, cough syrup and painkillers, as well as good old powdered cocaine. Pot and the other downers never did much for me. LSD had its uses, as did ecstasy and cocaine, but these were substances to be sampled during playtime. I had too much ambition to allow them to interfere with my career. And I'm probably lucky that I grew up in an era when heroin was unfashionable.

I first tried the stuff in 2001. By 2002 I still considered myself to have a non-addictive personality. I was twenty-nine, my career was going pretty well—a feature I'd written about the science behind traffic jams had bagged a prestigious nomination for Canada's National Newspaper Award, I was stringing for *Time* when that still meant something, and with the rest of my available hours I was building this 'zine I'd started, *Neksis*, into a cross-Canadian youth culture magazine. But then the general economic slowdown that followed the tech meltdown wiped out a whole host of our advertisers. Heading into the summer of 2002 I was looking for a grand artistic project to replace my 'zine. Crack was an ongoing source of fascination for two reasons. One was the role it played in the life of Natalie's mother. What was it about this drug that made it so much more alluring than getting your act together and having relationships with the people who loved you? The other thing fascinating me in this period was an area of Toronto called Moss Park, a bit of urban landscape a couple of blocks from the loft apartment where we then lived. Moss Park wasn't much—a couple tennis courts, a couple baseball diamonds, a hockey arena, some maples and oaks. But it happened to be the setting of a serious crack epidemic just as gentrification was scattering that same setting with briefcases and suits. The result was something like anarchy. I'd go there early in the morning to play tennis with Bay Street friends and watch the tweakers as they roiled through crack's economy: smoking, scavenging the base-ball diamond for change or wayward rocks, calling out to us for handouts through the tennis court fence. Sure, I'd walked through Vancouver's downtown eastside, and having grown up just across the Detroit River from another slow-mo disaster area, I was familiar with such lawless zones. It was just, I'd never before lived in one. I badly wanted to write about it. The novel I cooked up was about a couple, a banker and his graphic designer wife, and the way gentrification compresses urban strata. The couple lives in a loft that faces onto Moss Park; the wife grows intrigued by the layabouts, she tries crack, it becomes a problem, and then she tries to hide it from her husband. That's the conflict that powers the novel's momentum.

Clearly, there were elements of me in the graphic designer. Many afternoons in that period I just hung about the park, sup-posedly soaking up context. It was a simple matter to find someone to teach me how to smoke the stuff. I just asked around. Purely in the name of research, you understand. We got the screening from a bundle of cable wire that hung off an alley telephone pole, inside the block just east of Sherbourne, north of Shuter. I'd visit that telephone pole dozens of times in the teaching session's aftermath. What an awesome drug it seemed. For $20 you could feel amazing for about twenty min-utes. What a deal! A buck a minute rush. You inhaled, you ex-haled the distinctive cream fog, you felt great. Just great. No qualifications. Just great.

Oh, wait. You want more. That's the big *but* that comes with crack. Crack was a sentence that ends with an ellipsis rather than a period. But other than that there were good things about crack. I'm not the first to admire the existential economy in the plight of the crack addict. He's winnowed it down. He's dispensed with the rest of it, with all the other stuff we do to get us pleasure. Job satisfaction, the warmth that comes with enjoying time with good friends, the lift one gets from a family reunion, the contented admiration that comes from viewing the sublime. The crackhead has scalpelled away all the dross, the offal. It's just: satisfaction, warmth, enjoyment, lift. All that exists in the crack rock. Along with the imperative: more.

Things got pretty bad, the first time. Soon after it started I was lying to Natalie. Pretty much every time I left the apartment I was booting to Moss Park for a buy. I'd try to go see a movie by myself and skip out halfway through. I'd leave the house to work and detour parkward. I did a lot of crack smoking in the upstairs bathroom at this pub near the old place—the Imperial Tavern. This was before Dundas Square existed. The tourists hadn't invaded it at that point. You could go upstairs most afternoons and it was empty, just me and Brian the bartender. And the crack I smoked in the bathroom stall. I also did it a lot in the roof washrooms at the loft building where we lived. And then gradually it moved in with me, into our loft. This was difficult—the loft was only about 600 square feet. It was tiny, and yet I managed. I did it literally in the closet, our laundry closet. The loft was this big open space and then a hallway snaked out of the kitchen area to the entry way, and when the hallway turned right there was a little laundry closet that had enough room for one of those stand-up washer-dryer arrangements. Where the dryer was on top of the washer? I'd set the crack on the washer lid, heat the screen with the lighter, melt the rock onto the screen and hit the pipe. One thing about crack: the smoke isn't all that smelly. It's thick and its white and then it's gone: it smells sweet and then it doesn't smell at all.

Natalie was working night shifts and day shifts at this point. Three weeks of night shifts, three weeks of day shifts. The night shift stints were awesome. Twelve hours is a lot of time to fill when you're struggling to avoid doing crack, when you haven't told anyone you're doing crack. There was a point Natalie shifted from nights to days and I couldn't control myself. I did it anyway, while Natalie was asleep. One night, when I was sleeping next to Natalie, she woke me up, she was clutching me, I could feel the moisture from her leaky face through my shirt, her face was wet against my chest. "What's wrong? What's wrong?" I kept saying. She said, "I had a dream you were addicted to crack." *How'd she know?* I couldn't explain it, at the time; now I chalk it up to her subconscious correctly interpreting the cause of my evident agitation. How else to explain the late-night exits, and the insomnia? This was the first one, the first of many crack dreams. "Oh baby," I said. "Oh baby."

Some nights later Natalie woke up at 6 a.m. so she could be ready for her shift's 7:30 a.m. start. I was in the washroom. Previously I timed it better. I made it to bed before she woke up and I'd feign sleep for the hour or so she spent getting ready and by the time she was gone I'd actually descended into a disturbed sleep. This time, for whatever reason (hmm, because you were smoking crack?), I miscalculated. Natalie caught me in the aftermath. Pale, pinned eyes and the jitters, that's the picture I provided her. At 6 a.m. Nice wake-up call. I started crying. I said, "Honey, that dream you had? It's true."

I slept at my brother's awhile. I ended up going to counselling at Toronto's Centre for Addiction and Mental Health, at first one-on-one and then group, every Tuesday night, and then

I decided the group meetings were getting me down and I stopped going. I quit going to group because I'd been clean of crack for six months. Time passed where I'd go eight months, say, then fourteen months, and then Natalie was pregnant and suddenly crack was back—a cast member in my thoughts and dreams.

The reasons I smoked crack shifted between my first round of problems, in 2002, and the latest batch, in 2006. The first time, smoking crack was a way to commune with the city's downtown. I'd spent my adolescence romanticizing the people who lived in cities, and once I lived in a real city smoking crack seemed to be a form of urban communion—the most potent declaration possible that I was a resident of the same place *they* were. It was a way to stave off the sense that after two years of living in Toronto, I remained an outsider. Newcomer, interloper, whatever: smoking crack was my declaration that I belonged. In my head? The act of crack smoking amounted to copulation. It was a way of making Toronto my own.

Or maybe the first time was just crack being crack. Saying I did it for a book, that I smoked crack as research for a novel I was writing, that makes it honourable somehow, doesn't it? How devoted you were to your art, Shulgan! How *gonzo*. How *hardcore*. But that's not really being truthful. In retrospect I wonder whether I cooked up the novel to provide myself with an excuse to cook up the crake. Even without the novel I would have found my way to crack eventually. Debauch would have required it. Debauch, and its hunger for ever more transgressive thrills.

Debauch: that was the problem.

Debauch, and the way the thrill of it was wedded to this concept called man.

BACK TO THE SUMMER of 2006, now. I was in our kitchen washing the dishes. Natalie was sweeping the floor. She went,
"Ooof." I turned around. She had this look on her face and she
sank down into one of the kitchen chairs.

"What? What is it?"

"Nothing," she said. "It's just—" And the look on her face
traded for another look, a happier look, somehow suddenly
her face was giving the impression of *gleaming*. She said, "He's
kicking. Feel."

She positioned my palm just above her navel. We waited.
In silence we waited long enough that I started wondering how
long I had to wait before it was polite to get back to scraping
burnt penne noodles off our glass casserole dish.

"There," Natalie said, finally. "You feel it?"

"Yeah," I said.

And if it was possible her gleaming increased. She gleamed
more. "Isn't that *amazing*?"

"That is," I said. "It's just sort of like, blump. That's
amazing."

"That's our baby," Natalie said. She was looking at her belly,
but really, she was looking at the baby inside her belly.

I couldn't do that. I looked at Natalie's belly and all I saw
was Natalie's belly. Oh hell, I wish I did think it was amazing.
To Natalie feeling the movements of our little boy seemed to
be up there with a religious experience. Every time it happened
she seemed to feel as though she was being touched by forces
greater than reality. She gave off the impression of someone
who had just witnessed a miracle.

"Wow," I said. "It really is."

It was something in my tone that was off, I think. Natalie held both hands to her belly for another couple of moments. I went back to my penne scraping. And eventually she went back to her sweeping. But a silence existed between us now. For the rest of the night we communicated only when necessary, in one-word exchanges.

Every time I came home, that summer, Natalie seemed to be watching one of the baby programs that inundated the upper numbers of our cable subscription. Every day, it seemed, she came home with a new magazine. Or a book. Or a new developmental toy or a catalogue of kid-friendly draperies or a pamphlet for a line of organic, gluten-free carpeting. Suddenly she was a tourist vacationing through a strange new land, the land of baby supplies, she was skipping through an Oz of children's toys and clothes and she came home every afternoon bearing souvenirs from her travels.

Sometimes they were for me. She brought home a selection of books I was supposed to read: *The Birth Partner* and *The Expectant Father* and a couple of other titles I can't remember. These were guides for new parents, or specifically for new dads, and they were supposed to teach me how best to be a supportive and loving partner in this birth. And those books may do that. They may do that in a tone-perfect, informative manner that incorporates an ingratiatingly subversive edge to their educational paragraphs. I'll never know. I didn't read them. I didn't read *any* of them. I didn't even pick one up.

"I don't understand," Natalie said at one point. "What's the problem here?"

"What's what problem?"

"With those." She pointed to my bedside table, where the daddy books squatted, spines unbroken. "You devour books about anything and everything. And yet you haven't touched any of those. What's up?"

"They just—they're *boring*."

Natalie raised her eyebrows. "*That's* not boring?"

She meant the book I actually was reading: *A History of 20th Century Russia.*

"Look, I'll get to them."

Looking back to this time I can't help but think: What a dick. I should have been excited. Why wasn't I more excited?

"You must be so excited!"

This was my sister, Julie.

It was a Sunday morning in August. Julie and I were out at brunch. She lives next door to me, in an apartment in the neighbouring townhouse, but lately we'd both been so busy we hadn't seen each other much. The setting was one of those hipster breakfast places, where ironic tchotchkes cover the walls and the diners all sit on mismatched chairs waiting for coffees dispatched by hungover servers.

"What's Natalie's actual due date?" she asked.

"Second of September."

She leaned forward. She did something with her expression so she seemed to get even closer. And she said it again. She said, "You must be so *excited*."

"I'm not. Every time I think about it I feel sick."

"Why?"

"I was twenty minutes late getting here? I forgot my wallet? And I'm supposed to raise a kid?"

"Oh, you'll be fine. You'll be a great dad."

Yeah, well: Julie didn't know about the drugs. And she should have known better. Some years before, my sister had gone out with a boyfriend who was insanely jealous. Like, the kind of guy who followed her when she went out for a night with her girlfriends. We had these long conversations where she talked about how sweet this boy was, how the jealousy issues were improving, and then he'd do something insane and they'd have another fight and she'd end up crying on my couch and I'd tell her, "Julie, he's not changing. People don't change."

People don't change.

What if *I* didn't change?

Since Natalie had become pregnant I'd entered a phase where everything was more intense, including my drinking and drug taking. I didn't drink more, necessarily. I drank less frequently but each time I did, I drank more. I made every night out a big night out, and suddenly I was punctuating those big nights out with crack.

If I thought about it, when I thought about it, these nights out made me feel terrible. I'd labour under a layer of guilt like a storm cloud. The cloud stayed up there, dampening the lift I felt from good news. It was strange: Life went smoothest when I was beating myself up about something I'd just done. The redemptive phase was where I felt most comfortable. Once I strung a couple weeks together without a major fuck-up, I'd start to get antsy, and curious about the question—how was I going to fuck up this time? And when I did, in those bleary bloodshot aftermaths, I'd resolve never again to touch the stuff. Certainly not the drugs. Drink less, and quit the drugs, that was the idea.

One day that summer I ran a new electrical circuit from the breaker in the basement up to the bathroom on the second floor. Getting the wiring up there required electrician's equipment, like leader wires and fish tape. To access one of the leader wires I had to cut a hole in my kitchen wall on the main floor of the house. The spot where the hole had to go was right down by the baseboards between the countertop and the refrigerator. The actual hole I cut with a reciprocating saw—that's a really impressive-looking power tool you hold with both hands, a little like a machine gun. Where the muzzle would be there's a blade, a toothed thing that moves forward and back. With me crouched in the corner, the reciprocating saw bucked and skittered while it cut through the plaster and lathe of our antique home. It made a tremendous amount of noise. When I had two sides of the hole cut I looked behind me and saw there was dust and little chunks of plaster and lathe all over the kitchen floor.

Dust masked my face and created a feeling of grit between my teeth. I was three quarters of the way through my cutting when I felt the most intense pain at the top of my head. I would have sworn, usually, in such circumstances I would have dropped f-bombs like the blitz. But the pain had removed my ability to speak. I was speechless with pain.

What had happened was, the bucking of the reciprocating saw created all kinds of vibrations through the structure of the kitchen, including our countertop. The vibration inched toward the edge of the countertop our Kitchenaid cake mixer. This wasn't one of those lightweight plastic electric mixers you hold in one hand, above the bowl. This thing was heavy-duty. It had been a wedding present. It was expensive. It was all-metal and professional grade. It had a stainless steel bowl and three different mixing attachments and above that in a red lacquered housing there lived a heavy electric motor that powered the mixer's flagellation. The thing was so heavy you avoided moving it. When you did, you used both hands. What happened was, my sawing caused vibrations that moved the Kitchenaid cake mixer so far along the countertop that it tipped off the edge. It gathered momentum for two feet straight down. Then it hit the top of my skull.

It was strange. The pain was terrible. I've already mentioned that. I squeezed my eyes shut. I reached up and felt my scalp. There was a lump there. There was the sticky consistency of bloody hair.

And then, too, there was something that was separate to all that. Maybe it was the symbolism, the fact it was a wedding present that caused this awful sensation, but there was also an awareness that perhaps I deserved this. There was a sense, like:

Yeah.

That's right.

That's how I should feel.

AND THEN, YOU KNOW, just to make things *extra* awesome, Natalie's mom turned up. She made the usual noises about sobriety and moved in with Natalie's brother John until she could get enough money together to have a place of her own. Then came the weekend Natalie's siblings gathered for an annual camping trip. I would have been looking forward to getting out of the city—the more distance I had from crack city, the more stable I felt, at that point. Except there was a possibility Natalie's mother might also attend. She didn't, so that was lucky. But then I ended up messing things up. Nothing particularly spectacular. Just the garden-variety domestic discomfort that consolidated the way I'd replaced her mother in Natalie's life as a serious source of sketch.

The camping trip fell on the same weekend as the birthday of Natalie's sister, Jessica. Rituals like birthdays were important for Natalie. She brought cake in a cake dish all the way from home. The present was thoughtful and beautifully wrapped. Providing a perfect birthday was another gift from Natalie to her sister—Natalie hoped to stage an event as special as the ones their mom had given them during the early, sober years. This birthday was a tribute to a once-sober mother—as well as a defiant declaration to the current reality, of difference.

The problem was, Jessica's birthday dinner fell on the afternoon of the World Cup quarterfinal game between England and Portugal. I went off to the nearest small town to find a bar or restaurant playing the game—I found it at a public golf course. Beers out here in the middle of nowhere cost maybe $2, which felt like free to someone accustomed to Toronto prices. Then some bad luck: The match went into extra time, and even after that it was tied and so next it was the penalty kicks, which called for yet another round of drinks. By the time Cristiano Ronaldo put Portugal over England on the final penalty kick, it was 4:15, long after I'd promised to return.

The dinner was a little awkward but all things considered Natalie's silent treatment amounted to little in the face of the usual chaos of the camp dinner. By the time we all got our burgers and sausages and the potato salad on our paper plates everyone was so famished we just tucked in, almost in silence anyway. I had another couple of beers during the meal and so maybe there was a telltale stumble as I tried to help in the cleaning up. Natalie sent me a couple of looks over that part. Then I went to get the cake out and I didn't hold it right, so it lurched against the container's side. "Chris, I'll do it," Natalie said, manoeuvering her and her belly between me and the cake.

I stepped back. Natalie started to sing, and I sang, hell, everybody sang, and Jessica blew out the candles and the cake went back to the picnic table and I started heading there to help distribute the pieces and then, considering the slipperiness of the plates and the fact there was just enough cake for everybody, I opted for a change of plans. Instead I headed off on another errand, transporting all the presents to the picnic table, where Jess was, so she could open them.

"Honey," Natalie yelled, in a tone that didn't mean honey at all. "The presents go *after* the cake."

I stopped. The top parcel got away from me. It fell to the ground.

"What's it matter?" I shot back, but Natalie was already coming over to pick up the fallen parcel. My hands were full. She couldn't really bend over, because of her belly, so she kind of crouched and got hold of the parcel and when she stood back up we both saw the ribbon was muddy. Natalie freed one hand and touched the dirty bit. She put her head down. Even with the dozen beers in me I could tell not to say anything. When Natalie looked up again she said, "My family always does the presents *after* the cake." She gathered herself. And she said, more softly now, "Just sit down, okay?"

We headed back to the city the following afternoon. The two-lane rural road that follows Lake Erie's north shore seemed more appealing than the nearest four-lane highway, and so we headed east along the various concessions and County Road Whatevers of southwestern Ontario. Much of the time we spent admiring the view. The shore was defined by cliffs anywhere from ten feet to a hundred and ten. We went for miles without seeing a building or anything at all really except for the fields of soybean and corn and the occasional farm building, and shacks with handwritten signs like "Antiques" or "Blueberries $1 Honour System." Every so often we'd pass through an area of congestion, which wasn't like city congestion. More like a handful of houses set on a cluster of sandy hills.

"I wonder how much these places cost," Natalie said.

I looked at the place we were passing—a stone farmhouse that shared maybe an acre of lawn with a crooked barn, a parking pad and a couple of hundred-year-old trees.

"We could afford it, I bet," I said. "If we sold our house?"

"Sure," she said. "Except you'd go crazy, living so far outside the city."

"I don't know. Maybe it'd be good for me."

"It might be, you know. It would be like how you grew up."

"We could get a dog."

"You all ate your dinners together, right?"

"Every night at 6 p.m."

"And then your parents put you to bed."

"We got a story every night. Then my dad would lie on the floor in the hallway, next to my brother's room, and read the newspaper until we fell asleep. Or my dad did."

Natalie turned away from the window to look at me. "The first time I went to your house, I saw that photograph of the five of you, everybody in your sweaters, those pastel sweaters? I couldn't get over it. Everyone ate together and your mom made pasta just for me, because you told her I was vegetarian."

I smiled. "I remember," I said.

"The way you all got along together, I can remember thinking, you were like a family out of one of the books I'd read, when I was growing up."

I looked at her. I said, "Well, that was a long time ago." I thought I meant the sweaters—my parents and brother and sister and I were all dressed in Polo sweaters in that painting because that was the style then, back in the preppy '8os. But as our little conversational interlude faded, I wondered whether in fact Natalie understood me to mean something else. My side of the relationship was no longer the model side, the dream side. I wasn't the upstanding, stable component of our relationship anymore. There'd been a time when she saw me, and my family, as a bulwark against the evils of substance abuse. Now Natalie was struggling to create an environment for our child more stable than the one she'd had, with a mom who was around for the dinners and the bedtime stories. Natalie was trying to create for our children the childhood that I'd had. And I was fucking it up.

Here was how I was getting away with it: Natalie blamed drugs for messing up her mother. And, by extension, Natalie's childhood. And now that she was about to have the first of her own children, her husband was back into the drugs. On some level, I think Natalie thought it too awful to be possible. Could it happen a second time, to another generation? Just how cursed a clan could her family be?

-4-

LU$H LIFE

The month before Natalie's due date, I went with another writer, Ben Kaplan, to see the movie *Half Nelson*. In it, Canadian actor Ryan Gosling plays Dan Dunne, an inner-city school teacher whose drug of choice is anything he can get his hands on. Oh, and crack. Mostly crack. The first sequences are particularly great—an alarm clock keens, Dan's in his living room, he's still up from the night before; he stumbles into his bedroom to stop the clock's universal irritant. Oh, the chest stricture I got during the movie's perfect cocaine dialogue. Later, after yet another sleepless night he's all eye rubs and forehead palms while coaching his girls' basketball team and he's so clearly still out of it from the previous night, he's oblivious to his team, dude *yell* at them, shout some plays, get them fired up: *Be a coach*! Hey: You're not paying attention to what's *important*. When the girls lose something like 32–18 I was just disgusted with him. What an asshole.

Some of the shots amounted to kicks in my groin. Dan kneading his brow, thumbing his eye sockets, pinching the bridge of his nose; he's so clearly barely keeping it together. After the game, as he's supposed to be closing up the school, Dan heads into an empty girls' locker room to rock it up. The movie was pretty realistic, I thought. The sound particularly, that wet sizzle like butter on a frying pan. One of the basketball players returns, her dad forgot to pick her up, and she catches Dan—she pushes open the stall door and there he is, stem in hand. The first false note, for me, was Dan's reaction. It got the shame of crack right. He keeps apologizing. "I'm sorry, I'm sorry." But his freakout is a little much. The next thing you know he's on the locker room floor asking this thirteen-year-old to put a wet paper towel on his forehead.

Overall Gosling is amazing. His scruff of a beard, the sheen on his uncombed hair. His blue eyes always changing, they were up, they were down, they were having a laugh, the man has this zip to him and you can see how he's a great teacher and there's some children's book project on the side and yet he's letting the drugs fuck up the best part of himself and at one point I was ready to just leave, it was too—not disturbing, exactly. It was *unnecessary*. I didn't need to see this shit. I *lived* this shit.

"Some people change, Dan," an ex-girlfriend says to Dan. "Some people actually change."

"Yeah, not me," he said. "I'm still an asshole."

Half Nelson made me feel comparatively together. By the end of it I was defending crack against the movie's implied condemnation; the stuff didn't fuck you up *that* bad, I insisted to myself. And Dan, he's fucked up, too. *I* wasn't fucked up. I only did the stuff once every two weeks. Well, *about* every two weeks. And as soon as my kid was born I would stop. Simple.

EVEN THEN THE BIRTH seemed far off. Despite Natalie's hugeness. Which was alarming. Like, literally: you looked at her and you couldn't help but be alarmed. Was it *possible* for her belly to grow any more? I wasn't sure. She looked like an upside-down P with legs and when she exposed herself to the world, or, at least, our bedroom, I visualized what would happen if a sharp point ever prodded her—a table corner, a straight pin. Her belly was stretched so tight it looked like it would burst, less like a balloon than some massive cyst.

There came a moment in the shower when I realized: any second. When I acknowledged for the first time I was going to be a father. I just stared at the tile and wrongness ran over me. I felt like the character in one of those sci-fi films, when the protagonist gets stuck in an alternate reality: No! This isn't the life I'm supposed to be leading! My labour-delivery nurse of a wife recounted stories of babies born at thirty-nine weeks, thirty-eight weeks, thirty-seven. "So stay in contact," she said during a weekday conversation. "Keep your cell phone on."

That's when I broached the topic of Ben Kaplan's stag. It was certain to be a good one. Kaplan was as hardcore as I was. I could always trust him to stay out with me past last call. Often he knew better than I did where the week's after-hours was. In the middle of August the emails were flying among his writer friends. The subject line pretty much said it all: "A massive party event."

"No," Natalie said. "Absolutely not."

"Nater," I said, using the pet name with the descending second syllable. "Come on. Already I told him we couldn't go to his wedding." The date being Labour Day weekend, same as the due date. "He's a good friend. I should at least go to the stag. I'll come home early. I'll keep it to one beer."

"How many times have I heard that?"

"How many times have you had a baby due? It'll be fine."

On the twenty-sixth of August, Kaplan's stag started out a little weird and then quickly grew very weird. It was at the Little Italy second-storey apartment of another writer friend of mine. The turnout consisted of about a dozen writers and editors, music critics, and video producers, and the first moments were the usual battles for one-upmanship—who had just returned from which major cultural festival, and what exotic drugs they'd done there. To escape I went out to the balcony where I found the stag's only participant who wasn't a local. He was a big, blustery type and he introduced himself with a confidence I typed immediately as American. I forgot his name while we were still shaking hands. It turned out he was some distant relative—a cousin? He worked in sales, which I might have guessed, and he'd flown in from Miami a couple of hours before. That was all the information I had a chance to learn before he went inside. By the time I followed him in he was already sitting at the couch, leaning over the coffee table and laying out a line.

A dozen different conversations dwindled to silence. Among this set, doing a line of cocaine was a little like masturbating—something best done alone. In a bathroom, say. It's fascinating to me, how different are the conventions of coke use compared to marijuana. Can you imagine cokeheads going around with coca leaves sewn onto their baseball caps? Political rallies staged to legalize the consumption of cocaine? And yet here was this guy, this guy I'd just met, sitting on the edge of the couch in front of everyone and pouring out what really was an impressive pile of white powder. Without any self-consciousness whatsoever. With an adroit hand equipped with a credit card he chopped out the chunks and separated a single rail from the rest. He produced a bill. There was the roll up, the lean over, the sudden suck-in, and then he sat up. He looked around the room. He held the cylindered currency aloft.

"Next," he said, wiping his nose with his free hand.

There was a pause. The Canadian writers were conscious of everyone else while taking great pains not to look at anybody in particular. Whether *someone* was going to step up wasn't in question. I mean, this was a stag. Drugs wouldn't be the only vice conducted by our band of debaucherous Argonauts. It was just, nobody wanted to be *first*. Judging from the room's frowns, there were some who were thinking, maybe it was too early for coke. It certainly was too early to do coke *in public*. We were a stag at 9 p.m. We were just getting going. Some people had just arrived. Some people were only on, say, beer number *five*.

Muttered justifications filled the room with a warm baritone buzz similar to what fills the monasteries of certain chanting monks. The powdered mound was already tipped out. The coke couldn't get back in that Ziploc baggie. The powder was too fine. The Ziploc was too small. I mean, with the stuff out, with it on the table, there was no sense in letting it go to waste. Right?

What formed wasn't quite a queue. It wasn't that neat and tidy. What it was similar to was that awkward agglomeration of people that forms in busy supermarkets, where the aisles are too crowded, where everybody stands as close as they can to the cashier's chute and then nervously monitors whether anyone else is trying to cut. Between the lucky sniffer's turn with the $20 bill, there was a lot of coughing going on in that room at 9 p.m. on the twenty-sixth of August. A lot of jockeying for position. Some elbowing. Quite a bit of inching forward.

And I was a part of it.

My justifications had a different logic to them compared to those of my friends. My wife was pregnant. She was about to have our kid, our *first* kid. At any second. According to my vow, as soon as she had our kid, I was never again going to be able to do any type of cocaine. In other words, this was my last chance. Here, on the table before me, was potentially the last cocaine I would ever do. In my life! I *had* to do it.

And so I joined that shuffling, jockeying pseudo-line, and I sank into the couch as soon as a cushion became vacant. The stuff provided its usual illusion. The music grew louder and more boisterous. We did, too: cocaine turns Canadians into Americans. With the mound on the table, nobody wanted to risk leaving the living room for what was supposed to be the first spot on our long and eventful evening. We didn't actually leave until the coke ran out. And when it did, we went straight to the strip club. For Your Eyes Only; that was the name of the place where we went, and my memory gets particularly bleary for the two hours we spent there. The only image I remember from that aspect of the evening is a view of the Miami cousin stalled at the podium where the establishment took the cover charge. Most of the fellows already had handed over their money and were inside getting set for the raucous times ahead. Perhaps it was the expression on the Miami cousin's face, or just something about the mood by the entrance, but I moved closer. The bouncer was talking to the cousin. The bouncer was describing how respectful the club was; he called it a "gentleman's establishment." What was the problem? The Miami cousin was pretty turned out. He wore the costume of the summer for the thirtysomething male on the prowl—a blazer over a loudly designed designer T-shirt. On his legs were jeans. Half the guys in here were wearing denim. No problem. Whoops—then I spied them.

I spied them just as the bouncer pointed to a placard fixed to the wall by the cloakroom: "No Open-Toed Footwear." The Miami cousin was wearing flip-flops. He looked down in an exaggerated manner. He spread his hands, palms-up. He tipped his head back and raised his brows. Had he slipped the bouncer a twenty, or explained that he'd come all the way from Florida to come on this stag, maybe he would have made progress. Maybe he could have argued the case that down south, *everyone* went to the clubs in flip-flops. Maybe he could have said it was a case of culture shock. Instead, he did absolutely the wrong thing.

"Dude," he said in a tone that suggested he was bringing the bouncer round to his senses. "This is a *strip* bar."

And it was over. Tree-trunk neck moved behind him to nudge Miami toward Toronto's summer evening. The cousin tried to cajole. He coaxed. He wheedled. Finally he did dig into his pocket to produce his much-used $20 bill, unfortunately still rolled into a cylinder that suggested its previous use. Affronted now, the bouncer signalled to a similarly thick-necked co-worker for some help.

"Okay, okay, at least let me get my friends," the cousin said. One or two others from the stag were still hovering around the entrance. I don't know why it was me he chose. A moment passed between us. He suddenly bore the doleful air of an un-justly imprisoned Dickens character going off to the gallows.

"I think there's a bar around the corner," he said. "Would you tell Kaplan that's where I'll be?"

"Sure," I said. I headed back to the guys. "Ben's cousin, the one from Miami?" I shouted over the music into another writer's ear, seconds later. "He couldn't get in."

"Aww," the other writer said. "That's too bad."

Neither of us moved.

We ordered our beers.

The next dancer was beginning her routine.

We stuck around For Your Eyes until last call. There was some discussion of ending the night. And there was some discus-sion of heading to an after-hours club—something in Toronto's Parkdale neighbourhood. Which do you think I did? The after-hours club was certain to have coke. And it did. While there we also happened upon exactly the perfect accompaniment for any stag: We found a clutch of inebriated women on a stag-ette. And thus, the night ended where it had begun, with a half-dozen par-ticipants of the various stags and stagettes with their feet on the coffee table that had, hours before, held the night's first lines. A short time later the room's east-facing windows allowed in an unwelcome visitor: daylight. How I resented its arrival. Daylight was a consequence. It was a proof of the way I'd failed Natalie. So often a beginning, daylight in this context formed a conclusion—the end of my life as an untamed, masculine man. Along College Street the bakers and the street cleaners were getting their early starts, the pigeons alit on sidewalks looking for booty from the previous evening's drunk and disorderlies, and I passed them all encumbered with self-loathing as well as a more complex melancholy, that this might be the last time I'd feel this way.

MANY HOURS LATER I woke up to a house that felt vacant. Downstairs I found my laptop on the couch, which was a little weird. I tipped open the lid. Open on the screen was a Word document. Here is what it said:

"These are random thoughts but wanted to purge . . ." it began. "Let me just start by saying that I am just incredibly disappointed. YOU ARE BETTER THAN THIS!

"I could go into labour at any time. What if I went into labour last night and you were high on coke? I even explained my fears to you early in the night—that I was feeling vulnerable—You said you were just a phone call away—You're not a phone call away—you are a 'come down' away.

"What kind of father are you going to be if you are willing to go out till 7 in the morning when I am thirty-nine weeks pregnant? What would your friends/family think? Are you proud of yourself? Is this the kind of husband you want to be? Why is this such a temptation for you?

"You said you would not drink for the month of August—hmmm.

"We could have had a lovely Sunday matinee (as we planned), crossword in the park, Scrabble . . . No we can't still do that. I am upset and disappointed and you probably are too—Plus you will sleep late since you didn't get to bed until 7:30.

"You said you wouldn't be out 'crazy late.'

"You are defensive when I insinuate that it is maybe not the best idea to go out partying with these guys one week before my due date.

"You come home and are dirty and sweating and your body is pulsing, you're breathing heavy and fast and crawl into our bed—our safe place that I have prepared to give birth in and for our baby to sleep in.

"We have to deal with your resultant changes in mood over the next couple of days. What if I go into labour in the next few days?

"What if my water broke last night or I started bleeding or there was an obstetric emergency and you were high?

"What would you think of someone who did the same thing. . . . What if your sister was thirty-nine weeks pregnant and her husband was out till 7 a.m. partying? What would you think of him?

"Did you think about us at all while you were out? Maybe before you did that first line? Did we even cross your mind?"

RABBIT, RUN

They made a big pile in our family room, my avowals of abstinence, my apologies, my promises of never again. Oh, and by
the way—what *had* I been thinking? The proximity to the birth
worsened my deed, but it also leavened the consequences. Neither Natalie nor I were prepared to confront the return of my
drug problem at that particular point in time. Other matters
seemed more pressing, such as our impending responsibility
for another human being. Yes, I had used cocaine. That was a
fact between us. But it suited both of us to frame my misdeed
as a one-time affair, a symptom of temporary insanity brought
on by this pregnancy's imminent fruition.

Natalie came around. What really did the trick was my
pledge that things would change once the baby was born. At
that point, we both genuinely believed that. My wife wondered

whether I was having a mid-life crisis. But to say that is to decorate this period with gum-chewing molls in miniskirts, and sports cars with bullet acceleration. Well, I didn't have the money to buy a Porsche, and if an affair might have done me good, might have pulled my attentions from the drugs and the drinking, I was too wasted when I went out. Seduction requires a propensity for rhetorical flourish, in my experience, or at least the ability to string a couple of words together, and by the time 10 p.m. rolled around I was usually too drunk to manage that.

The impending birth of my son loomed for me like a kind of death. That's where this mid-life crisis business might fit. If that burst of carpe diem that strikes men in their 40s is brought on by a confrontation with mortality, several decades on, then my own crisis felt comparatively more serious: the event destined to cause my own little death was about to happen any *day*.

My sister and her boyfriend, Isaac, returned from a six-month-long trip through Southeast Asia. My sister had been bitten by a mongrel dog on a Thai island. They danced to Shanghai techno and ate porcupine in Ho Chi Minh City. In Hanoi they drank snake blood at a restaurant slash butcher shop where an attendant was skinning a cat, right there in the open, next to the reptile cage. Horrible, right? As well as exotic. Natalie and I had never gone on a trip so exotic. In fact, we'd never travelled at length anywhere together and now, it seemed, we never would.

Think of the language we use to describe the act of a male starting a family. So, the buddies say, you're *settling down*. It's a fucking surrender! No wonder we resist the white flag! Greek mythology had it right. The first father of it all, Uranus? He imprisoned his kids underground, except then his son Cronus escaped and castrated the old man. Cronus was no better; he didn't bother hiding his sons. He *ate* them.

There is a practice in society of celebrating those rare cases granted the foreknowledge of impending doom. The terminal cancer patient gets one last party before the pain gets too bad. There are toasts and tearful goodbyes. I wonder whether the blind binges I subjected myself to in the summer of 2006 amounted to an equivalent—my own private send-off for my concluding career as a carefree male.

The due date of Sept. 2 came and went. People called us up or mentioned it when we met them for various social engagements. "No baby yet, huh?" they said. "Not yet," we'd say. "Maybe he's not ready yet," they'd say. And every time, I would think, maybe he knows *we're* not ready yet. I mean, Christ. We were chronically short of cash. And although I had lots of things on the go—feature stories for men's magazines, a book proposal being schlepped around town by my agent, some meetings with a producer in town about doing a feature-length documentary—I didn't actually, you know, have a regular job that provided, like, regular income.

On the seventh of September, a Thursday, I accompanied Natalie to the midwife's so that Natalie could undergo the following fearsome-sounding manoeuvre: a stretch and sweep. It was designed to trigger the onset of labour, and as we rode the streetcar home from the appointment, a contraction struck. Natalie tightened her grasp on my forearm. Responding to my worried look, she shook her head. "It could just be a Braxton Hicks," she said. Which meant, I knew, because they had happened before, a contraction that happened before labour actually was getting going.

We made it to our streetcar stop. I helped Natalie off the steep back steps of the streetcar. She leaned on me for most of the block-and-a-half walk home. After umpteen reassurances

that she'd call me if something eventful happened, I left to do
some errands (dropping magazines off at my agent's, meeting
the documentary producer for a coffee). I called Natalie before
I went home. No painful contractions yet, although she was
having a craving for a slice of pizza. Of a particular kind. She
wanted Pizza Pizza pizza. I returned home bearing the requested
slices. We watched the first half of a Steelers-Dolphins NFL
game. And then we went to bed.

The contractions persisted throughout the next day. They
came and they went. She'd have three, and then two hours
would go by and she wouldn't have any. Otherwise, life pro-
ceeded as normal. Would I fuck up somehow during the birth?
My anxiety was of such a quality that the issue wasn't *whether*
I would fuck up. It was *how*. I had a premonition that Natalie
and I would get in a fight. I had never seen a couple get in an
argument during the birth stories that Natalie watched on the
television. But I could see us doing it.

Friday I tried to get some writing done, couldn't, headed to
the library, tried to get some writing done there, couldn't. Natalie called me around three and asked me to come home.

"Is it happening?" I said.

"I'm not sure. But I just really need you here now."

Soon the two of us were sitting on our couch. We watched
the green digital time display on the cable box in an effort to
time the contractions.

"What is a contraction, anyway?"

"It's a clenching."

"A painful clenching."

"Eventually. Right now it just feels weird. They're like period cramps."

Natalie grimaced. I looked at my watch.

"Nine minutes."

The lights were off. A breeze blew from the back door to the front. Outside through the open windows we could hear the shouts and the engine noise of our oblivious neighbourhood. An incongruity existed between the routine outside and the events in here. I had the sense uniformed officers should be on the sidewalk wrapping our lot line with police tape. Directing traffic. And where were the news helicopters hovering atop their spotlights?

"What actually happens, if it *is*, like, labour?"

"We call Jen."

Jen was our midwife.

"And then what?"

"We change the sheets on the bed. The plastic sheet? That goes under the fitted sheet."

I watched the digital clock flip from a one to a two. It had now been ten minutes since Natalie's last contraction. "What's that for? The plastic sheet?"

"The blood. Mostly the blood."

"Sure. Right. Of course."

More silence. We sat facing one another on either ends of the couch. I squeezed Natalie's foot. Natalie kept her eyes closed. Her hands were on her belly, as though she wanted to prevent it from popping. I think I dozed off.

"Do you want to grab something to eat?"

This was Natalie. I *was* hungry. We decided to go up to Little Italy, to a restaurant we'd always wanted to try: Olivia's. It was a slow walk. Natalie waddled. I held her hand. As we crossed College Street we passed a pair of restaurants, one on either side of the street.

"It feels like everyone is looking at us," Natalie whispered.

Everyone *was* looking at us. Both restaurants had patios, and the patio diners' eyes were fixed on Natalie's enormous belly. We kept walking. Natalie eased into a seat on Olivia's patio. She ordered fettucine alfredo and a Sprite. I ordered linguini primavera with chicken, and, incredibly, in retrospect, a beer. (Seriously, Shulgan? Seriously?) As soon as the waiter left Natalie reached across the table and gripped my forearm. She said, "Woo-*uf.*"

That's what it sounded like, anyway. Her head went down. I went to stand until I realized Natalie wasn't going anywhere. From a half-standing position I reached over the table and squeezed Natalie's shoulder. There was time to sink back into my seat before Natalie looked up. She said, "Whew."

"We should go."

Natalie looked around. She whispered, "We just ordered."

"Natalie, you're having *our kid.*"

"We don't *know* that . . . Just wait. Wait until the next one."

People brushed past our table bearing large objects: an amp, a speaker monitor, a cello in its case. They were preparing for the evening to come. I was, too. I considered whether to take a stand on this one. Should I call the midwife myself? I didn't want my son to be born in a Little Italy restaurant. And then I thought, this isn't my game. It's not my thing. My job is to support Natalie. I wasn't the general in this battle. I was infantry. I was a private. And I would do as I was told.

I waited for my primavera to show up, and when it did, I tucked in with the knowledge that I might not eat again for a while. Natalie didn't eat much at all. "I'm just glad . . ." Natalie said, then paused.

I said, "Another one?"

Natalie's hand found its way to my forearm. She gripped me. I looked at my watch. "Fifteen minutes, this time." This contraction seemed longer. Or maybe it was just that I was having to endure Natalie's fingernails on my forearm. A white silhouette showed on my arm where her hand had gripped. "Okay," she said. "Okay."

"Baby, let's go, seriously," I said.

"It could go on like this for hours, you know."

"Let's go on like this for hours *at home*."

Waiting for the waiter to bring the bill was interminable. Natalie had to stop on the sidewalk in that gauntlet of patio diners but this time no one seemed to notice, maybe because it was too dark. Even at this point, Natalie didn't feel any urgency. She thought we were in for a long night. To keep her attention occupied we talked about getting a movie. We walked a block out of our way toward the video store, where the aisles were so narrow it was tricky for Natalie to wander through the racks, because her belly brushed against the boxes. I chose the Noah Baumbach movie *Kicking and Screaming* and the first season of *Veronica Mars*. Even as I paid for them, the movies seemed like a bad idea. Several times on the walk home Natalie stopped, gave my arm the death squeeze, then continued at a progressively faster pace. We made it down the final block home only with Natalie leaning heavily on me.

Inside the house, we settled in the nursery, with Natalie in the rocking chair where we planned to soothe the baby.

I asked, "Do you want a glass of water?"

"No."

"*Us* magazine?"

"No."

"The light on?"

"*No*. Just sit here with me."

I set myself on the chair's ottoman. I held Natalie's hand. I stroked her thigh.

"I don't like that," Natalie said.

I stopped stroking her thigh. Natalie opened her eyes. She said, "I think we should call Jen now." It took me a minute to find the phone. Once I returned with it, Natalie was standing at the nursery's dresser, swaying her hips from side to side. She made the call. It was a short one. "They're regular. . . . Five or six minutes . . . I'm fine . . . No, nothing." She hung up. "She's coming over," she said.

I realized this was happening.

We changed the bed between contractions. Jen arrived at 10:30 p.m. bearing an oxygen tank and a black bag of other equipment. Seconds later, a back-up midwife showed up to assist, along with a student, who was there to observe. Jen dispatched me to fill a pot with water, to boil the facecloths and towels, a sterilization procedure. It was at that point I noticed the rain. Thunder, lightning, the evening had all the hallmarks of a good September storm and it's an indication of my focus that I didn't consider the possibility this was some kind of metaphor. As midnight hit Natalie's contractions were accompanied with swearing. "Oh fuck," Natalie said more than once. "Fuck. Shit."

I'd installed the new shower just a few weeks before. Now Midwife Jen suggested Natalie take a shower. Perhaps it would ease her discomfort. Natalie stripped down. She got in the shower, yelled for me, and soon I was in there in my boxers applying pressure to the bottom of her back. That was the moment her water broke. Natalie inserted a "mother" in front of her "fucks," and other adjectives besides, and Midwife Jen decided it was time to get her to the bed and suddenly the both of us were shower wet on our sheets that crinkled thanks to the plastic underneath. I went up by Natalie's head, where she cranked on my forearms through each contraction. Five or six passed this way, and Natalie grew more and more alarmed at the pain. She was not in control here. Evolution was the big cheese guiding this process, evolution and instinct and biology and whatever else you called the body's involuntary musculature. What seemed just as bad as the pain of the actual contraction was the knowledge that there was nothing she could do to prevent the next one from coming, and hurting more. Natalie ceded control of her body to biology. Her involuntary muscle system was conspiring to expel our baby from her body, and what was most alarming was how little control she had over the process—she was an audience member watching a storyline that nevertheless came with all the pain of the protagonist's role. And if Natalie, then four years into her career as a labour and delivery nurse, felt alarm at this biologic possession, during a process she had witnessed easily hundreds of times, then I could never begrudge other women for doing what they could to wrest control from nature, through such tools as epidurals and Caesarian sections. I mean, this was crazy. The noise in the room was pretty much a soliloquy of pain. It was Natalie chanting: "Oh fuck, no fuck, Jen, fuck, no no no, oh my God, I can't do this, fuck fuck fuck fuck fuck."

Jen suggested Natalie get on her hands and knees. I was at the side of the bed, now, by Nate's head, offering my arms for her to grip through each pain cycle. It was about 1 a.m. "Can you see him?" Midwife Jen asked me, and for the first time I really went in for an unobstructed view of what might as well have been a crime scene, there was so much gore. I shouted for Natalie's benefit, "Wow, he's right there!" Without being conscious that I in fact could see my boy's head. Then I skedaddled to my old position. Another contraction. With Jen's help Natalie got up into a position they both called the Irish Kneel, she was sort of up on one knee. Jen called me back for another view and I saw what looked like a little fist-sized ball. It was the baby's head! And, wait a second, also his arm! Jen got me to put my hands under there and his fist came out pressed against his face, geez, and he plopped into my palms, slimy, bloody, wailing. I brought him closer. He had two eyes and a mouth and a nose. He had two hands and two feet. And he greeted the world with a roar.

"He's perfect," I blurted, ignorant of cliché, existing for the moment without irony or any other shields. Jen got me to cut the umbilical cord, a process that involved squeezing a pair of snips through what felt like somebody's forefinger. Free of his cord, our little boy now, an individual connected to no one else in the world but through the bonds of love and family. Next was some business about delivering the placenta, the actual sac that housed him in the womb, and one of the other midwives was saying something about burying it in a hole three feet deep under a tree, excellent fertilizer, and neither Natalie nor I were paying attention because now Natalie had the boy, our perfect, lovely boy, and then the midwives went to stitch up the, Christ, the tear in Natalie's vagina and Natalie handed him back to me. So it was that I was sitting on the edge of the bed holding this person, this boy, this crying and flailing creature, aged five minutes and weighing nine pounds and three ounces, twenty-two inches long, with black hair and Asian eyes and huge hands, born 1:47 a.m., Sept. 9, 2006.

So it was that I was holding him as he fell asleep for the first time.

WE NAMED HIM MYRON. Full name: Myron Fletcher Shulgan. The surname actually was the toughest part. Natalie didn't take my name when we married. So back in the early part of our pregnancy there was the usual discussion in such situations about hyphenating our kids' surnames. Natalie really pushed for it. Finally, for what I think was the first time in our decade together, I just put my foot down. "His last name is Shulgan. *Just* Shulgan." Amazingly, it worked. "I saw you felt strongly about it," Natalie explained, later, when I asked about her capitulation. But I still wonder whether she acquiesced because she worried about my lack of interest in all things baby and pregnancy. I wonder whether she hoped giving me authority over the name would increase my ties to the child.

Proceeding now in reverse order we come to the middle name. This was where I wanted to put Natalie's last name. That was where *my* parents put *my* mom's maiden name: Murphy. But Natalie appeared to regard the name's middle regions as some unfashionable suburb compared to the really top neighbourhoods of first and last. So we ultimately used the centre blank as a back-up—a second stringer in case, I suppose, something happened to the starting quarterback. The Fletcher didn't really mean anything. It was just a name we both liked. "Fletch" just sounds cool. Say it: "Fletch." Doesn't it? Fletcher means "arrowmaker." Also cool. Plus, there's the association with the Chevy Chase character in the '8os. And what's cooler than Chevy Chase was in the '8os?

Our chosen name generated no small amount of controversy. "Do you *really* like that name?" whispered a cousin of mine. She wasn't the only one. Plenty of people asked what we were *really* going to call him. "I just want to make an impassioned plea," one relative emailed me, "please think very hard about not naming your child Myron as a first name. It sounds foreign and goofy. It sounds like an old guy. It separates the child from his peers when he has such a name. Think if you were named Rudolph or Hector or something—would you like it?"

Wait a second. Are you kidding me? Compared to a Wonder Bread conformist moniker like Christopher? Yes I would like a name like Rudolph. And Hector? How great would it be to be able to introduce yourself with a diminutive that's a synonym meant for an exclamation of casual indifference, an attitude of insouciance, of devil may care, of come what may? "Heck." And doesn't "Heck Shulgan" sound great? I so can't wait to give that name to my second son (if we have one). "Hector Rudolph Shulgan." Fantastic.

In fact, I never considered giving my son any name *but* Myron. I did it because I have a great association with the name. It's the name of the best man I know: my father.

I love my dad's name. Perhaps because I like my dad so much. I mean, I love him, sure, but I also happen to dig him as a human being. He is a neat guy—a singular combination of hard and soft, of cool and conventional. He is blunt, sometimes to a fault, but he's also a sucker for sentiment. No one else appreciates a good story like my dad does. It doesn't matter what form it takes—a song, a film, a book, an anecdote—when he comes across a good one, he takes some time to appreciate it. I learned my first elements of good storytelling from the sessions he used to conduct during long car trips. I can remember driving north for ski holidays along Michigan's I-75 highway in our wood-panelled Grand Marquis station wagon, one of my dad's hands on the steering wheel, the other pressed against the rewind and play buttons on the tape deck. The aim was to work through a song until we knew and understood every line of every verse. We did it with dozens of songs over the years. Maybe hundreds. But the ones that taught me the most were such albums as the Rolling Stones' *Let It Bleed*, the Big Chill soundtrack and, best of all, Bruce Springsteen's entire oeuvre. Springsteen's 1982 album, *Nebraska*, could choke up my dad like nothing else. Particularly the song "Highway Patrolman," the theme of duty expressed succinctly with its penultimate line: "Man who turn his back on his family, well he just ain't no good." Which sounds weird, here—Springsteen's colloquialisms plunked down amid my narration. But within the context of the song? It rips out your heart.

My dad didn't really have a dad, if by "dad" we're talking about the male figure who is always there for you, as my dad was for my brother and sister and I. He didn't talk about his childhood. He was born in the Detroit neighbourhood of Hamtramck in 1946. His dad was Nikolai—"Nick." About whom I know very little. I recall some mention that Nikolai had served in the U.S. Navy during the Second World War, in the Pacific. That he had a bad time of it. And that when he returned to Michigan he concentrated more on providing himself with alcohol than providing for his family. My grandmother's name was Mary Sozonchuk. She and her family emigrated from Belarus to Canada in the '30s. When she married Nikolai she moved to Michigan, to the Polish burg of Hamtramck, then when the couple split in 1953 she bounced once again across the Canada–U.S. border to Windsor, where she and her two boys lived with her parents. My dad spent his adolescence in the eastern European ghetto that existed around Windsor's Drouillard Road, known as "Ford City" because it abutted a complex of generating stations and engine foundries owned by Ford

Motor Company. Mary died of cancer when my dad was seventeen and from there he worked at a variety of jobs, including one at the Ford Foundry, where blast furnaces liquefied and poured the metal that became automobile engine blocks. My dad's job involved knocking a sledgehammer against recently cast engine blocks to pound off sand left over from the moulding process. With such jobs he put himself through university and law school.

The proximity of others' problems with substance abuse pushed my father farther away from it. He likes a Scotch now and then, but the strongest pharmaceutical remedy he takes is Bromo-Seltzer for the occasional upset stomach. Many years ago, when a skiing accident shattered the sphere in his shoulder's ball-and-socket joint, he even refused to take Tylenol 222s. While liberal on such topics as gay marriage, he is conservative when it comes to drugs. Cocaine? Even marijuana? These, to him, are the realm of the cowardly and the fallen.

My mother also takes a pretty hard line against drug use. Born in 1947, she comes from a conservative background. Her mother is an intelligent sparkplug of British origin, the daughter of the local butcher, who conducts herself with a grace I associate with Queen Elizabeth II. My mom's dad was a fiercely proud Irishman whose family ran a sheet metal shop. The Murphys were small-business men in an auto factory town. My mother, a nurse, was the first in her family to get a postsecondary degree. She interrupted her nursing career to parent my two siblings and I. She did the laundry, made the meals, she packed the lunches, and shooed us to school. My dad also made family his priority. Early in my adolescence I can recall a conversation with him when he divided life into three spheres: family, friends and career. Success, he said, was possible in two, but not three, of the spheres. In other words: focus. He followed this ethic. He worked sixty-plus hours a week in our youth and yet most nights made it home for dinner and bedtime stories. It was friends he cut off. During my youth he saw two or three at holidays or vacations. He had given up friends to concentrate on work and family.

What I wonder is whether fatherhood intimidated me to the extent it did, precisely *because* my dad provided such a good example. Where did he get it? He didn't have an example from his father. I never saw him reading a fatherhood manual. I kept thinking about the time he caught me shoplifting. It was a Saturday morning at Windsor's only real shopping centre, Devonshire Mall. We were pulling out of our parking spot for the highway ride back to Puce when my dad looked over in the front seat and caught me examining something. "What's that?" he asked. I felt danger's buzz. I was caught. "A book," I answered. It was *Prince Caspian*, the second volume in C.S. Lewis's Narnia series. That shoplifting the Pevensies' adventures among fauns and talking lions contradicted the spirit of the Christian allegory was lost on me. I'd just completed *The Lion, the Witch and the Wardrobe*, and my eleven-year-old self hungered not so much to discover what happened next, but to reside once again in that fantastic land where a child's choice could affect the fate of a kingdom. Narnia's paperback editions popular in my youth were wonderful, with ornately painted covers that depicted gleaming swords and shields somehow more real than objects in my own world. Thanks to such covers, these were books I craved to possess. Probably, at some point in the day, I'd begged to go to Classic Books. Probably my dad, a voracious reader himself, had lingered in the new releases while I pushed deeper into the store, where the children's sections lined the rear corner wall—and where I surreptitiously tucked the Narnian monarch into my belt, under my shirt.

My dad executed the four turns that brought us to our original parking spot, and turned off the car once we were in the old place. "You're going to have to return it," he said, without any note of condemnation in his voice. He kept the disappointment he must have felt out of his tone. Nor did he provide me with any additional mission details as we retraced our previous exit path. I considered flight. The Sears at the end of the mall sold mattresses. I could live in the department store, like Corduroy, the bear from the children's story. I seemed locked into our path; in retrospect, the paralysis I felt was not that dissimilar from what would grip me decades later in the Eaton Centre, during the incident of the black Bonhomme.

As we approached the scene of the crime I expected my dad to march me into the store, to request of the cashier a word with the manager. But no: some feet from the entrance he set himself on a wood planter that afforded a direct view into the store. A step or two toward the bookstore's mouth and I turned back toward him. Don't make me do this, my expression said. He just raised his eyebrows and jutted a chin toward juvenile fiction. Avoiding the gaze of the cashier at the kiosk on the store's right side, I tucked the slim spine back into my belt and walked a path calculated to maximize my distance from any appraising adult. I peeled the paperback cover from my perspiring belly. A glance down the aisle and I fumbled to get the book between *Wardrobe* and *Dawn Treader*. No one noticed. Minutes after I had executed my first theft and become a shoplifter, I had also executed my first un-theft. I had also become an un-shoplifter.

My dad's actions struck me, they still strike me, as acts of perfect justice. Police or a scary encounter with anyone managerial smacked of overkill. There was the fact of loss of control, there, too—what if they did something daft, like actually pressing charges? Instead I'd been forced to do something I hadn't wanted. There was the punishment. Returning the book was scary. It also deprived me of the book's possession. "I know you're better than that," my dad said during a long ride home made longer by the silence that filled the car. He never again said anything to me of it.

Perhaps because his relationship with both his parents ended early, my dad loved his three children with an intensity that suggested he feared that our time, too, might be limited. My father's love for his children is the purest thing I've ever experienced. It is an elemental force. It is fierce and it is powerful and it exists without judgment or boundaries. I believe my brother and sister would say the same thing. I don't recall feeling a need to prove myself to my father. Somehow, early on, he just accepted that each of his three kids were basically good. When each of us messed up—and we did—we always felt like we could appeal for his counsel or guidance without fear of harsh judgment.

Regardless of whether the problem was something of our own construction, regardless of whether the problem was caused by asinine behaviour, he responded with justice and a character of impartiality. He may have told us he thought what we had done was stupid, but we never got the impression he thought *we* were stupid. He went to every high school football game either of his sons ever played—a remarkable achievement for a lawyer dealing with the scheduling requirements of trial work.

So long as I could care for my son the way my father cared for me, I figured I'd be okay. I'd be better than okay; I'd be great. On one level, calling my son Myron was a bit of flattery, a bit of tribute. It was a gift designed to honour the best man I knew. But there was also a pragmatic motive. It was a reminder for me—a way of incorporating my relationship with my father into the relationship I had with my son. Naming my son Myron was insurance, a gambit through which I aimed to inject some of the love that went from Dad Myron to Son Christopher into the relationship between Dad Christopher and Son Myron.

MY PARENTS' NUMBER was the first one I called once we cleaned up after the birth. They were so excited they wanted to hop in the car right at that moment.

"Mom, it's three in the morning."

"Good, we could be there by seven."

"No, wait, you need to sleep."

"We won't be *able* to sleep."

"*We* need to sleep. Don't leave until seven. Please."

I left the news on my brother's voice mail. We had a great conversation with Natalie's dad, now living in California, and he sounded as excited as though he'd just won the world championship of whatever. And once they heard the news, Natalie's brother and sister resolved to drop everything to drive up from Windsor the next day. And then I headed downstairs.

"But it's three in the morning!" Natalie protested.

"On a Saturday. Maybe they're still up."

I mentioned my sister lives next door to us, right? I knocked on her door. I went back inside and tried to get them by telephone.

"Oh my God, Natalie's in labour," Julie said before I could say anything into the receiver.

"Sort of. She was. We had the kid."

"Oh my God, we're coming over."

"He's so *cute*," my sister said five minutes later, and then her boyfriend Isaac put the same thing a slightly different way: "What an unusually adorable child." There was some discussion about which of us he looked like. I looked at him. He had a red face, eyes like slits, a crumpled nose. His head north of his brow was squished out into this tubular shape—a result of the squeezing that occurred during delivery, which would disappear after a couple of weeks. It was crazy to compare him at that moment to one of us; he still looked like an alien. Specifically, he looked like the Dan Aykroyd character on *Saturday Night Live*. He looked like a conehead.

My sister leaned in to get a close look. It looked like she was smelling him. "Is there *supposed* to be hair on his forehead?" she asked.

"Sure, it's normal," I said. I turned to Natalie. "Right?"

My wife, the labour and delivery nurse, nodded. "Lots of them have that. It goes away in a few days."

Then came a moment that grew familiar as we displayed Myron to the rest of our family and friends. The process was a little like the examination of a museum exhibit. Remember that at this point, Myron was two hours old. He was asleep. And when he woke up, all he wanted was breast milk. The point being, he didn't *do* much.

"Well," Julie said.

"You guys go to bed. Go to bed, we'll see you in the morning."

They left. And there. That was it. There was no one left to tell, not really. There was nothing left to do. No more preparation. At that point, I'd seemed to have left the province of angst and self-doubt about whether I felt ready. Whether I felt ready was immaterial. It was done. I was a dad. And Natalie was a mother, but then, she'd been becoming a mother for the previous nine months. Mother was a role she grew into as the fetus grew. I had no such luxury. Besides death, is there any other life change that happens so quickly? Myron was born at 1:47 a.m. Pow: I was a dad.

Natalie had Myron in her arms. She set him on the bed. She set out a blanket so its rectangle looked more like a diamond, did a few folds and suddenly Myron was all swaddled up in the soft cotton with only his head sticking out.

"Wow, where'd you learn to do that?"

"Work, duh."

"Is that okay? Isn't it too tight?"

"He likes it, being swaddled. It's supposed to remind him of being in the womb."

Natalie set our son in the wicker basket we'd been keeping in our room in preparation for just this moment. We stepped into each other, so we were side by side looking into the bassinet. We watched our son breathing. The air current made a little whistling sound as he inhaled. Outside rain spattered against the window glass. It was an autumn rain, just cold and windy enough to make us feel glad for our shelter. I put my arm around Natalie. My drug problems, our unpredictable financial situation, my overall absence of any responsibility to speak of: those felt as though they were from another time, the problems of another person—a person who had never felt the thrill of supporting a human being as it emerged from the womb.

"Wow," Natalie said.

"How cute he is?" I asked.

"No," she said. "I was just thinking, I can't believe he came out my vagina."

FORTY DAYS: that's how long Natalie wanted. Although our family of three was much smaller than the one housed in Noah's vast wooden ark, we did pretty much the same thing: we cut off ties from everyone else and floated, solitary. Noah's aim was survival. Ours was getting to know our newcomer. The midwife ordered Natalie to stay upstairs, in bed. I hustled between storeys one and two bearing placemat-covered cookie trays crowded with juice glasses, cut flowers, and the reheated harvest of our freezer shelves.

My first big decision concerned whether Myron should be circumcised. Natalie leaned toward no. As a nursing student she had seen the procedure botched. A doctor used a safety pin to pull the foreskin into the clamp, then cut too much. It was a bad scene. But since I was the one with the penis, she left the decision to me. As though compensating for my previous apathy, I worked hard on the research. I had studies from the American Medical Association. I digested academic reports chronicling the possibility that circumcision affected HIV-transmission rates. And I happened upon the dozens of online communities of hardcore partisan parents who were bent at all costs on protecting every last penis from what they argued, quite often in all caps, amounted to genital mutilation.

I understood their arguments. The more I thought about it, the less difference there was between circumcision and the sort of mutilation that happened to little girls in some parts of Africa. Except male circumcision doesn't damage the male's ability to orgasm. And I was circumcised. And so was my brother. And his son. And my brother-in-law. And *his* son. In fact, as I researched, I discovered my hometown of Windsor, Ontario, had a circumcision rate more than three times the national average—approximately 50 percent of the kids in Windsor get circumcised versus 13.9 percent across Canada. Probably because the town is surrounded by Michigan, which has the highest circumcision rate in the United States, at about 85 percent.

I called up female friends and asked them the sort of penises they preferred. I did the same thing with gay friends. No preference, came the answer from both sides. Penis is pretty much penis. And I spoke to a friend of mine, the only guy I knew who had spent significant years as a sexually mature male in either state. My friend went uncircumcised until he was twenty years old, when persistent infection led to his doctors' decision to go for the pruning. What followed was a period of ten days when he had to avoid, um, arousal. Did I mention he was twenty years old? My friend also described in great detail the hygienic difficulties foreskin presented. Once I read up on *that*, I found my decision fairly easy. I didn't want my son to grow up thinking his penis was dirty. I wanted him to feel about the same thing toward it that I felt toward mine: free-floating affection.

Myron's appointment happened Wednesday, the 20th of September. He was just eleven days old. We went up to Natalie's floor at the hospital. Natalie picked a friend of hers to do it, a pediatrician. Natalie waited in the waiting area. I took Myron into the little room where the procedure would happen. The doctor wondered whether I wanted to wait with Natalie. "Sometimes the parents find it traumatic," he said.

The *parents* find it traumatic? The *parents* aren't the ones getting their penises sliced with a scalpel. I thought: if I'm putting my baby through circumcision, I'm going to put myself through watching him get circumcised.

And I wasn't the only one. Two medical students also watched. The doctor narrated what he was doing as he did it. I had to hold Myron down on the operating table. He was wailing. The doctor pulled Myron's foreskin over a bell-shaped metal clamp. From somewhere else he produced a scalpel and cut around the clamp's edge. Some Polysporin, some bandages, and within a total of maybe five minutes, it was over.

That was by far the most traumatic thing that happened during Myron's first month. Aside from that, it was bliss. No, really. After the first flurry of Myron-showings, I locked the front door. And turned off the telephone ringer. Without visitors, without phone calls, with a baby who slept more often than not, the parents had more time to ourselves than we'd had in months. I left the house once daily; I picked up coffee at our nearby coffee shop, then nipped over to the convenience store to pick up newspapers, books of Sudoku puzzles, and crosswords. We spent significant portions of the day in bed. On the second day, I toted the television upstairs, set it on a chair, balanced the DVD player on top of the both of them and kept the slot loaded: *Veronica Mars, The Philadelphia Story, It Happened One Night*. The crossword documentary, *Wordplay*.

But the most important thing we did was talk. In fact, more than anything else, we talked. During this period Natalie and I got along better than we had for years. We both were relieved to discover that we liked our counterpart's parenting style. We made a good team. Natalie turned out to have a confidence in her maternal demeanour. She just knew how to do things—to get Myron latched for breastfeeding, for example, or the best way to rock him to sleep. She was a no-nonsense diaper changer, a generous provider of breast milk, and, most of all, she impressed me with her capacity to love our child. I think I impressed her, too. I changed diapers, too. I was the game player and the silly noise maker. Even an accidental smile on Myron's part could activate my tear ducts. My usually clumsy fingers grew adept as I threaded his legs and arms through the tiny holes in his peculiarly named infant clothing: the bunting bags, the onesies. Other dads I'd seen held their kids like they were carrying something breakable. Which, give them credit, they were. The point—they looked awkward. But Myron fit into the crook of my arm like I was moulded for him. His skull just fit the space under my chin, a little like the coastline of South America fit under Africa's. He fell asleep on me all over the place. On my chest, as I read a book. On my crossed legs, as I typed on my laptop. Each time he closed his eyes his arms brought his hands up to his face, balling his hands into fists and his fists pressed in close to his cheeks, like a boxer. I could sit for hours with him on me. If I exuded some sort of vibe that encouraged him to sleep, his sleeping self had the same effect on me. Natalie would come upon us all the time, flaked out, on the couch, on the rocking chair. Something about Myron seemed to set me at ease.

We fell in love with these new facets of our counterpart's personality. Natalie fell in love with Chris, the father. And I fell in love with Natalie, the mom. A month after Myron's birth there was an evening that sums up the way I felt throughout this period. It was perhaps 8 p.m. Natalie had dozed off on the couch. I sat at the end opposite from her, her feet on my lap, Myron swaddled into the crook of one arm. He too was asleep. The stereo's playlist shuffled between Okkervil River and the New Pornographers, the volume turned down to a murmur. I was reading the Alison Bechdel graphic novel, *Fun Home*. Something took me out of the story for a moment and I looked around the room. I took in the scene. And for the first time, the part of the house where we were at that moment really did feel like a family room.

-6-

SOMETIMES A GREAT NOTION

Notice I haven't talked about drugs during this time. And I'd
love to tell you they weren't a problem. How simple that would
be, so in accordance with the way we train ourselves to think,
so in fitting with our prejudices about parenting. I had all the
usual hallmarks of a good father. I changed my kid's diapers. I
stumbled into the nursery when he woke up in the middle of
the night. I rocked him in his chair until his sobs grew farther
apart, then disappeared altogether. If I was concerned enough
about my son's welfare to care for him at 3 a.m., then that same
concern should mean that drugs and alcohol no longer held
any allure, right?

I wish.

The birth of my son hadn't suddenly and miraculously
cured my desire to go out and party with a capital P. It wasn't

like that at all. During those days, the desire to do them built up like the steam in a kettle. In fact, it was worse. There were times that Myron was crying and Natalie and I both were cranky and I felt trapped in our little six-room row house. The cry Myron developed in his second week was remarkably effective at grating on my nerves. I mean, that's what the baby's cry was supposed to do, right? Grate on his parents' nerves. The better it does that, the better that cry summons the food and attention the baby craves. Myron had some remarkable crying spells during those first weeks. Some of them were astonishing. I'd look at my baby and be astonished that anything that small could make a sound that loud.

It would be easy to describe my life, then, as a double construction. That would have an insulating effect. It would keep pure my existence as a father, and my relationship with my son. But do double lives really exist? Isn't the notion of a double life a construct that simplifies actual human complexity? We don't want to believe there's good in evil people because we tend to think of ourselves as good, and if there's good in evil people, that means there's also some evil in good people. That held true for me. The fact is, my drug dabbling had progressed too far to be dispatched by any nine-pound mass. I was thinking about drugs and alcohol at moments when I should have been concerned only with parenting. They were the finish line. The relief.

I've mentioned that my sister lives next door, but I haven't fully explained the layout of my residence. I live in the end unit of a row of four century-old brick townhouses. My sister has an apartment on the main floor of the neighbouring unit. Above her lives another neighbour. He's a white guy, maybe thirty-seven years old. He's single. A serial entrepreneur, he works hard developing whatever business he currently has on the go—as I write this, his latest gig is in the telecommunications field. The time before that he owned a Subway franchise. And his social life is a lot like what mine would be if I'd never met Natalie. It's active. Thursdays he hosts a poker night. Sundays are football. And one weekend night, usually, he's out until the bars close, and then he has people over to his place. The music goes until five or six, sometimes later.

I know this because I can hear the music through our upstairs wall—the wall we share with him. One Friday evening during those first days of Myron's life, I was rocking Myron in his nursery. A soft light glowed on the table next to me. Above the crib I'd turned on Myron's mobile, and thanks to the white noise machine that Natalie had bought, the room was filled with the sound of crashing surf. I could also hear various thuds and bumps from the other side of our upstairs wall. It wasn't all that loud. It wasn't enough to wake Natalie, for example. But it was loud enough that I could hear it. I also could hear the shouts and guffaws of drunken men and women. But by far the dominant sound coming from the neighbouring apartment was the music. Specifically, Elton John.

Now, I don't harbour any ill will toward Sir Elton. As I understand, he throws a good party. And I think it's cool he married a Canadian. I like his fashion choices. Anyone who wears that many sequins has to have some guts. But at 4 a.m. on this night in September, I felt very strongly about Elton in a way I never would have expected. The banging and crashing from the other side of the wall stopped as Elton sang about a blue jean baby, an L.A. lady, the seamstress for the band . . .

The party stopped. It stopped so that everyone over there, it sounded like, could follow the song. It stopped so that all of them could sing along. Opposite that plaster lathe, through those construction studs, was a bleary zone where thirtysomething guys and girls were drunk enough to be belting out Elton at full volume. And as I sat there with my baby in my arms at 4 a.m., I badly wanted to be on the other side of the wall, too. I wanted to be drunk. Never before had I wanted to sing along to Elton; now I positively ached to be belting out "Tiny Dancer" along with everyone else.

My house had been overtaken by bottles, by swaddles, by Baby Bjorns and bath toys. These artifacts feminized the home's interior. Look, I know it was baby stuff, and boy baby stuff at that, but decades, hell, centuries of cultural memory that considered babies the rubric of women now encouraged these rooms to feel foreign to me. I felt a little like a beaver regarding the golf condo development that sat on land that had once hosted his lodge and dam. Who was expected to want to live in unit 9A. Well, gosh, thanks, but hey—I liked the old set-up just fine. Hey: mind if I go wander in the bush for awhile? Chew some trees? Our house felt foreign to me. This new *existence* felt foreign to me. I ached to be myself for awhile. To hang with people who knew me babyless as a fully functioning male. I needed to go out and be a man. Be a man, that is, by going out and getting really, really drunk. A bender of Hemingwayesque indulgence seemed the most effective way to assert my masculinity.

And hey, look at that, an opportunity presented itself. Natalie and I received an invitation to a friend's party. It was the thirty-second birthday of a fellow writer, the restaurant critic Chris Nuttall-Smith, and Nuttall's wife was throwing him a little shindig. Natalie and I discussed going. Part of me wanted to bring Natalie. And Myron. We were a family. It would have been fun to get out, all three of us, to have people *ooh* and *aah* over Myron and then get out of there at a decent hour. How appropriate to our new existence.

Except I couldn't bring Myron to Nuttall's party. He and his wife had been trying to have a kid for awhile now, and I didn't want to rub Nuttall's face in my ability to procreate. Oh, and look at that, not bringing Myron to the party meant one of us would have to stay home. But I was Nuttall's friend. So . . .

"*You* go," Natalie said. "I still feel a little delicate, anyway."

"You sure?"

Something flashed across Natalie's expression. Irritation. Huh: she'd wanted to go to this party, too.

"Chris," she said. A word of warning.

"Hey, you know that research trip I have coming up, to New Brunswick? Maybe you guys could come with me."

"What, in exchange for this?"

Of course not, I said, although a quid pro quo was exactly what was happening. The one condition Natalie levied involved me sleeping on the couch, when I came home, if I came home drunk. By this time Myron was spending much of most nights in bed with us. It was easier to breastfeed that way, Natalie said. And she didn't want an inebriated me rolling over on her son and inadvertently suffocating him. Of course I agreed to that stipulation. I didn't want that either. And so, on the thirty-fifth day after Myron was born, I was sprung, I was solo. For the evening: I was free.

(Yeah, good point: we didn't quite make the full forty days. Well, I tried.)

Misgivings existed. As a father I allowed myself to drink. Smoking drugs, however, was offside. Nuttall lived on the east side of town, then, in Cabbagetown. Between my place and Nuttall's it was only a short detour south to Moss Park and the near east side of Queen Street—the land of crack. Did I do anything to safeguard myself from my destructive impulses? Go with a non-drugging friend? Make arrangements to crash on Nuttall's couch? Naw. The only reason for that, I surmise now, is that I wanted to leave the possibility open. The faint possibility. Had I bet, I would have bet I wouldn't have done the stuff. Crack seemed a long way from the existence I'd lived these last thirty-five days. I was pretty firm with myself. Drugs and fatherhood didn't mix. And yet, I went with a bike. I rode my bike solo to Nuttall's, an arrangement that guaranteed I'd leave solo as well.

NUTTALL'S HOME was a post-war two-storey brick home renovated by Nuttall himself into an open-concept modernist domicile, where every framed article and bookshelf advertised its occupants' effortless membership in the intelligentsia. I always felt a bit intimidated in his place, in the way one does when confronted by evidence that another's taste is better than one's own. About a half dozen people already were there by the time I locked my bike to his porch railing. I handed over a birthday present for Nuttall that strikes me as remarkably appropriate, given what I got up to that night: Ken Kesey's *Sometimes a Great Notion*. By that point, it had been years since I'd begun telling people Kesey's second novel was my favourite book. I reread it recently and was alarmed to discover prose full of "hysterical crashing" and a river "like an aluminum rainbow, a slice of alloy moon." And that's just on the first page. Huh—the book I'd gone around for years saying was my favourite? It was terribly written. In my youth I guess I'd ignored the prose in favour of the way the story stands as a study in masculinity. The book chronicles the conflicts that exist around the two stepbrothers in the Stamper family: Eastern academic Leland and his brother Hank, an Oregon logger. Leland represents a tamed, civilized, more sophisticated type of male, while Hank is the rugged, unreformed individual. Both become immersed in a dispute with the rest of their dying Oregon logging town, where most want to unionize. Hank's against it. He won't have any union committeeman dictating what he can or can't do. He's too much a lone wolf, too much an individual. In fact his stubborn streak infects even the perverse ungrammatical phrasing of his motto: NEVER GIVE A INCH!

The novel poses the question whether it's possible to fully exercise one's masculinity within anyone else's social framework. It set up responsibility to others as contrary to a man's responsibility to himself. And it suggests that subsuming one's own interests as an individual is inherently unmasculine. I wonder, now, about my choice of present. Why then? Was the gift an unconscious reflection of the similar struggle then happening within me?

Nuttall thanked me for the book with, I thought, a grimace, an expression that indicated, perhaps, the height of the pile alongside his bed. He showed me toward a punchbowl that contained a Brazilian concoction, a nice segue to Nuttall's recent fabulous trip to South America, yet another place I'd never been. By the time we finished discussing Ipanema and the strange yen toward plastic surgery of already beautiful Brazilian women, I'd transferred three glasses of the stuff from the crystal tureen to my stomach. "Go easy on that stuff," Nuttall reminded me before turning to greet the party's latest newcomer.

A house full of unfamiliar faces loomed. I spied a writer friend, Josh Ostroff, and inserted myself into the conversation he was having with a girl I didn't know. "I'm just saying," Ostroff was saying. "We use North America when we just mean the U.S. and Canada. Not Mexico. There should be a new term that means the English-speaking countries of North America."

I'm making that up. I can't remember what he was saying as I joined them. I handed Ostroff a beer, which he probably nursed, given that Ostroff can nurse a beer like no one else I've ever met. Dude is the world's slowest drinker.

Regarding his conversation partner, the girl I didn't know? Probably jeans, probably a top. Certainly, she wore clothing. But the most noticeable thing about this woman were the Orphan Annie curls that topped her. She bore some of the same girlish innocence as the comics character, although to mix things up her blowsy loops were the shade of wrought iron rather than Annie's strawberry blonde. As I recall she worked as a copy editor at *The Globe and Mail*, where Nuttall's wife worked, too.

Once we exchanged names and occupations there was a pause in the dialogue, which Ostroff filled with a question about my baby—"How's fatherhood?" Which was a natural question, considering this was the first time I'd seen him since the birth. And yet, the mention of my new status did something to me. Now I was conscious of Little Orphan Annie's gaze. It was as though Ostroff had disclosed I worked as an accountant, or a Baptist pastor. The label he'd just affixed to me—new father—had a stereotype to it I didn't want. So rather than talking about the vulnerability I felt whenever Myron acknowledged my existence with a coo, or the novelty of the pride I'd discovered in myself that I'd actually been good at caring for Natalie during her first few delicate weeks after the birth—rather than any of that, I reacted against the fatherhood label. "It's great," I said. Then I reached out and touched the copy editor's curls. "But not as great as your curls—are they natural?"

She flinched, probably at my hand's proximity to her face. This was too intimate a contact for someone she'd known about sixty seconds. She recovered well, though, and replied with a testament to their realness, simultaneously taking a step backward, away from me.

"Shulgan, when did you start drinking, exactly?" Ostroff asked.

"I don't know," I said. "What time is it?"

"Dude, it's only ten o'clock," Ostroff said.

"What?"

"Dude, it's only ten o'clock—how'd you get so *wasted*?"

Hard work! This was my first opportunity to drink seriously in what felt like ages and I was going to use it. There was a sensation of catch-up. Of making up for lost time. As well as the time I was bound to lose in the future weeks of child care and sleep loss. And on top of that, an instinct to overcompensate. Father? Not me. I was *fun*! I was *reckless*!

"I love girls with curls," I said. (Not even particularly true.) "Yeah," I said. "It's a fetish of mine." (What? No it's not!) "In fact," I said, as Ostroff blanched and looked around for exits, perhaps because experience warned him things were bound to get worse before they got better. "In fact," I said, "The girl I was with this afternoon? Well, on the Internet? She was on my computer, as I masturbated? *She* had curls." Perhaps this is painful for you to read. Trust me—it's more painful for me to write it. Gaa! And yet, I continued: "Yeah, there's this website, it's just for guys who like girls with curls, that's where I was. Hey! You should model for it."

No I wasn't. No there isn't! No she shouldn't! It wasn't true! None of it! Well, probably there is a curl-fetish site somewhere on the Internet. And there may have been some veracity to the verb/date linkage of masturbating/that afternoon, since the romance had been lacking since Myron was born. As was natural. But no predilection for kinked hair existed in my catalogue of preferred kinks!

Blackout descended, thankfully, as I'm not certain I could bear the embarrassment of what else I said to the poor girl. My next bout with sentient thought included an awareness of crushed velvet on my cheek. Headache failed to prevent me from recognizing the dim outlines of my family room's furniture. The cable box advertised three minutes after six. Standing made me aware of an ache in my inner right thigh. I investigated by unbuckling my pants, where I spied a bloom of purple and green about the size of a ten-dollar T-bone steak.

The bruise announced itself with each step up the stairs. In the bedroom Natalie and a pillow formed boundaries around my boy on the bed. Jeans and shirt removed, I slid between the cool sheets. Natalie touched my chest. "Thanks for sleeping downstairs," she said.

It felt... nice. Being there with my baby and my bride. I've written about the relief I experienced when I left the house and was sprung from the pressures of fatherhood and family man. Does it complicate matters if I describe another relief, of equal intensity, that happened when I *rejoined* the family? Because that happened, too. That's what was so fucked up about this time. Immersed in family, I craved a respite in debauch. Immersed in debauch's aftermath, I craved a respite in family.

"What time did I get home?" I asked.

"Two, I think."

I nodded. Not bad. Not bad. I woke up several hours later. Say, around nine. When I went back downstairs Natalie was in the kitchen with Myron in her lap. I kissed her. I scratched my head. I asked, "Why is my bike in the front hallway?"

She shrugged.

"You dragged it in last night, when I let you in."

"You let me in?"

"You said you lost your keys. You'd been in a fight, you said, and you lost your keys."

I went out to the front hallway to look at my bike. It rested at an angle joining parquet floor to painted wall, a line Pythagoras would love. It didn't belong in this setting. I kept it locked to the metal frame on our porch. And yet, here it stood, an artifact from an earlier time, and for a moment I played archeologist, attempting to deduce how it had moved here, and why.

Blackouts tell us things about memory, which seems strange—the learning of something from its absence. Had these incongruities not announced themselves, I doubt I would have been aware that I'd lost four hours of my life. And yet, here was a bike I had no awareness of putting there, and a bruise I had no awareness of receiving. Were there other blackouts that didn't leave such incongruities behind, and so passed into history unnoticed by memory? We like to think of consciousness as a continuous spool. But us binge drinkers, we can wonder whether it's not. Whether we all have gaps. Ellipsis. Lacunae. Musical rests in four-quarter time. Perhaps what we consider continuous spools are only illusions, similar to the way a digital audio source of a CD, and its chopped-up, super-fast bits, are able to replicate the continuous stream of analog reality, simply because we aren't aware of the gaps? We think memory is analog—but perhaps it's not. Perhaps it's digital.

My front rim was bent. Most of it looked like a normal bike tire. And then a slice of it was angled off plane, probably sixty degrees. There was no doubt about it: the rim was ruined. After I wrestled the frame out to the front porch, I discovered something else. I looked in my backpack, and around the first floor. Yep, definitely: my bike lock was gone, too.

Like Lt. McNulty on a homicide, I interviewed the witnesses. I called Nuttall. After the usual apologies, I grilled him about the evening that passed. Once the party started breaking up, he said, a few of us went to a bar, a place called Ben Wicks. Later, once I found a credit card receipt from the place, I had a flash of me there, waiting for a beer at the bar. There was an image of Nuttall's wife giggling at something I said, although possibly it was at me, and how drunk I was.

"What time did I leave the bar?" I asked him.

He thought about it.

"One a.m.?" he guessed. "Shulgan, if I'd known you meant to ride your bike home, I'd never have let you go."

I almost didn't hear that bit. Can relief roar? It may have, that moment. The bruise, the bent rim, the missing bike lock, the existence of a blackout so black. Many might be disturbed by such details. Not me. I was relieved. And even that might be understating things. I was almost exultant. I'd worried whether I smoked crack. With my history, I figured I'd probably had. But the timeline made it unlikely. Between the time I left the bar (1 a.m.), and the time I arrived at home (2 a.m.), there was only one hour. One hour for me to stumble back to Nuttall's house and retrieve my bike. One hour for me to fuck up my bike, fuck up my thigh, get home. The timing was tight. Too tight. Surely the timing meant I hadn't bought drugs. I hadn't smoked crack. I hadn't had *time*. My vow to quit drugs with Myron's birth was unbroken.

THE FOLLOWING Tuesday evening, I volunteered to try to get Myron to sleep. He was basically freaking out when Natalie handed him to me. Five minutes after she went downstairs for her respite, the boy and I had a moment. He made a sound mid-sob, like a hiccup, and when I looked down to check on him he seemed to be watching me. Did he realize, at that point, who I was? Naw: I'm sure he didn't have a concept for father, not yet, but I think at that point he realized *something*. How dadlike I felt, having been present at such an early epiphany. He was asleep some seconds later.

Once I set Myron down in his crib, once I'd checked that the baby monitor was on, once I got the doorknob closed without it clicking so loudly that it woke him, I basically floated down the stairs. Natalie was folding laundry. The TV was on. It was *Dancing with the Stars*. I joined her in both the watching and the folding. This was the year that Mario Lopez was a contestant. Mario Lopez and his partner were dancing. I remember having my hands in my pockets and standing and watching, torn between a desire to go up and read in bed or to spend some time with Natalie. And then at some point I must have removed my hands from my pockets. I rolled something between my thumb and forefinger. It felt like a pebble. At some point, I looked down at this pebble. I jammed my hand back into my pocket. I looked at Natalie. She was watching Mario Lopez.

"Do you want something to drink?" I asked Natalie. She didn't. I went into the kitchen. Behind the fridge, I pulled my hand out and looked at what I just found in my pocket. It looked like a large, uncultured pearl. I touched the tip of my tongue to it. The telltale numbing. I leaned against the kitchen counter. I stared at the opposite wall. I should mention here I don't have many pairs of jeans that I like. I tend to have one pair I *really* like and I tend to wear that pair for long stretches at a time. I must have been wearing these jeans Saturday night. There was no other explanation why there should be a piece of crack in them. Somehow, that night, against all probability, I had obtained the rock. Quite a big one. And somehow, it had stayed in my pocket, undiscovered, like the unexploded ordnance British schoolchildren found after the Second World War.

The little rock might as well have glowed for the way it illuminated recent events. Up until my faux-geologic discovery, I'd sought to explain the few flashes I'd had from Saturday night with one of two theories. The first, that I'd bent my bike rim myself. Wobbly me weaved my two wheels into an unforgiving surface, a parked car, a parking block. I'd walked the bike for a time, then flagged a cab. Easy. Occam's Razor suggested this one. Except it didn't explain everything. I'd told Natalie I'd been in a fight. I had an image of me wielding my bike lock. So: scenario two. Perhaps someone else had bent the rim. Perhaps, upon colliding with something, a witness attempted to wrest the bike from me. In the ensuing struggle belligerent me threatened somebody with the bike lock. Which I subsequently lost.

The pocketed crack suggested a third possibility. I'd clearly detoured south from Cabbagetown, to Moss Park. I'd clearly procured crack. The proof was in my pocket. Had I somehow managed to procure the crack without cash? The credit card receipt suggested I didn't have any money. But getting crack out of a drug dealer without money is approximately as likely as getting type AB from volcanic igneous; that is, blood from a stone. Perhaps I just hadn't paid enough. Or been too drunk to figure out how to pay. Whatever had happened, there'd been a dispute. Somebody kicked me in the thigh. Wielding my bike lock got me out of the situation. I'd dragged my bike, flagged the cab, gone home—and my drunk self just plain forgot to smoke the crack.

Wow. An equipped drunk with a drug habit forgets to smoke his stash? You *know* he's wasted.

From the fridge I retrieved the evening's third beer. In the family room I slid onto the couch, next to Natalie. Once I finished that beer I had another. And another. This was a scene of what should have been domestic bliss. Watching TV with my wonderful wife. Folding laundry as my baby boy slept upstairs! In a fugue of my own creation! This was an evening the likes of which indicated success. We were doing it! We had this thing down cold! We were being parents, and not bad ones at that! And yet: *five* beers, Shulgan? And yet: I was setting excuses. For example, I smacked my lips. I said, "We have any chips?" And: "Maybe, it's ice cream I feel like." Knowing well we had neither, knowing the consummation of uttered desire would spring me through the front door.

"Are you coming to bed?" This as Natalie packed piles of half-folded boxer shorts on onesies on sleepers on tiny socks. Of course I wasn't. I was going to get something. Why couldn't I go upstairs with her, to spoon her to sleep? A little affection was just what she needed. She, too, was feeling lonely. She, too, had to feel confined in the pressures of parenthood. But no.

The local 7-11 didn't have the required equipment. The closest Asian convenience store was closed. Turned out I had to sprint all the way to Ossington to find a bodega whose cash counter included the proper display of ginseng syrup vials. I bought two. Usually I didn't buy the vials with a lighter, figuring to avoid the embarrassment, figuring the store clerk could determine what the white boy was up to. But on this night I didn't have time. The purchase ate the better part of a five. I sprinted the seven blocks home and had turned up my street before I remembered I should buy ice cream as well. Breaching the front door with my booty, I tried to be quiet. Natalie was a light sleeper. Would she wonder why it took me forty-five minutes to go to the corner? Perhaps I'd met someone. Perhaps the old Italian man from down the street had accosted me, as he often did, and subjected me to one of his harangues in which I nodded frequently to disguise the fact I understood perhaps one word in ten.

I had a thing about smoking crack in the house. I never did it, nor had I explored why I didn't. It was more complicated than simply wanting to avoid getting caught. It had something to do with sullying my domestic domicile with a side of myself I didn't want to acknowledge existed. Here was another sign what I thought of as a habit I controlled was once again growing into something more serious. My walk to the basement was interrupted with a shiver. Despite my seven-block run I felt a bloodless cold similar to the onset of pins and needles. Our basement is a windowless chamber divided into three sections, the furthest of which was my office, an area Natalie called the dungeon, for its dank air, which suited me for its distance from the rest of house. I could write there knowing I wouldn't be disturbed. The distance could also serve other purposes.

I bit off the soft metal top and emptied the sweet syrup in the laundry bin. I never kept the crack pipe because, as you'll recall, each bout with the stuff was supposed to be my last. This meant I'd made lots of crack pipes over the years, and I'd come to take pleasure in the ritual the task involved. With practised adeptness, I poked through the vial bottom. Now it was a fat little irregularly shaped glass straw, about the dimension of half a cigar. Creaking somewhere above in the house stilled my movement. Natalie? No, it sounded as though it was my sister next door. The cable wire entered the house in the basement and led to the cable modem on my office desk. I unscrewed the wire from the modem and unwound a length of black electrical tape, which disguised the numerous times I'd harvested screening from this wire. Scissors helped detach shielding from cord. Working faster, now, I burned off the chrome, then pushed the mesh into the vial top's narrow opening.

First there was the anticipation because that's part of it. With my fingernail I pinched off a bit of the rock, a small chunk the size of the Pop Rocks candy that, when you put it into your mouth, sounds a bit like heated crack. The lighter's flint cylinder pressed into my thumb pad as I flicked it once, twice, then held the flame under the screen, heating up the metal fibres, counting to ten to be certain my anticipation didn't rush the process. The heated mesh I pressed against the pinched-off bit. A glance at the vial's end revealed the crack rock melted onto the mesh. This next bit required some coordination; bringing the glass vial to lips, and the flame maybe a quarter-inch from the vial's opposite end, I inhaled, sucking the flame onto the rock and the melting rock into the pipe mesh. A wet sizzle signalled the rock's sublimation from solid to the smoke I sucked in, in, in. The pipe heated up if you kept the flame on it too long. I've burnt my lips to blistering thanks to that. Same with thumb and forefinger. Other times, the heat cracks the glass of the pipe and there's the pain of interrupting the chain-smoking to make another. So I didn't keep the flame on for the whole of the inhaling. I flicked the fire back and forth across the mesh, on and off, flirting with the flame and the rock and the crack as I sucked. The sweet chemical perfume of burning cocaine. I seemed to rise with the inhaling, as though the substance I sucked was lighter than air, as though I was a balloon inflating with helium. The heart pounding apparent at half capacity and growing worse as my lungs filled and by the end my diaphragm was expanded to superheroic proportion, tense like a Charles Atlas pose, every muscle in the torso stretched and out and on and finally I took the pipe from my lips. Hold, hold, hold. A flashing instant when reality flickered into non-existence. And exhale, a long, slow puff of thick white smoke.

Crack is all about that first breath. It's about the rush of the actual action rather than the high you get from it. The high is pretty good. It's fine. Imagine a great mood and that's pretty much what you get. Don't get me wrong—that's pretty nice. But it's the action that distinguishes this drug from any other. It's the smoking, the taking, as though ecstasy was all about the swallowing, as though coke was all about the snort, as though mushrooms were all about the chomp chomp chomp. Oh, and then: more please. I parcelled it out. With my eyes on my watch I separated the doses with time, five minutes at first and then as my self-control evaporated I was lucky to make it to a minute. Maybe 20 minutes later I conducted my last smoke standing above the toilet in my basement, in, in, in, I dropped the pipe into the toilet and flushed and *exhale*, my last one ever, I promised myself. Oh, I considered heading out for more. But this was only a $20 rock, and the inconvenience was pretty extreme. Now I faced maybe an hour or two of self-loathing before I'd be able to get to sleep. That was a taboo that still stood—I would not crawl into the sanctum occupied by my wife and child while in the grip of a crack high. (Big of you, Shulgan. Big of you.) To distract me from my self-loathing I got out my journal and pen and began writing. Every so often I put my finger to my carotid artery, to check the pulse, measuring in ten-second increments and multiplying by six. I recorded the number in the journal's margin, vowing to write out this bizarre tale until my pulse was back into its normal range. When I started the writing my pulse was above 120. An hour later it was seventy-one.

Bed.

7

ROCKBOUND

Look, it sounds like crack was the problem. You drop an issue like crack into a story and the story becomes all about crack. Crack was *a* problem. Clearly. But it wasn't *the* problem. It was symptomatic of the problem. The problem was the paradox, the glitch, the incongruity I had in this idea called man. Not that I was thinking much about paradoxes at the time. I didn't do much thinking about my situation. Most times, whenever I was sprung, whenever I had time to myself, it was self-annihilation I pursued rather than self-knowledge. There were other things on my mind besides self-analysis.

For example: October. Natalie called me home from the library. Myron had been fussy, we called it, for much of the afternoon, and she needed a break. "Just let me go for a walk, around the block, to clear my head," she said. And then she was gone. *She was gone.* But wait a second. I didn't have the necessary equipment for the task she had set me. I didn't have *breasts.* Christ, could he wail. My kid's in distress. Do something! Somebody, do *something!* With my boy in my arms we wandered from living room to dining room, back through the living room, then a wing around the kitchen. Repeat. Myron in these moments was the living embodiment of my failure as a parent. Dude was dangerous. I couldn't stop him from crying. I had him face up to me and his face rouged and his brow furrowed and every muscle he had was hard with strain and anger and Christ the little guy could writhe, you really had to keep tight to him as he twisted and arched and maybe if I, wait a second, huh, that works out nicely—he seemed to fit in okay on his belly, my hand running up through his legs, my palm spread out on his chest, I could almost handle him one-armed, a little like a running back with a football, bouncing to the dining room to the living room to the kitchen, wearing a groove into the floor, but, owp, he's tearing up again, these crying jags as cycles that progress from sob to tears to wailing to full-blown white-hot rage and then coughing, Christ, it's almost regurgitation that comes from this anger, and then a sigh, and then he's calm.

Upstairs to the rocking chair. I cradled him with both hands, I got him into a bit of a swaddle, not the tight rope-binding exercises in which Natalie was able to constrict him but a fairly decent full-body covering all the same, and we rocked forward and back, my toes just pushing enough to give us the required momentum, and still he pushed against the cotton fabric like a baby bird escaping an egg. Forward and back. Counting helped—counting *anything:* the swings of the rocking chair, usually, although sometimes it was how frequently I made the trip from my bedroom to the nursery and back. His cry moved into a range I hadn't heard the human voice reach, wow, how'd that sound even come from that little chest cavity? What's the quaver Tiny Tim sang in? Falsetto? Something like that was going on here, a waver between tones not unlike that used in certain industrial alarms or automobile security signals, the sorts of noises unleashed on the world for the express purpose of maximal irritation. Didn't they pipe baby cries into the cells at Guantanamo? If they didn't, they should have . . . He hit it once every cycle, only for a few seconds, thank god, because it is quite literally unbearable, you hear it and the unwilling reaction is to turn to the side and tilt your head as though that makes the tone less likely to penetrate the aural cavity. In my head, it seemed, there was a rattle and somehow the noise reached into my head and *shook* it. Myron's cries were so powerful they yielded in me a physical response.

In the rocking chair, now: forward and back, forward and back. Thirteen, fourteen, fifteen . . . He wore a fresh diaper. Nate said he wouldn't take food. I checked for biting insects or noxious substances or small edged implements hidden within the folds of his skin. Naw, what was causing this displeasure was existential angst of some sort, this kid genuinely just seemed to find existence unpleasant, life was a punishment to him and he would wreak revenge by making our lives unpleasant so long as he was around. Here, I imagined him calculating, was my vengeance for you causing me to exist. The discomfort of enduring a baby crying compared to the physical sensations during the final few kilometres of marathons. Forward and back, forward and back, thirty-seven, thirty-eight. . . .

Natalie returned. He latched onto her breast and snuffled for some minutes before falling into a troubled sleep. He'd be silent and then out of nowhere he'd startle, his eyes opened wide, he'd crumple into displeasure at the realization that he's alive, and he was *angry* about it. "Those fuckers!" he thought. "I *am* alive."

Natalie raised the prospect of colic. My initial reaction was relief.

"There's a name for this?"

A name suggested there was some cure. Right? If it's been diagnosed.

"Wait," I said. "What is colic? Like, what's it caused by?"

"They don't really know," Natalie said.

"Well, what is it?"

"Yeah, that's what I'm saying, they don't know."

"Well, babies who have colic, what do they have?"

"They cry incessantly. Like, without stopping."

"But what *causes* the crying? What's the underlying condition?"

"There is nothing else. That's it. Incessant crying, colicky baby."

"That's ridiculous," I said. "That's just a circular definition."

"Some people think it could be gas."

We discussed possible cures for this gas issue. I went out and got something called grippe water, which smelt faintly of dill. Some of it dribbled down his chin. Did he swallow any? I have no idea. But in the days that passed, Natalie went to her doctor and her doctor brought up the possibility that the colic was caused by something she was eating—something getting to him through her breast milk. "Like what?" Natalie wanted to know.

"Well, it could be dairy," the midwife said. "That's one possibility." And so my vegetarian wife who received protein only through the consumption of dairy foods like cheese and—well,

no, pretty much at this point that was the only way she got any
protein. And yoghurt. And now the midwife was telling her to
eliminate both from her diet. Well, okay. Suddenly we were eating a lot of beans. Lots of lentil-salad lunches. Natalie found
this whole grain that had protein in it, quinoa, like keen-wah,
and suddenly we were eating exclusively this stuff that apparently grew only in certain isolated mountain valleys in the An-
des. Sure, it helped Natalie drop the baby weight. What it did
not do was affect the baby's crying. After every evening of 2
a.m. crying jags Natalie went back and parsed her diet for of-
fending morsels. Ah—she slipped up and tipped a dollop of
milk into her 6 a.m. coffee. Or perhaps it was the jalapeno that
somehow got into the cheeseless burrito.

Sometimes I participated in these detective sessions.

"Those corn chips?" I shouted, in a raised voice, in Myron's
room, as the twelve-pounder wailed in Natalie's arms. She
handed him over to me.

"I doubt it. You think it could he hummus?"

"When did you eat hummus?"

"At lunch. When I was out with Amy."

I sat down in the rocking chair.

"Well, why the hell did you go and eat hummus?"

Back and forth, forward and back. Later the same evening I was in the rocking chair and back at the counting: one
seventy-two, one seventy-three. Natalie left the bedroom and
shut the door, to keep the cries inside. She headed down the
hallway, then down the stairs. My wife was so exhausted she
slept on the couch. Because Myron and his wails were too loud
to let her sleep in our bed.

Can I disavow that little shiv about hummus, one paragraph up? These were hard times. We were sniping at each

other. Other times, I wondered whether the kid's crying maybe, perhaps, just possibly, had nothing to do with my wife. I failed to see any cause-and-effect relationship that linked Natalie's diet and the kid's tears. The fucker just wailed. His default setting was wail. He woke up wailing and he fell asleep wailing and even his sleep contained sobs.

At the time I was reading Lionel Shriver's novel, *We Need to Talk About Kevin*, which is a remarkable and remarkably well-written work of art about parenthood that I recommend all new parents never read. Burn it if somebody gives it to you for a present. Don't even pick up the back cover to scan. Forget I even mentioned it. Also avoid *The Omen* and *Rosemary's Baby*. And also miss the copse of similar thrillers that have come out more recently, such as *Orphan*. Anything that contains the theme of evil child born into the world. Look, I know there's all that cultural opinion about the cuteness of babies and how adorable they are, but when you and your sleep-deprived self are stuck in a rocking chair with a bundle of anger at 5 a.m. and your wife is sleeping fitfully a floor below, on the frickin' couch, because she can still hear the kid in the bedroom, then your mind starts to wonder some strange things. They call them defenceless. But that's bullshit. Evolution has armed them with weapons as powerful as sabre teeth and adamantium claws. Who's that X-Men character, the Banshee? Armed with a wail that can inflict 6d12 hit points of pain? Well, how's this for a super power: my kid's cry could drive his mother *insane*.

Two hundred and eight.

Two hundred and nine.

Holy fuck! Just go to sleep, child! And if you've tried everything, if you've spent hours walking your home's upper floors, if bedsores develop from the time you've pressed your ass into your rocking chair, then you find that frustration creeps into even the most devoted parents' mind, and you started to understand the instincts of those maligned babysitters found guilty of terrible things to otherwise defenceless kids.

Three hundred and forty-three.

Three hundred and forty-four.

Colic. Don't talk to me about colic. The word means nothing! Just to spread the frustration around, just to give my baby a break, I spent some of those late night hours directing rage and various other bilious emotions toward whatever doctor invented that well-rubbed chestnut.

He's crying uncontrollably? The lady at the park asks, then suggests, maybe he has colic?

Which, translated, means: "He's crying uncontrollably? Maybe he's crying uncontrollably."

It doesn't make sense! They asked whether we'd tried hot compresses? A soother? A Portuguese widow down the street suggested a little rum. We didn't try that. Although I was tempted. We tried everything else under the fucking sun. Did I mention my wife was starving herself?

Is it possible waiting to have kids until after thirty is not the brightest idea the world has ever seen? We're so together by that age, supposedly. We took the time to put the headphones on the pregnant bulge and to read the nighttime stories in utero, and if we did all those things we expect the baby to be perfect because we've been perfect, and then the baby isn't, no baby is perfect, they're frickin' babies, they don't know shit. And so when they wail uncontrollably for nineteen-fucking-hour stretches, perhaps we're just not prepared for it. Do I have a lot of rage? Yes, I have a lot of rage, I'm sorry.

But wait a second. You weren't perfect. You're *not* perfect. And maybe *that's* it. Maybe it's you. Maybe the kid knows.

The kid knows!

The kid knows what a fuck-up his daddy is!

Listening to the banshee's wail, it's like you get so . . . clenched. Muscles in your face tense up. Your torso clenches. Maybe the angle your head usually sits at skews a little bit, and sooner or later you're looking like some Dr. Jekyll / Mr. Hyde bullshit, after an hour of the eardrum busting it's difficult to deny you're in some sort of altered state. Has anyone done any research into this? The physiological responses to baby cry? Somebody should.

Death by baby wail. What a cruel and unusual punishment *that* would be.

Four hundred fifteen. Four hundred sixteen. We spent a weekend at my parents' house. Early in the visit the cleaning lady was working on the next bedroom when Myron had one of his fits. "That baby—something's not right," the woman told my mom.

"Yeah," I said, when my mother told me. "We wonder whether he might have colic."

YEAH, THERE WERE other things on my mind besides self-analysis. But every so often, something happened, some glimmer that suggested: dude, you're fucked up. That the paradox existed. These glimmers happened during a series of trips we made beginning in November 2006, when Myron was about ten weeks old. The first happened because the men's magazine where I was a writer-at-large assigned me to cover a trial in a New Brunswick fishing village set on the Bay of Fundy. The

trial was set to last a week. Natalie balked at being left solo in
Toronto with our wailing whelp, our mutual bundle. And at
that point, we had a little extra cash for the plane ticket so we
figured we'd make a getaway out of it. A vacation.

Ha! No vacation was a vacation when you bring along a
ten-week-old baby. Particularly when that ten-week-old baby
was the Colic Kid. Factor in the fact there wasn't much to do in
November in the village of St. Andrews By-the-Sea. This was a
Maritime fishing village sustained in the summer by the tourist
trade. Off-season, there was a commercial strip papered with
the words "Closed for the Season." I was at the courthouse
from 9 a.m. until about 4:30, covering the trial, and since I was
waking up at 4:30 a.m. to type up my notes, I was pretty bushed
in the evenings. Meanwhile, Natalie was bushed all the time.
To try to give Natalie a bit of a break I went for long walks with
Myron. This was something I didn't frequently do in Toronto.
I'd tried. Walks were one of the suggestions people gave to
beat the colic, and so once or twice I loaded my boy into the
stroller in his onesie and his bunting bag and, huh, hey, yeah,
look at that, the sidewalk expansion joints set up a drum beat
that soothed the savage beast. It was to Kensington Market I
went, the first time, one of my favourite places in Toronto. It's
got a reputation as a hipster enclave but it's more a sprawling
oasis for countercultures of all sorts. Before the kid, I went
there once or twice a week, to drink at Ronnie's, buy steaks at
European Quality Meats or Montreal-style bagels at My Market Bakery. And yet, on this trip to my favourite haunt, as I
pushed my stroller past heads of all kinds, I started feeling a bit
strange. Shopgirls in the second-hand stores watched as I strug-
gled with the stroller to navigate paths through their clothing
displays. The skinheads outside the anarchist bookstore, the

potheads outside the head shop, the baseheads outside the soup kitchen, they dismissed me not with a gaze but the absence of any recognition whatsoever. I wasn't *worth* being recognized. Apparently I no longer belonged there. The next time I took Myron out for a sedative walk I avoided Kensington and went south, to Queen Street, which turned out to be worse than Kensington, so far as hospitality to new parents went. (Bear in mind this was a few years ago—the whole world's become a lot more baby friendly since then, including Queen Street and Kensington.) Back then, Queen Street was so inhospitable to babies the shopkeepers frowned on babies even in the *baby* shops. Natalie was with me, once, as we walked along Queen. At one point, she'd wanted to go into a shoe store. I pushed the stroller in among the displays like the captain of an ocean-going freighter. The shop clerks all seemed to be about fifteen years old. And maybe I was imagining it. Maybe it was the fact it was closing time on a Saturday night. "Can I help you *find* something?" asked a clerk in a keffiyeh, and the emphasis on *find* implied that rather than being in the act of finding, we were in fact doing something else—wasting his time, perhaps, or invading the store with our establishment parenting. The shame I felt was similar to going to the mall with my mom in my mid-teens.

"Let's just go," I hissed to Natalie when the clerk was gone.

Walking with Myron was a different experience in St. Andrews. Our cottage, the so-called Red Cliff, was a romantic little cabin at one end of the main, bayside stretch, decorated in the Nantucket style, that is, sided with cedar-shake shingles painted burgundy. A deck encircled the side that fronted the bay, and if you set your elbows on the railing at the right time of day you could look straight down into salt water. The place's best feature was the fireplace, set in the middle of the home's divided square, with openings facing into the single bedroom and the living room. The smell of burning logs hit me as I entered the front door after a day at the trial I was covering. Natalie and Myron were asleep on the couch as I came in, and I studied them a moment in the afternoon sun. Myron's face peeked out from the wrap slung around Natalie's neck. His conehead was gone. He looked like a cartoon character, these days, with his dashed, dark eyes. Maybe something out of Tintin. As I leaned over to kiss him those eyes opened; my tie had tickled his face. Natalie's eyes opened as I straightened. She looked down at our yawning boy.

"Oh," Natalie said, disappointed. "He just fell asleep."

"Stay there, I'll take him out for a walk."

I traded my hard shoes for runners, my suit for jeans and a hoodie. When I returned to the main room Natalie made as if to unsling the wrap so I could wear it. But I wasn't ready for the wrap. I understood the theory of babywearing, that it was better to pull the infant to your skin rather than keeping him away at arm's length, as happened when you transported him by stroller. But to me the wrap felt a little too much like bondage. I felt the same about those baby backpacks. I thought they looked ridiculous on men. The effect was similar to castration; the male baby wearer might as well have worn a T-shirt, *I've been fixed.*

"I thought I'd take him in the stroller."

"Bring the rain cover, then."

"Why? It's not raining. Have you seen it outside? It's beautiful."

"It's windy. And it could start raining any minute."

And just like that we were on the verge of a fight. My impulse had been for a quick jaunt and the apparent requirements of element protection were delaying things. I put him in a bunting bag and when I went to move Myron toward the stroller Natalie handed me *another* bunting bag, this one with a nylon shell. Christ.

"Thanks for this," she said, softening. "He's been crying most of the day—I think maybe it's the garlic from the tomato sauce?"

It was nearly five by the time I breached the front door, and nearly dark. Dusk lent a warm glow to the surrounding homes. In Toronto the streets would be clogged with rush hour's effects. Here, on the shores of Passamaquoddy Bay, things were deserted. One could hear a single car from a range of several blocks. My boy squawked. I lifted the portal in the rain shield and recorked his mouth with the soother, a new addition Natalie acceded to only reluctantly because it seemed to help with his colic. Er, his nonstop crying. Car gone, mouth corked, the only sound was the wind, the bay's distant bell buoys, and the whisper of the dead leaves I disturbed in the gutters.

It was a straight shot of a few blocks along the main road from our house to the downtown strip, and soon I was lingering before shop windows. The off-season tourist town felt like the early scenes of a zombie movie. Post-apocalyptic. I had the sense it existed purely for us to view it. A video store was the first business I found open. Myron and I went in, less to look than to get out of the wind—Natalie'd been right about the bluster outside. I found a rental Natalie and I both might like, the first season of *Big Love*. Next we tried a wool shop by the pier. The place was full of the thick wool cabling and tweed that tourists imagine Acadian fishermen don for their oceangoing jaunts. I tried on a tweed driver's cap and modelled it for Myron. He seemed to appreciate the new look. The shopkeeper came around to get a look at the stroller's contents. "Oh wow," she said. "How old?" This was different from the treatment babies drew in Toronto. At the next shop we entered I actually took Myron out of the stroller, which earned even more accolades than before. All the praise juiced me enough to go out on the pier with my boy. Seconds later I lifted Myron from the stroller so he could appreciate the view. A fisherman's pickup pulled off the wharf as we walked on. Back home, baby-encumbered me might have kept my gaze on the stroller handle. Here? I looked at the driver and waved.

Myron was asleep when I returned to Red Cliff. I left him in the stroller while I set the bags on the counter. "You went *shopping?*" Natalie asked when she came in to kiss me. "You *hate* shopping with Myron."

"I hate shopping with Myron *in Toronto.*"

Part of this welcome wagon involved the off-season. It may have been weeks since these shops spied a tourist. I had the sense some of the stores were open less to conduct some capitalism than out of a desire to provide their owners with something to do. Me, my baby, we represented something new, so they appreciated us. But the fact was, style was different out here. A kid was an accessory with currency. Out here, kids did not preclude you from hipness. And I responded to this—on the last half of our little amble I might as well have been a Shriner on parade, I was so proud. Hey—in St. Andrews, I was proud of my boy. That's nice, Shulgan, but doesn't that imply you're *not* proud of your boy in the city? That, in some way, back in Toronto, he *embarrassed* you? Him, and the whole role of fatherhood? Well, yeah. I guess it does.

IN RARE, SPARE MOMENTS, I indulged my fascination with the tides of Passamaquoddy Bay. Often, the name of this village, St. Andrews By-the-Sea, was a lie; often, the sea was gone. The tides of these shores were some of the highest in the world. Around twenty feet twice a day these waters surged up and down, from low to high in six hours. At low tide, even from the wharf, one might search in vain for the brackish bay. Without water to balance them, the fishing boats lurched drunkenly off-centre. And then the tide came in faster than a foot's depth change every twenty minutes. You could actually watch the water move. Most striking was what happened to a wooded peninsula near the village, which I'd happened upon during an exploring session with Myron. They called it an island, Minister's Island, because for half the day water submerged the land that joined the peninsula to the mainland. The "island" fascinated me.

One afternoon I wanted to show it to Natalie. We loaded Myron into the rental car, a little front-wheel-drive import, and went for a drive. A Tudor-style resort hotel, the Fairmont Algonquin, topped the hill above the town. Some blocks past the hotel I braked within sight of the peninsula. We were on a street called Bar Road; the pavement stopped just about where we were, but the tire tracks extended out, tracing a rumpled route between mainland and island over the sea floor's recently revealed gravel and sand. The car was poised on what must have been the high-water mark. This was low tide, and past the pavement's end I planned my route along the bottom of Passamaquoddy Bay, to the opposite shore, a hundred yards away.

"Honey," Natalie said. She dragged it out: "Huh-*kneeeeee...*" It was a warning. I studied the tire tracks that led out into the sand. Here and there was a clump of seaweed. Natalie knew what

I was thinking. The "honey" was a warning not to try it. The "honey" said the gravel could be crossed perhaps by 4x4s, but our gutless little four-cylinder rental could get bogged down among the quicksands. And the honey reminded me of the baby buckled into the backseat. How long did we have before this isthmus was submerged? Natalie's "honey" said we didn't know.

But there's this weird thing with me. It's how I imagine Tourette's. It only happens with certain kinds of impulses, and the impulse I was struggling with now was a classic example. I had the impulse to drive across the isthmus. And I knew if I didn't do it, it would bother me. "You're a coward," something would whisper to me. "You're not a man. You're too chicken to do it."

Natalie glanced back at Myron, asleep. Her hand was looping into the handle on the roof just as I hit the accelerator. The downhill start helped get us up to speed, but from the first moments I knew it was a mistake. The troughs created by previous vehicles threw us around like we were driving over tree trunks. One threw us to the right and I spun the wheel left and floored it and I felt the little import front-wheel drive spinning the tires without any effect on our overall direction until, *slam*, we lurched out of one trough and into a new one. Natalie was moving left and right with the car. Halfway on I could see the end would provide us with trouble. The isthmus ended in a steep incline. If we were going to get bogged down anywhere, it would be there. I pressed the accelerator all the way in. The thumps grew louder. Now keeping us out of the divots required the frantic skippering of a rally car driver. The engine whined, our tires spun, and by the time we tipped up at the end, we had the momentum the car needed to climb the sand hill to pavement.

"Stupid," I said as I braked. "That was stupid. I know."

Natalie was paler than usual. She kept her hand on the roof handle.

I wheeled the little car around and drove to a spot that afforded a view of the mainland through the aged leaves. Out of the car, now, a few paces toward the sea bank, I felt the light, the wind, the ground beneath my feet. It felt pretty much the same as the mainland. And yet, something was different. From the car, Natalie called out to me. "We'd better get back. The tide's coming in." Her lips pressed tight together as we headed back down for the return trip along the sandy ribbon. So did mine—any of these ditches could have sucked us in and the way the tide changed around here there was a good chance the waters could have beaten my attempts to free our rental. Myron would be fine; we'd just walk him out of there. But still.

"What?" I said to Natalie's quiet.

"I was just wondering when you were going to quit that stuff," Natalie said once we were on the other side. "Proving yourself."

I flushed. "Christ, can't we have some fun once in a while? I wasn't proving myself."

"No?"

"I just wanted to see what it felt like."

"What's your verdict?"

"Neither. It doesn't feel like an island. It doesn't feel like mainland. It's neither. It's both."

ISLAND/MAINLAND. Kind of a random issue, the nature of this local land mass, and yet I thought a lot about the question while we lived those two weeks alongside the surging tides.

(The trial lasted an extra week longer than the lawyers had predicted.) The question plagued me, I think, because I was struggling with other dichotomies, including one related to this trial I was in New Brunswick to cover.

What spawned the trial was a riot on a sparsely populated island set about an hour's ferry ride south of here, in the middle of the Bay of Fundy's mouth. Grand Manan Island was home to approximately 2,500 people, most of whom made a living from the sea—potting lobster, weir-fishing herring, gathering the high-grade dulce, a form of seaweed, that grew on the island's west side. In good summer months, a fisherman might work 80 hours and bring in five grand a week. And in the long winters, when gale waves cancelled the ferry, when a rime of salty slush iced every outside surface, that same fisherman might not leave his house for days. The money, the isolating weather, the fact that Grand Manan didn't provide all that much to do, made the island's population well-suited for a drug epidemic. Soon after a Nova Scotia mainlander named Ronnie Ross arrived, word began circulating that a new drug was available: crack cocaine. A rash of burglaries ensued. Islanders tied the thefts to the drug problem. It seemed someone was pawning booty for crack.

The islanders appealed for help to the local RCMP detachment, an already overworked four-officer band. Then, in the summer of 2006, just as my own substance abuse was growing into a problem in Toronto, islanders in the Bay of Fundy began pursuing extra-legal measures to push Ross from the island. One night a crowd gathered across the street from Ross's house. Ross called some of his own friends to his house. Both the anti-crack contingent and the Ross side equipped themselves with a small arsenal of hunting rifles and less conventional armament, such as baseball bats and, on Ross's side, a broom handle tipped, with the help of duct tape, with a carving knife. The confrontation started shortly after midnight. It began with a schoolyard-style rumble that saw Ross's eye blackened by his across-the-street neighbour, the twenty-four-year-old scion of a prominent Grand Manan fishing family, Carter Foster. Rifles fired from both sides of the road. Combatants scattered. Someone set fire to Ross's house, and the volunteer fire department extinguished the blaze. Then someone set fire to the Ross place a second time, and when the fire engines returned, the anti-crack islanders set road blocks to prevent them from reaching the Ross place, which collapsed into flame. Ross left the island that night, never to return, and the island's drug problems eased.

The trial I was covering concerned the fate of Carter Foster and four of his anti-crack islander friends—a group the media called "the Grand Manan Five." Two were charged with arson; another three, including Foster, caught weapons-related charges. The case had attracted attention across the United States and Canada, particularly after *The New Yorker* examined it in a feature. I understood the draw. Here was a case of regular people succeeding where law enforcement had failed. Here was the rare case where vigilante justice may have been warranted. I was less certain of the appeal the case held for me personally. Natalie also had some concerns when I told her about it.

"Is that wise?" Natalie asked, when I told her of the trial's subject.

"Why?"

"Your history. Why would you want to have anything to do with crack?"

"It's fine," I said. "Besides, you and Myron will be there with me."

As the trial progressed I mulled over the appeal. Why did I want to write about it? Was it just the connection to crack? Did *everything* about the drug fascinate me? I don't think it's explained so easily. What fascinated me was the dichotomy between the two sides, between Carter Foster and Ronnie Ross. I spent a lot of time during the trial studying each of the two men. Foster and his friends looked a little like a hockey team at a charity reception; uncomfortable in white button-down dress shirts and ties they wore without jackets, over khakis and running shoes. When they went outside it was on with the parkas or Gore-Tex shells. Their supporters were lobstermen and high school teachers, skiff captains and church ministers, and they filled the pew-style courtroom seating with buffalo plaid and denim.

Ross, only a witness in this court proceeding, was easy to notice because he was trying so hard not to be noticed. At the end of his first day in court, he turtled his head down into his jacket, so that what little hair he had made a fringe for his collar. Taking care not to nudge up against anyone, keeping his gaze on his toes, he threaded his way past the cops, the lawyers and the media swirling outside the courthouse in day's-end conversational cliques. Fists jammed into stonewashed front pockets, he was down the courthouse steps and well on his way toward the sidewalk before I finished my own goodbyes. My tie fluttered out of my suit as I ran. Natalie waited for me in the car and it was the briefcase on the floor, a kiss for Natalie, and a glimpse toward the backseat at sleeping Myron before the car fully settled from my weight. "Sorry I'm late," I said. "We have to do something—we have to follow Ronnie Ross."

Natalie shifted the idling engine into drive and twisted to check her blind spot before pulling out. I nodded toward the figure with his fists in his jeans, on the opposite side of the village road.

"*That's* Ronnie Ross?" she said. "That guy with the white socks? And the Tevas?"

I hadn't noticed his footwear.

"Him, yeah."

"He looks like such a dork."

"Yeah, well. You think you could follow him?"

Skinny legs, but they had some speed. Already Ross was a block ahead. The next block ended in a T-intersection at Water Street. He turned right. We drove around the block and parked farther along Ross's path, so I could see Ross walking toward us in the rear-view mirror. It was here that I wondered about the wisdom of tailing an alleged crack dealer with my baby in the back seat. He was coming alongside us just as Natalie twisted in her seat. "Don't *look* at him," I hissed, but she wasn't, she was fishing around on the floor under Myron's car seat and placed a soother on my sleeping boy's lap. Ross walked by without noticing us. We watched him plod along until he turned into a motor lodge that backed onto the bay.

"What a dump," Natalie observed.

"Yeah, well. Probably the Crown's paying his way. He probably didn't have the money to upgrade. He's not exactly rolling in the dough, you know?"

"Hey, Natalie said. "Easy. You sound a little defensive."

Later I'd drop off a letter for Ross at the hotel, arguing why I was his best option for an exclusive interview (he did talk to me, although not exclusively). More pressingly, why was I making excuses for Ross? Did I have something invested in Ross as a certain type of character? What a dump, Natalie had said. He looks like such a dork. These insults concerned Ronnie Ross, but they stung me. What *had* I expected? In retrospect, I see that, before I met him, I had personified in Ross the allure I felt from crack. Ross, to me, *was* crack. So what did crack look like, as a person? My notion wasn't quite as well formed as that. But these are things that wouldn't have surprised me: tattoos. Greasy denim. Sunglasses and a mohawk. Manson eyes. At least some portion of Manson charisma! All this should have helped me identify crack's allure. This should have prompted me to explore the appeal crack held for me at that moment in time. It did not. Instead, at that moment, I felt some injury from Natalie's insults at Ross and, simultaneous to that, some injury from Ross's banal reality. I felt a bit betrayed by Ross. With his Teva sandals and socks, with his windbreaker jacket and stonewashed jeans, with his bald head and nothing frame, he seemed at this trial to be only a frightened and lonely middle-aged man. One who quailed whenever anyone attempted to engage him in conversation, as I did, several times through the course of the trial. Perhaps, I thought at the time, Ross wasn't such an outlaw. I wonder now, however, whether he was *exactly* an outlaw. Whether the outlaw as a societal role involves none of the glamour to which I'd ascribed it; whether outlaw as a role also included sadness and solitude, particularly when the outlaw was my age or older.

WHEN THE TRIAL broke for the Remembrance Day holiday weekend, Natalie and I made plans to conduct our first visit to Grand Manan Island. Saturday morning dawned with a quality to it, where the leaves, the cars, the sidewalk, everything, existence itself, seemed to *emit* light rather than just reflect it. Packing up meant we didn't leave until 9 a.m. on the winding road to the ferry terminal at Blacks Harbour. We played peeka-boo with Passamaquoddy Bay through the trees and the rock cliffs. I stopped at a general store for a newspaper. A van in the parking lot proved to have homemade, er, *van*-made donuts. Remarkably delicious, promised the gap-mouthed proprietor, and they were. The remaining curves were punchlines. It seemed a joke that a town that looked so close on the map could seem so far away as we traced the coastline's every bay. Our rental car was one of the last to roll on the ferry. All those sleeping cars and vans on the cargo level seemed liable to wake any second. I thought about Stephen King's *Christine* and kept Myron tight to me until we stepped over the portal at the top of the steep stairs and into the real world, or at least the pro-cessed world of the ferry cafeteria with its hamburgers like drink coasters and arcade of ancient video games.

Natalie left for the bathroom, leaving me with Myron—an act, ten weeks into this father thing, that still elevated my blood pressure. "It's called the Grand Manan Five," she said when she returned. "The ferry, I mean. That's funny. Hey, there's a poster by the bathroom, about whales. Maybe we'll see some."

"You're excited about this," I said.

"I've missed you."

It would be Tuesday morning before I'd have to go back to court. The long weekend stretched before us. We took turns holding Myron while the other parent went close to the railing to examine the whitecaps and the rollers for telltale fins. At one point, Natalie frowned. She sniffed the air. I had Myron and she leaned in close as though to examine his pants. She sniffed.

"Is he . . . poopy?"

At that point I was still getting over the public utterance of words that referred to feces. I particularly disliked the juvenile euphemisms. Natalie took Myron out of my arms and managed to spread out a cotton-and-plastic sheet in the cafeteria booth. Myron's cries attracted looks from across the deck. What code did it violate, besides mine, besides those of propriety and decorum, to change a baby in the middle of a cafeteria? I stared hard at *The Globe*'s Saturday crossword and tried to concentrate on twenty-three across. The diaper changing upset Myron. To calm him, Natalie began breastfeeding, and when I looked up I caught a guy across the cafeteria, watching. I put down the crossword.

"I'm going for a walk."

"Honey," she said. "This is what it's *like*."

We looked at each other. She looked away, through the window. Her eyes widened. She pointed.

"Look."

Tails, two of them, attached to black upside-down boat hulls, they looked like, except then you saw the spray from the blow hole. Three. No, four. The fourth came up and out of the water in a remarkable sequence I'd seen in nature documentaries but never in person. When it hit the bay's surface it sank below and a moment passed before the water rushed to fill the empty space and met in the middle and splashed up. The friends performed tail slaps, as though in appreciation.

The whales broke the tension between Natalie and I. I reached for her hand. She gave me a squeeze back. A tyke at another table of tourists shouted "land" a few moments later. Grand Manan Island came up out of the sea like a larger version of the creatures we'd just seen. I drove over the ferry's great metal tongue and onto actual road.

"Isn't there like a town or whatever?" Natalie said.

"I thought *this* was a town."

The map had a dot where the ferry docked—North Head, they called it, but it was only a handful of picturesque homes set on rolling meadow and the odd exposed scab of rock. We set out on the road, driving south and wondering about what it would be like to live here. "Castalia" was the first town we passed. I recognized the name from court testimony.

"Cedar Street?" Natalie said, twisting to follow the road sign. "Isn't that the one you're looking for?"

"Yeah—let's come back to it. Let's grab some lunch first."

To picnic, we wanted secluded meadow; we drove for what seemed like ages through rock or deep forest. A little past a marked settlement called Seal Cove, we came upon a lighthouse that warned ships off Grand Manan's southern tip. Around that was a spread of government land, cleared of trees and recently mown. We spread out a blanket a little distance from the gravel pad where we parked the car. Natalie unpacked the food while I retrieved Myron from the car and took him out to get a view of the sea.

"What do you think he's doing?" Natalie asked, meaning a fishing boat we could see. I shrugged. "Lobster?" I guessed. With the sound of our chewing for company the three of us lounged on the blanket. There was a feeling of rightness. Over the past week I'd grown increasingly anxious. I was hearing about events that had happened in a land I'd never seen and I'd doubted my ability to recreate it in my magazine piece. Now that I was here I was starting to understand.

It would be wonderful in the summertime. The hunting and the fishing and the sports and the summer people and the bonfires and the barbecues and with an occasional ferry trip to the mainland I could see how this rock would be the epitome of a *Blueberries for Sal*–sort of existence, all dogs and picnics and pink cheeks and breeze. And then came winter.

Oh, it wasn't just the dark—in early November, we could see the effects of that well enough. It was the damp and the way it picked you up and wrung you out. The heat dripped from your core and kept you in bed or on the couch, inside at the very least, there must have been winters here when people avoided passing their front doors for the whole of February, particularly when storms in the Bay of Fundy cancelled the ferries, particularly when the slush sucked your boots and froze them to the ground. Christ, if the stuff was a problem for me with my stand-up friends and full schedule then could you imagine how tough it would be to kick crack when you're a single islander with a bank account full from a five-grand-a-week fall?

IT WAS AROUND NOON when we returned to Cedar Street, and the setting felt a lot different from the image I'd built from court diagrams and witness testimony. From the start of Cedar Street by the island's main road, the woods closed in, Sleepy Hollow-style, and then at Ross's address there was a clearing that only grudgingly opened for a handful of homes.

The remnants of Ross's burned-out house left a footprint about the same size as a mobile home. I parked on the gravel pad that used to be the driveway. "Coming out?" I asked, and Natalie looked around to where Myron was, early into his afternoon nap, and shook her head. How little space a home occupied, when it had burned and collapsed. What had been Ross's two-bedroom home was nothing but a pile of fire-blackened lumber. With pad and paper in hand I moved around the lot like a stage actor hitting his marks, as I imagined the events the testimony had described, and allowed the context of place to fill them with greater meaning.

Navigating the rubble, I envisioned the first confrontation between Ross and Foster, with the resulting flight into the Ross home and the rifle reports that sent bullets crossing between their homes. Creeping through the underbrush behind the Ross home was difficult for me in daylight. Encumbered with gas containers at night, as Foster's buddies had been, must have made navigation more difficult still. I imagined the rear igniting with that trademark *whoomp*. It was 3 p.m. when I finished my scrawling. As dusk approached, Myron woke and fussed and Natalie pulled him into the front seat for some breast milk.

A car approached on Cedar Street. I tensed; the islanders weren't known to be friendly, particularly to reporters. The car stopped right behind our car, blocking any exit. A woman came from the driver's seat. Her mouth was tight. "Can I help you?"

"Hi Sara," I said, recognizing Carter Foster's girlfriend from the trial. Sara lived with the leader of the anti-crack contingent in a neat home across the street, I knew. She flinched at the sound of her name. For a second time she went over me, shoe to hat.

"You're from the trial."

"Yes."

"The one from Toronto. From the magazine."

"That's right."

"Everyone says it's better for the boys if we avoid you people. The media." She stepped backward. She stepped away, to go, and then Myron gave out a gurgle and Sara looked into the car's open window, at Natalie and the swaddled bundle.

"Hi," Sara said, her voice softer. "A boy?"

Natalie nodded. She rearranged her top and got out. Sara peered at Myron, now just a foot or two away.

"You must be so tired of the media," I said. "Always looking around.'"

"No, go right ahead. I do wish we could talk. But some of them have been pretty hard on us. Of you, I mean. The media. And the police. Nobody knows what it was like, living across the street from a crack shack, worried about going to sleep at night because he said he was going to burn *us* out."

"Probably you sleep better, now."

"Not yet. Once the trial's over."

Natalie said, "It must have been awful."

Sara looked at her, back to me. "Your baby's darling."

"Is there anyone we could talk to? I get one side from the trial," I said, "But I'd like to hear it from your perspective, what happened. Maybe a friend, somebody not involved in the trial?"

Sara uncrossed her arms. With my notebook and pen she wrote out contact information for several friends. She watched us as we drove away down the little country road.

A lot of the return ferry ride was downtime. Myron slept and Natalie dozed and I spent long minutes staring at the walls, rearranging the paragraphs I'd already written and filling in the holes with the context I'd absorbed today. I got up and paced past the cafeteria and out, onto the upper deck. I thought about the moment with Sara. The sight of Myron and Natalie had softened her; she had me pegged for a family man. It took only the fact of Myron for her to decide I was a good guy.

What was it about seeing a man with a child that prompts such a change in female perceptions? How absurd: I had only to donate a DNA speck to create this child, and suddenly I was regarded as a safe creature, a civilizing creature, a stable figure worthy of trust and confidences. Something rankled about the way the mere fact of Myron wrought my transformation in Sara's eyes. I didn't want to be so easily converted from dangerous to safe.

The trial dragged on until the end of the following week. Ultimately, the jury issued what amounted to a split decision. The two arson charges stuck, but Carter Foster himself was found guilty of only the minor offence of improperly storing his rifle.

The evening we returned to Toronto, I went out to dinner at Little Italy's Bar Italia to celebrate my brother's thirty-first birthday with a tableful of friends—other parents, mostly, all professionals with solid jobs. Loaded with mixed drinks and wine, I made up my midnight excuse, I was tired, travelling with a baby is exhausting, and then escaped to wander the streets of Queen West until 5 a.m., smoking crack.

8

THE ROAD

An equilibrium developed: a night's transgression, two weeks atonement, a night's transgression, three weeks atonement. In this manner I passed my boy's first year. You might be surprised to discover that this time featured moments of incandescent happiness. In moments of privacy, on weekends, on evenings, my boy and I shared experiences that opened aspects of myself I'd never suspected existed. Soon after he left the colic phase— oh wait, yeah, shoot, I forgot to tell you—he left the colic phase! Around the five-month mark, just one day, he woke up and, well, he still cried, he was a baby, of course he cried. But now the crying was prompted by reasons, discoverable reasons. He left the land of sustained and unexplainable crying with his soother as a souvenir. We never would have survived the trip without that soother. And now, bouts of crying had causes. Soother gone? We found it, he stopped crying. Empty belly? We fed him. He stopped crying. Dirty diaper? We traded his diaper for a clean one. And he stopped crying.

Having emigrated from the land of non-stop crying (a.k.a. colic), Natalie now felt more comfortable leaving the young boy with me. And I discovered soft. I discovered tender. I discovered affection and I discovered hurt. I discovered all these things in an intensity I had never known. Natalie on maternity leave was the monarch in our familial court. She set the timetables and the routines of morning and night. She established the laws that saw me home, most nights, for a six o'clock dinner. If Natalie held the leadership position, then my role in that first year was fool. That's what turned me around on this kid, when I discovered what I contributed: fun. Through toe chews and stomach zerberts, through peekaboo hands and air tosses, it was me, the jester, who could elicit the smiles and giggles.

I was best with my boy in private auditions, when the casting couch was occupied by no one else but him. His mom I wanted around, to provide solace in the bosom, in case he cried, so the optimal arrangement, our best moments, were the stolen ones after waking or just before bed, when Natalie was off, brushing her teeth, say, or in the shower and I could kneel amid our pillows and press his heels into my eye sockets (peekaboo!) or alternately, flibber my lips with his toes. In time it took only the sight of me to get him giggling.

Would I describe Myron's first year as a happy point in my life? Oh hell. Oh, I don't know. It was intense. There were moments of beauty and warmth. Lots! Afternoons in the park on a blanket as a family, where we arranged our diaper bag and clothes strategically to provide each of us with pillows. I had a paperback, Natalie a copy of *Us* magazine. And Myron wandered between the two of us. The blanket soon proved too limited a habitat for our fast-developing boy. He extended an arm onto the green sea that surrounded our raft. Another arm, and he crawled fully into the grass. He looked back at me, as if to say, this cool? I shrugged. He was off, speed-crawling with remarkable velocity until a stray branch stopped him to allow for some investigation. I set down my book. I made my diesel engine noise—*rrrrrrrrr*. And I rolled closer to him until I had him within grasp and we were a steamroller together, him on my chest, me using my arms to keep him close to me during the rolling and to prevent me from crushing him when I went on top. He giggled at that. He giggled more when I stopped while he was on my chest, the two of us now some fifteen feet from the blanket, and he reacted to my closed eyes with a nose tweak, a pinch of an ear. And I opened my eyes with a mimed expression of astonishment and he surprised himself, he *was* astonished, we did this several times until another noise attracted Myron's attention, another guttural *rrrrr*, Natalie's approaching steamroller, and now it was the three of us on the grass.

Myron walked at ten months. One afternoon, well, actually, the eighteenth of July, I was at Robarts Library, working on my first book, when my cell phone buzzed and showed the home number. And buzzed again. Natalie's consequent text drew me from the stacks, where cell phone use is banned, and down to the main floor, where I heard the news that Myron walked four steps by himself. Didn't just walk—walked *four* steps! By himself! I rushed home and we engineered various incidents and situations where Myron might conceivably opt for vertical ambulation instead of crawling—rearranging the furniture so that the coffee table was just a single step from the couch, say.

Good times. Except, hell, another afternoon at the park, a Saturday, and there was our little square and other park loungers spread their blankets so the Bellwoods lawns were a checkerboard of fabric and turf. We dozed. Myron woke. I felt him bumble off the blanket. It was hot, and humid, the sort of day you sit and you sweat and there's a gap between thought and movement as you ponder ways to minimize exertion. I altered the position of my forearm just enough to spy the boy crawling off and exploring the territory around us. The spiral course took him nearer the closest blanket, which belonged— to whom? I moved my head. Two figures, both flaked out horizontal, one of them attached by leather strap to what looked like, with my limited knowledge of dogs, some kind of husky. Myron really was quite a sprinter when it came to crawling. He burbled to himself. With soporific detachment I watched Myron close on the dog. The dog was still. It may have been asleep. Myron extended his hand.

The dog snapped his jaws toward Myron's hand. Full-blown panic, that's what Myron shifted into, and I was there picking him up and the nearest girl was up and pulling her dog away and Natalie was up, now, too, she extended her arms as I brought my boy in for a hug. No one except me knew what had happened, no one except me knew that I had watched as my only child approached a strange dog, watched, and did nothing, basically, because—I'm not sure. Laziness? The reader's desire to find out what came next? Or perhaps a more benevolent reason: an uncertainty about the line between autonomy and caution. Between self-determination and parental prevention. This was me, attempting and failing the trick of letting my kid explore and yet not letting him stray too far.

The dog could have bit off his hand! The dog could have bit off his *face*!

"They fuck you up, your mum and dad," Philip Larkin's poem goes. Yeah: But Larkin never explores the parents' view. It doesn't talk about how *bad* they feel about it. A reconstructed nose, a fretwork of faint lines on the boy's cheeks. Shulgan: you were one or two inches away from a dog's jaws providing you with a lifetime souvenir of your inability to parent.

The dog's owner explained, "He doesn't like kids." She was apologetic, but something in her tone suggested I was crazy to let my son so close to a strange dog. I agreed with her. What had I been thinking? For days afterward I walked around, wondering: what if I just wasn't cut out for this, this responsibility called parenthood? I kept fucking it up.

So yeah, there were lots of good times, and some bad. There were times when without question I was a family man, a devoted dad, no question whether I was domesticated. But something like Newton's third law seemed to be at play here. For every swing toward settling down there was an equally erratic swing toward the opposite. Almost invariably, these opposite swings included drugs. I was thinking about the stuff again, counting the days from the last jag and anticipating the date when an absence of accountability provided me the freedom to do it again.

This was not addiction. Not *simple* addiction, anyway. The dynamic involved was more complex. What else could explain such willful and reckless stupidity? I had lots of opportunity. I had to travel a lot, to research my book, and if I was away I travelled with a sick feeling in my stomach, as my sober self wondered what business drunk Chris might get up to under cover of darkness. The old souvenirs from my earlier troubles were showing up again. The lip blisters. The sores on my thumbtips and the scabs around the fingernails. The persistent cough and the thickened voice I figured came from smoke-coated vocal cords. All of it was coming back.

There was a three-night trip to Costa Rica. I was there to profile an Internet gambling mogul, a British Columbia entre-preneur named Calvin Ayre, who had parlayed a portfolio of gambling websites under the brand name of "Bodog" into a fortune that landed him on the cover of *Forbes* magazine's bil-lionaires issue. I flew into San Jose to then follow Ayre to a coastal resort where Bodog was staging a no-holds-barred brawling tournament. This should have been just what I needed. It should have been enough without drugs. The research trip started with an afternoon at Ayre's compound just outside San Jose, where bikinied women flashed their silicone alongside brawny security staff. Ayre's pad was an example of the bach-elor's life as imagined by an avid reader of *Maxim* magazine, one that grew more extreme the next afternoon on the Pacific coast, at the tournament.

Unlike the mixed-martial-arts brawls conducted by the UFC, Ayre's bouts occurred in a standard boxing ring. But what a boxing ring. The stage was constructed on the sandy Pacific beach, so that the wet slap of body blows competed with the sound of the surf. A light breeze riffled palm fronds. Because this was a spectacle intended for a televised audience, there weren't many spectators; just the fighters, their cut men, their wives or girlfriends or children, and a trainer or two. And Ayre, who presided over each match from a throne, on a dais of palm and bamboo, one fist clutching a Bloody Caesar, the opposite hand stroking whichever bikini-clad babe happened to be near-est; there seemed to be a harem around. The fights progressed smoothly throughout the day; brawny males bashed each other, blood dripped to the mat, victors raised their fists and flunkies wiped clean the canvas as the next combatants threaded their way through the ring ropes. The girls changed, the fighters changed, at some point Ayre traded Caesars for a different mixed drink—and yet Ayre stayed the same, cheering the damaging blows, admiring the ring girls, and sucking back his alcohol. At some point we broke for dinner at a long banquet table. I sat next to Ayre and across from a broad-shouldered almond-skinned guy in a black short-sleeved dress shirt, with sunglasses pushed up high on his crew cut. Ayre was turned away from me, deep in conversation with the guy on his left. I extended my hand across the table to the crew-cut guy and introduced myself. He gave his first name but I didn't catch it. I asked him to repeat it.

"*Hoist?*" I said. "How do you spell it?"

Willingly, he went through it for me—R, O, Y, C, E. I got it—the R was silent. You pronounced the R like an H.

"Ah, Royce. Like Royce *Gracie.*"

"That's right—Royce Gracie."

And something clicked. I recognized him. "*You're* Royce Gracie? *The* Royce Gracie?" He nodded. "Dude," I said. I was speechless. "When I was in university? We watched you in UFC I."

He winced. "You make me feel so old," he said in halting, Brazilian-accented English.

Look, there are very few people on Earth who could make me starstruck. But Royce Gracie was definitely on the list. Everybody knows about Ultimate Fighting Championship today; hell, CEO Dana White's been on the cover of *Esquire*. But back in university UFC was a bit of a freak show, a weird amalgam of boxing and other combat sports. The first one was supposed to settle those schoolyard debates about who was tougher—it was a tournament that included boxers, Olympic wrestlers, Thai kickboxers, karate black belts, and maybe the strangest one of them all, a comparatively little *ghi*-clad practitioner of something few had heard of back then, Brazilian jiu-jitsu. That was Royce Gracie. And Gracie cleaned up. He beat everybody at UFC I, and then continued to dominate at the next couple of UFCs with a fighting style that favoured complex anaconda-like wrestling holds that could break arms and legs or simply cut off blood flow until the unfortunate victim passed out. Gracie came from a Brazilian family that made its income travelling from town to town in the Amazon river basin, challenging all comers at events and charging to watch the resultant spectacle. North Americans who have heard of Brazilian jiu-jitsu have heard of it because of Royce Gracie. Certainly, he's among the reasons mixed-martial arts is the phenomenon it is today. Few men on earth possess the sort of male cred that Gracie has. Brett Favre might have it, if he was more decisive. Bruce Lee? Pat Tillman? Tyson, minus the sex assault charges? And Gracie turned out to be ridiculously nice. We talked throughout dinner. Ayre seemed to have paid Gracie an appearance fee to be there. I got the feeling he felt a little out of place; he seemed glad to have someone to talk to.

Early that evening I rode a chartered helicopter back to San Jose. And as I watched the coast's jungle give way to the more arid mountain landscape of central Costa Rica, I felt a strange emotion: regret. The girls, the fights, the liquor, Royce fucking Gracie: today might as well have been an orgy of male culture. It should have been just what I needed! Just the thing to counteract the emasculated, trapped sense that built up during my family man day-to-day. How I wish I could have gloried in what I saw that day! How much easier it would have been, had I been able to ogle the bikinis and swish the liquor and revel in the broken noses. But when I saw a silicone-enhanced breast I didn't admire it; instead I wondered about the bearer's self-esteem. Although I was too male not to feel a thrill at the sight of a kick to the face, my next thought was guilt at my enjoyment. One of the fighters wore a T-shirt that bore his daughter's name, as inspiration, he said, and the way this low-opportunity California kid was exploiting himself for Ayre's televised event only made me sad.

I returned to my hotel room toting a feeling of sketchiness, a feeling I got when my own internal limits went ill-defined. As an experiment, purely, you know, as an exercise in whether it would work, I searched the grocery store in the mall opposite my hotel for a ginseng vial, with no luck, then scoured the shelves for similarly sized vials, eventually settling on small bottles of peppermint extract. I bought two. The corner of the bathroom sink faucet served to knock the bottom out of one of the bottles. The screening I found by cannibalizing the hotel room's television cable cord. Purely as an exercise in whether I could do it, you understand. I stuck the customized container in the pocket of the pants I donned to go out to dinner. Had you asked me whether I would smoke crack that night, even after the pipe construction, I wouldn't have been able to give you a definite answer. I didn't know whether I could bring myself to do it. I didn't know whether I had the power to avoid it. At one of San Jose's entertainment compounds, where a high wall encircled a warren of variously themed restaurants and nightclubs, I had a dinner of chicken and rice and then went from club to club, looking for other fun. My fourth conversation was with a bouncer whose English was OK. Sure, he said, he could find me some cocaine. Hey, I said, as though the idea had just occurred to me—what about crack?

"Crack?" he said in his accent.

"Rock cocaine?"

"Crack," he said, and nodded.

He asked for twenty minutes and I spent it wandering the rest of the complex until I found myself facing the opening this bouncer had protected. I turned around and performed a reverse of my previous loop, this time stopping in a reggae-themed kiosk that, improbably, sold Canadian beer—Labatt's Blue. I forced myself to drink slowly. I peeled the label from the bottle. When gravity failed to deliver any more of the bottle's golden liquid I left and accepted the two rocks from the doorman for $40.

Sure, it would have been smarter to wait to smoke the stuff. But I lacked the self-control to bear the ten- or fifteen-minute cab ride back to the hotel. There was a bathroom I'd spied during my wandering. It was off by itself, off by the rear corner farthest from the compound entrance. The only people around were a couple of uniformed staff by the back gate. In the dank room's single stall, and perched on the toilet, I thumb-nailed a chunk of crack into my palm, then set it on the flattest portion of my thigh.

A noise above me caused me to look up. The stall door opened and exposed my seated self to the uniformed staffer, who, I realized, now looked a whole lot like a security guard. He pulled me forward—I remained fully pantsed—and fast hands were pushing into each of my pockets.

A grunt of triumph signalled the discovery of my pocket contents. There was a gesture I interpreted as a request to open

my fists. Pipe, rock. He took the rock and walked out to his partner, who I now saw was standing by a service exit. The only
word intelligible in the next bit was "crack." Apparently the
term is universal. I considered flight. Maybe five feet separated
me from them. But I'd be running *into* the compound, which
didn't seem like a smart idea. And my brain seemed not to
grasp the enormity of what was happening. I hadn't just been
caught with cocaine in a third-world country. Not *me*. Not upstanding, successful *me*. This was a misunderstanding that would
dissolve as soon as—what? There wasn't time to discover. The
pair opened the rear entrance and, whoa, right there was a
smaller man in a more serious, scarier uniform whom the security guards treated with respect. He lounged on a police car,
gesturing his arms in a conversation with a guy in a soccer jer-
sey. When the security guards brandished what they found on
me, the cop's arms crossed and he devoted his grim attention
my way. Here, now, did my awareness arrive. This was no misunderstanding. These men had caught me with crack. In Costa
Rica. My wife and my baby dissolved to a darkened cell. Who
could I call? I couldn't call anyone. There was no misunderstanding to sort out. These men had caught me with crack.

The cop was snapping his fingers. He seemed to want
something. I handed him my passport. The security guards
looked from my picture in the billfold to my face, then to the
police officer. The police officer looked to his left, in the space
between his car and the compound wall, where, I noticed for
the first time, an old woman sat on a blanket that bore various
sundry items. He stepped over to her. I tallied the cash I had
remaining in my wallet—maybe $140 US? It wasn't nearly
enough for a bribe, of that I was sure. But I could go to a bank
machine. Maybe I could get more. How much did I have in my

account? Maybe I could get a cash advance on my credit card. The police officer turned back to me. He tried something in Spanish and I shook my head. "You come with me," he said. "Or—"

At the "or" he stopped. I braced myself. He turned to the woman and mouthed something, and she answered with an urgent, fervent nod. "You pay her—" And he named a figure.

I thought I'd misheard.

"*How* much?" I said.

He couldn't possibly . . . Was he fucking with me? But no: again the look at the woman, again the nod, again the figure: "Twenny dolla."

Twenty bucks?!

They waited, as though in suspense, as though they expected me to deliberate about a tough decision. Surely they were fucking with me. I removed my wallet, extracted a $20 bill and extended it slowly toward the cop. He gestured to the woman. I stepped forward. I reached toward her. She snatched it and stashed it somewhere in her garments. The police officer's arms uncrossed. He returned to his former posture. The security guards gestured for me to return into the compound. I gave a cautious wave. I walked down the corridor toward the more populated parts. And I realized: I still I had the pipe in my palm. Finding more crack was as easy as finding a cab driver fluent in English. We went out in some barrio to get it. The second time around, though, I waited until I returned to my hotel. The next morning was supposed to have been a day off, something I'd reserved for a possible tour through the Costa Rican jungle canopy. Instead I changed my flight to fly home early that afternoon. I couldn't bear another night in San Jose. No, not that: I couldn't bear another night alone.

FAMILY MAN, drug freak. I was the sort of dad a law-abiding islander in the middle of the Bay of Fundy could tell was trustworthy with a glance. I was the sort of psychopath who so didn't trust himself he fled Costa Rica for Toronto—*in February*. It was work on my book, play with my kid, work on my book, play with my kid—and then blam, what I considered an explosion. I didn't start thinking about this cycle until the end of Myron's first year. Thinking about it meant it was happening and I wasn't yet ready to concede that. And then, toward the end of the year, it was all I could think about.

The twelve-month maternity leave provided by the government and my wife's excellent benefits package—that time was coming to a close. Natalie and I spent anxious afternoons discussing how to manage her return to work. Someone else would have to look after Myron. That seemed wrong, somehow. Unjust. It felt as though someone was taking our kid from us. How I wished I made enough money for my wife to avoid working, but I didn't. Natalie found a nanny who fit our child-rearing philosophy. And we opted for an arrangement that would limit the extent someone else would care for our child. Natalie would return to the labour and delivery ward working steady night shifts: Seven twelve-hour shifts every fourteen days. This arrangement caused me a significant amount of anxiety. I'd blown through other taboos: I wouldn't do drugs after the kid was born. I wouldn't smoke crack in my new house. I wouldn't buy crack in my own neighbourhood. Each one of those self-imposed limits evaporated in the lighter's flame. What if I couldn't withstand the temptation? What if I did crack while Natalie had entrusted me to the care of our child? Not doing it while watching Myron was something like my final taboo, the ultimate test that would *really* show me for the degenerate I was, the last barrier between me and just completely not being cut out for fatherhood.

TWO WEEKS BEFORE Natalie returned to work, we went on vacation to Natalie's dad's house in California—actually, in Topanga Canyon, between Santa Monica and Malibu, just north of L.A. The time we spent with Natalie's dad, John, and step-mom, Maria, was unlike any of our previous visits. I get along well with John. He's a voracious reader with taste that's similar to mine, and we trade recommendations about books we've read recently. Maria's a bit of a different story. The trouble had begun several years before at the reception after her wedding to John, an open-bar affair at a swank little boite in North Vancouver, where I'd first been introduced to Maria's mother, a smiling little Greek garden gnome of a woman, whom everyone called YaYa, including Natalie when she introduced the two of us. I let out a little giggle. "YaYa," I said as I clasped the old woman's hand. What a lovely word for a grandmother, I thought. Try saying it yourself: "YaYa." Isn't it great, the way it trips off the tongue? It's the sort of word you want to keep saying. And I did, each time I saw her: "YaYa." Bear in mind this reception happened at a little restaurant. I'd be talking to someone, and there'd she be. Also bear in mind that for some reason I was doing this thing where I couldn't say it twice the same way. So there was the conversational *yaya*, and the sonorous *yaya*. I whispered it. I sang it baritone. I sang it bass. I rapped it like Jay-Z, and I rapped it like Snoop Dogg. She liked it. Well, at *first* she liked it. Then some uncertainty crept into

her expression, and another couple of times replaced that uncertainty with fear and the next thing you know, Natalie's hand
was clutched around my upper arm. "What's this thing with
you and YaYa?" she asked.

"YaYa," I said. This time like a Munchkin on mushrooms.
"Knock it off."

But by this time it was hopeless. Was this a temporary case
of Tourette's? Ah, more likely, it may have had something to do
with the open bar. Another couple exchanges and Natalie was
pulling me toward her sister.

"I need the car keys," Natalie said.

Jessica looked at me. I shrugged.

"YaYa," I said.

So things didn't start out well between Maria and I. And
through the years, during our annual visits, she grew no warmer.
She didn't like my tendency, during vacations, to crack my first
beer around noon, sometimes precisely at 12:01 p.m. She didn't
like that one New Year's Eve, after one of those afternoons that
started precisely at one minute past noon, I asked her nephew
whether he could score me some cocaine. Plus, Maria was one
of those people who took her Scrabble very seriously. I beat
her once. She didn't speak to me for the rest of the visit.

And then Maria's attitude toward me changed on this trip.
First off, I didn't drink much. I was a bit freaked out about Myron in this unfamiliar house that hadn't been child-proofed.
And I was intent on giving Natalie a rest before she returned to
work. For the first time since the weeks after his birth, Myron
and I were together pretty much all day, every day, for seven
days. I had my own reasons for the intense dad–son time—it
was a dress rehearsal for the consecutive nightshifts to come,
one conducted with Natalie nearby in case I required emergency

intervention. This changed a number of things, the least of which was Maria's perception of me. One morning around 6 a.m., Maria padded across her Spanish revival home's adobe tiles to make coffee and found me on the couch with Myron in the crook of my arm. "It's like he fits in there," she said.

Their place was high on a mountainside. It faced west toward the Pacific, which glittered with sun flares maybe a dozen miles away. To get there you turned up one of the canyon roads that branches off from the Pacific Coast Highway between Malibu and Santa Monica and then hand-over-hand turned the steering wheel up dried mountain gulches, past cycling teams working on hill climbs, past Ducati-straddling film execs. It took about forty-five minutes to get from the highway to their house. Once you were up there, L.A.'s halogens and fluorescents strung permanent yuletide displays along the south ridge. And yet between the ocean and the home one spied only tumbleweeds and dry creekbeds. Maria warned me about leaving Myron on the ridge that formed their backyard.

"Why?" I asked.

She nodded out a window. "Coyotes."

Wait: what? On previous visits such dangers contributed to the allure of the place. Every hillside felt inhabited with history. Charles Manson made these hills his stomping grounds in the late '60s. One of the Manson family murders happened near here. Thanks to the canyon's starring role in T.C. Boyle's *Tortilla Curtain*, I imagined the lives of the Mexican labourers who lived in the gulches. There was a mysticism among the sage and the creosote scrub, a sense that the territory around us represented a catch-all for social detritus. "The big ones eat the little ones, up here," says a character in a Topanga Canyon cabin in Robert Stone's great book, *Dog Soldiers*. "All summer these people sweat fire, all winter they sweat the floods. Shit creeps out of the night under those sundecks, and they know it . . . Fucking L.A., man—go out for a Sunday spin, you're a short hair from the dawn of creation."

Perhaps it was just the unfamiliar setting. Perhaps it had something to do with America's comparatively greater economic polarization. But compared with Toronto, things seemed less civilized around here. And it bred in me a protective ethic. My eleven-month-old son and I explored every bit of that remote compound during our week there, and with untamed carnivores foremost in my mind I kept him within range for a quick scoop up. I heard somebody say once that letting a kid loose into the world was like unzipping your pants and taking a testicle for a walk. And for that week in Topanga, that sounded about right.

Topanga was the place where my old ideas of masculinity and fatherhood, already moribund, began to crumble. The image I have in my head here is of grand statues, one representing "man" and one representing "father" and of similar dimension as the Colossus of Rhodes—I see the monuments developing cracks, perhaps stress fractures, perhaps the effects of physical blows, and eventually things fragment and topple into the harbour below. Maybe this is getting a little Jungian. But look, the fact is, I had these ideas about fatherhood and manhood, and they were exclusive—the sort of man I wanted to be didn't accommodate this notion I had of what it was to be a father. And then, over the course of some months, those old ideas changed. And the start of that process occurred in Topanga.

The final catalyst for this change was a novel. I had the novel with me almost as much as my boy, that week. The novel's what kept me company when Myron slept. The last pages I raced through late one night in our bedroom. Myron breathed alongside me. Past him was Natalie in her usual nocturnal posture—on her side, her legs drawn in toward her chest, her hands pressed between her thighs. After the last page, I pressed my palms to my forehead. "Oh god," I said. "Oh Jesus Christ."

Natalie stirred. In addition to my whispered epithets I probably also let out a few groans, and Natalie stirring was an indication I was being too loud. When I stood, this moisture ran out my eyes and down my cheeks and I wiped it off, then shuffled out through the bedroom's patio door and into the breeze of a Topanga mountainside on an August night. For a while I just paced back and forth on the balcony, railing to railing. I'd wipe off my nose, wipe my eyes, groan, look off into the desert, then go through the cycle again.

The book was *The Road*, by Cormac McCarthy, the story of a father and his son walking through post-apocalyptic America. It's kind of fashionable to hate on the book because of the Oprah book club connection, but I would argue that Oprah has pretty good taste in books (pick me, oh god, please, pick me) and anyway, fuck that, *The Road* is amazing. The book absolutely wrecked me. It changed the way I perceived masculinity, and fatherhood. That was good. The way I perceived masculinity and fatherhood was kind of messed up. Before we talk about how these things changed, it probably makes sense to talk about how they developed, how things became messed up in the first place. A situation, oddly enough, that has a lot to do with Harrison Ford.

"IS IT PLUGGED IN?"

"Yes, it's plugged in."

"And the TV is plugged in."

"Of course the TV is plugged in."

"Switch the thing on the back, the antennae thing."

"I did already."

We were in the house in Puce. My eleven-year-old self was on our blue canvas overstuffed chair. My brother was on the couch and my parents stood, frowning and bickering while they stared at the Sony Trinitron television's static-filled face. Outside, winter hurled itself against our lakefront windows. The deck, the lawn, the beach, all of it hid under the white layer that extended far out into Lake St. Clair. Seconds passed. I could feel each one. "Well, *somebody* do *something!*" my brother shouted, and he ran from the family room out into the hall, slipping around the turn on the tile floor and past the stairs, the front hallway, around through the kitchen and back onto the family room carpet through the opposite entrance he'd just left, to reassume his position on the couch.

It was 7 p.m. on a Friday night and the popcorn mounded warm and buttery in bowls on the coffee table. Paper towels everywhere—as coasters protecting our mahogany coffee table from four sweating glasses of Coca-Cola. Another four towellettes floated free, intended to wipe the butter from our lips and fingertips. Everything was ready. The only thing preventing the evening from starting was our technical ineptitude.

The previous weekend my parents had gone to a party at a friend's house in the city. They told us about it the next morning, the way the friend's television was equipped with a device that allowed him to play movies, whenever he wanted. The movies came in cartridges. The friend broke one out. Michael Jackson's *Thriller*, as I recall. They told us about the way you could use the device to stop the movie whenever you wanted.

If you missed something you could just stop it and back it up. Or if there was a boring part? You fast-forwarded it, just like a tape in a stereo.

In deference to our begging, the following weekend my mother rented one of those devices, a VCR, from Maidstone Township's latest retail operation, a video store in the nearby town of Belle River. People today have difficulty selecting which movies they want to see. I see them. They shuffle through the video store aisles. They nibble on fingernails. They scan the backs of the Blu-ray boxes. Folks, you have nothing on a village kid on his first trip to the video store. You have to understand, I was eleven years old. The closest cinema was a half-hour's drive away. Movies until that point were a once-a-season special occasion. So I wandered the wall displays savouring my ability to select whatever I wanted. *Tron* or *2001*? *Airplane!* or *Police Academy*? *Escape to Witch Mountain* or *The Watcher in the Woods*? Or what about that under-recognized Disney classic, *Condorman*? It was *agony*, I tell you. The only thing that got us out of the movie store was the knowledge that the longer we took, the less time we would have to watch the movies at home.

"Do you want me to bring out the VCR for you?" the clerk said, and my mom nodded.

"I wouldn't want to break it."

My brother and I stepped back, to get out of the way, and the older boy hefted the cushioned suitcase-sized thing and staggered with it out the door. My mom rushed forward to swing out the wagon's back gate. The clerk eased his cargo into the back.

Same time we did, my dad arrived home from his office in the city. I put my pajama pants on backward, I rushed to get in them so quickly. My mom got started on the popcorn. My dad prepared to hook up the VCR. There was some business involving a screwdriver at the back of the television. What followed was my father's whispered cursing. Then cursing at considerably higher volume. My dad turned to my mother. "Your fingers are smaller," he said. My brother took a piece of popcorn. "Wait for the movie," I hissed.

My mom found the power button on the VCR and pressed it. She pressed another button. Still static.

The four of us stared at the screen. Eventually my brother reached forward. "Don't touch it!" my dad managed to get out, but it was too late, my brother was messing with something, he switched the Trinitron's top dial from channel 2 to 3, and suddenly we could see Harrison Ford pouring sand from a bag before a golden bust in the opening scenes of *Raiders of the Lost Ark*.

"Nice one," I said to my brother. We flopped onto the mattress. My dad hit the rewind button. My mother passed out the popcorn bowls. My brother adjusted his blanket, and I settled in for a viewing experience that for decades would define the way I saw myself.

THIS WAS A REMARKABLE moment in the history of art. Here was the beginning of the end. Here was the advent of our current crisis. Here was a step toward the downloadable everything that today delights and confounds. Dude: you could watch movies at *home*. And we did, we made events of them, in those early winter weekends my parents handed over their $50 or whatever it was and for 48 hours we ignored the frozen lake and its winds and crammed as many cassettes as time permitted into the ever-hungry electronic maw.

Those horizontal occasions, the comforters, the couch cushions, the parents bookending the kids, the movie on the TV screen and the winter wind outside: these early home movies formed some of the best times of my youth. They also contributed to the formation of my masculine ideal. Think of the heroes who populated the movies of the '80s. This was an era when Hollywood celebrated the lone wolf, the outlaw anti-hero, the troubled, the tragic, the flawed individual nevertheless working on the side of the right and the good. James Bond, Rambo, and most of all, the vulnerable anti-heroes played by Harrison Ford, who may have had the most successful box-office run of all time with the movies he starred in from 1977 to 1984—the *Star Wars* trilogy and the first two Indiana Jones movies. If in 1985 you were to consult a list of the all-time highest grossing movies, four of the top six would have starred Harrison Ford, who helmed the year's biggest grosser in each of the years 1977 (*Star Wars*), 1980 (*The Empire Strikes Back*), 1981 (*Raiders of the Lost Ark*), and 1983 (*Return of the Jedi*). The only one that missed the top ten was the Raiders sequel, *Indiana Jones and the Temple of Doom*. Born as I was in 1973, I was too young to watch most of these movies at the cinema. But the apex of Ford's career was perfectly timed to encourage his archetypes to resonate in my young mind when I saw them during our family movie weekends. Over and over I watched Indiana Jones use torches and chutzpah to fend off asps and cobras in the Well of Souls, or Han Solo sprinting into the Millennium Falcon's cockpit ahead of the Empire's stormtroopers to gun his ship into the solace of hyperspace. How devastated I was, the Christmas my brother received as a gift Han Solo's laser blaster. My blaster was Luke Skywalker's, who in comparison to Solo seemed so conventional. Han Solo had that hip, anti-establishment vibe—he was the maverick pilot who existed apart from the Empire and the Rebel Alliance. Ford brought a similar élan to his archeologist character in the Steven Spielberg-directed *Raiders*. His characters were swaggering freethinking rule-breakers with no emotional ties. Rarely were they depicted in relation to a home or a conventional job. Their loner status was so central to their identities even their names were signifiers of their exceptionality: Indy, and Han *Solo*.

"How come you haven't found some nice girl to settle down with, raise eight or nine kids like your friend Sallah?" Marion Ravenwood asks Indy at one point.

"Who says I didn't?" Indy shoots back.

"Ha!" Marian says. "I do. Dad had you figured out a long time ago. He said you were a bum—the most gifted bum he'd ever trained."

That's what I wanted to be—the gifted bum. Didn't we all?

SO IF FORD was the seminal component in my development of the masculine ideal as outlaw, how did I establish my notion of father? Well, teenage sexuality with Mr. Villaire started the ball rolling, when an educational system intent on preventing teenage pregnancy encouraged me to regard parental responsibility as a kind of death. And then pop culture helped. My peers and I were suckers for the counterculture marketing of the '80s and '90s, which encouraged us to use consumerism to distinguish ourselves from the suburban mainstream, to borrow a line of thinking laid out best by Thomas Frank in his book, *The Conquest of Cool*. Think different, the ads recommended, regardless of whether they actually used those exact words. Such youth marketing advocated rebellion. It commodified dissent while encouraging it. It praised actions that subverted mainstream values. What counted, under this counterculture, was anything that, as Frank noted, "distinguished us from the mass-produced herd."

Thus, I skateboarded and listened to "alternative" radio and the "indie" rock of such bands as the Pixies or Pavement, as well as the "gangsta" hip-hop of N.W.A. and the Geto Boys. These cultural genres defined themselves as opposed to mainstream culture even as they formed it. No wonder the generation raised on Harrison Ford's anti-heroes persists in a state of arrested development. When all of youth culture is "indie" and "alternative" the mere act of aging is interpreted as acquiescing to the mainstream. Amid such a milieu, it seems natural that I resisted the ultimate statement of conformity: that of starting a family.

We expect guys today to become a certain kind of engaged father—the dishwashing, diaper-changing parent who knows not to discipline with spanking. This, in the face of a pop culture weighted heavily toward depictions of the engaged father as wimp. How many archetypal fathers does pop culture have that aren't ninnies or nincompoops? Atticus Finch? Well, that's going back some years. And Atticus was pretty hands off; he let his live-in maid, Calpurnia, handle much of the child rearing. But okay, let's allow Atticus. Who else? The Coz from *The Cosby Show*. Dan from *Roseanne*, and their sitcom-dad followers. Okay, fine. And if a U.S. president can be regarded as a part of pop culture, Barack Obama strikes me as a pretty decent daddy archetype—a male so sensitive he got misty-eyed during his first campaign when he pondered the sacrifices the electoral race would pose to his family. But still—Obama, Atticus, the Coz:

comparative rarities. More often, when a real man is depicted within a family setting, it's an occasion to depict some tension. The family prevents the real man from asserting himself.

Two of the more critically lauded films released in 2009, the year I wrote most of this book, offer remarkably cohesive examples of this phenomenon. Recall the sequence in *The Hurt Locker* when Staff Sergeant William James completes his tour of duty in Iraq and returns home to his wife and infant son. What follows evokes Updike's story from his 1960 novel, *Rabbit, Run*, an account of what happens once young father Harry "Rabbit" Angstrom flees his familial responsibilities: "The clutter behind him in the room ... clings to his back like a tightening net," Updike writes. Nearly a half-century later, a similar tightening clings to James' back. Unfulfilled with his dishwashing and child-rearing responsibilities, as all real men must be, James makes like a Rabbit and runs by signing up for another tour of bomb-disposal duty in wartime Iraq. *For real men, wartime Iraq is preferable to family life.* And what is Wes Anderson's film version of the Roald Dahl classic *Fantastic Mr. Fox* but an allegory of the tension between father and man? Feeling stifled within the domesticity of his fatherhood role, Mr. Fox asserts his wildness by heading out on illicit nocturnal missions to the farms of Boggis, Bunce, and Bean—placing his remarkably understanding family in danger in the process. My reaction to that one was not unlike what hit me during *Half Nelson*. I didn't need to see this shit. I *lived* this shit.

Culture tells us over and over again: Real men cannot be good fathers. The roles exist in opposition to one another. Fathers, the odd times they're depicted in pop culture, tend to be bastions of lameness and conservatism. They're not real men. At best, they're dull or out of touch; at worst, forces that stomp on the hero's individuality. They nag about hair cuts, going to college, not going to college, getting a real job. Few social roles have been more maligned, whether it's Will Smith proclaiming parents just don't understand, the hypocritical smoking dad of the Beastie Boys' "Fight for Your Right to Party" or the oblivious Audi-driving patriarch faked out by a thermometer to a lamp bulb in *Ferris Bueller's Day Off*. The engaged father we expect today conforms well to the family man archetype criticized by the alternative culture that raised my peers and me, that regarded the family man as an object of contempt, the antithesis of the fully formed male.

"Do you want the family man or the swingin' man?" Henry Rollins asks in the anthemic spoken word introduction to the 1984 Black Flag album, *Family Man*, the cover of which depicts a background of presumably murdered family members dominated by a foreground of a man placing a handgun to his temple. "Family man with your life all planned, your little sand castle built, smilin' through your guilt . . . Here I come family man. I come to infect, I come to rape your woman. I come to take your children into the street. I come for *you* family man . . . Saint dad, father on fire, I've come to incinerate you, I've come home."

Father on fire: thanks for that image, Henry. That was me. That was me.

THEN CAME *The Road*. The story is little more than a father and son walking across territory where nothing lives but a few human beings, many of whom have resorted to cannibalism. Encouraging their archetypal nature by never revealing their names, Cormac McCarthy depicts the duo hurrying south through some unidentified section of the United States as they try to beat the coming cold of winter. They encounter various dangers, mostly from the cannibals roaming the ashen wilderness. With little warning, a "roadrat" holds a knife to the boy's throat until, with a single shot, the father kills the interloper. To mollify the boy, who remains shocked by the violence days after the incident, the father addresses the son. "My job is to take care of you. I was appointed to do that by God. I will kill anyone who touches you. Do you understand?"

Eventually, the boy does. Here is an example, so rare in our culture, of a father depicted as a hero *purely for the act of caring for his child*. Nowhere else had I ever come across a story that so glamourized paternal protectiveness. That so glamourized fatherhood, good fatherhood, loving fatherhood. Here was a circumstance when the mere act of parenting was heroic. I don't think there's a moment when McCarthy explicitly depicts the father giving the boy a kiss, or even a hug. And yet at no point do we doubt the father's love for the boy. It shows in every act the book depicts. *My job is to take care of you*. And the father does. In a looted supermarket the father happens upon a long-overlooked can of Coca-Cola. He gives it to the boy, who has never tasted the stuff. "It's a treat," he says. The boy drinks. "It's really good . . . You have some, Papa." Only once the boy insists does the father accept a cursory sip—he wants the boy to be able to relish the rest. It's a beautiful moment.

Plenty of people think the book is overly bleak. Bleak it certainly is—in the most distasteful sequence, the duo comes across an infant, skewered and roasting over a cookfire. One friend who was turned off by such moments compared the feeling he got from reading the book to stabbing himself in the eye. But the book had me from the first page, and upon rereading the story much later I would realize what caused me to identify with it to the extent I did. It was something on the story's second page: "They set out along the blacktop in the gunmetal light, shuffling through the ash, each the other's world entire," McCarthy writes. And elsewhere: "He knew only that the child was his warrant." I identified with the man's sense that his boy was his redemption, that the boy was not only the best thing about him, but the best thing about his world. That the boy represented a hope for a better self.

At one point on the duo's journey they catch a glimpse of another boy, and the son beseeches his father to go back for the young man, to help him. The father doesn't because there's only enough food for the pair of them. He believes that if they assume responsibility for a third person, all three of them will die. Through this sequence we see that the father is so focused on his boy's survival that he's at risk of losing his humanity. He's become inhuman, which, within the context of the book, may be the ultimate sacrifice. (Throughout, death is depicted as surrender; in the post-apocalyptic wasteland, death is the easy choice.) McCarthy's work is a portrait of the paternal spirit at its most ruthless. As I surveyed the ridgelines of Topanga Canyon, I ached to make some similar sacrifice for my boy. And for the first time I wondered whether fatherhood might not amount to emasculation—might instead feature a power all its own.

WE RETURNED FROM vacation late one Sunday night, and Natalie returned to work for her first night shift the following evening. As dusk fell, we ate a dinner of linguine with pesto, a green salad, and a chicken breast for me. I listened to the CBC's *As It Happens* as I washed the dishes. Natalie gathered her scrubs and her lunch of the evening's leftovers. I loaded Myron into the stroller, Natalie slung on her jacket and the three of us strolled the two blocks to the streetcar stop. The approaching streetcar sounded like an electric current. Natalie hugged Myron, kissed me, then leaned in close to my ear. "Call me later, K?"

"Around 10," I said. I breathed in. It's one of Natalie's best qualities—the smell of her neck.

I crouched down. Together my boy and I waved to his mother, to the sight of her torso as it navigated the streetcar's narrow interior aisle. Already, her existence as a wife and a mother was being shunted aside as she donned the armour necessary for work. She side-stepped and shimmied her way into a seat on our side, at the back. She leaned over the person next to her, to get closer to the window, and gave us a wave.

"Bye Mommy!" I shouted for both of us. Realizing what I had just shouted at top volume, I looked around to make sure no one had witnessed my profoundly unmasculine goodbye. They hadn't.

I missed Natalie, but you know what? I felt liberated by her departures. Myron wanted to push the stroller himself. I walked behind him; I picked him up by his shoulders when he stumbled down to a knee or a full-blown faceplant. For the walk across Dundas he went willingly back into his stroller. In future months he would learn to resist this; to ask to press the button that signalled the pedestrian crosswalk; to hold my hand as we crossed the steel of the tracks and over to the other side. He was mine, he was mine, he was mine. Once home, we parked the stroller in the front hall and climbed the steps. We wrestled on the bed at our own pace.

Natalie was regimented in her evening routine. Everything was about getting Myron to bed with the story going for 8 p.m.

I didn't care about schedules; not these days. The novelty of quarterbacking this process myself was too new. I lingered over each play; I relished every aspect. There was no cell phone. No website to distract me with instant messages. It was only this boy and his dad. Many of these wrestling moves my dad had done to me. We rehearsed the standard stuff, like stomach zerberts and the deadly chin. Suplexes and bodyslams I'd robbed from professional wrestling were sprinkled through our routines. And more exotic moves beside. The airplane, where Myron leaned his chest against the soles of my feet and then I raised him up, so he was four feet up suspended on the support of my legs. He'd try to wriggle away; my challenge was to keep him up there.

Bath time was easy, in those days. Stripping him with wrestling. Washing his feet and hands, his arms and legs, no problem. The hair washing was the worst part of it, particularly if I knocked his head with the wand-rinser. The bath's climax, my boy's rage. Okay, maybe bath time was the hard part. Still sniffling as I bundled him into his towel. The diaper, the olive oil we used as moisturizer, the waistband velcroing required to fasten the Pampers size 4, all of it happened with my boy still mad at me. His grudge disappeared during the first story—Seuss, or Munsch, in those days. Then by the second story he'd corkscrew into the crook of my arm. We were friends, we were brothers, we were father and son, we were two people falling in love.

His first word, uttered clearly in October, was "Daddy." We were walking on one of our morning excursions to the corner store, to buy the newspapers, the *Globe* and the *New York Times*, and my boy's eyes were on the ground. He scanned the sidewalk. He came to one of those divisions between slabs; what do they call them—expansion joints. An orange cigarette butt rested in the slit. He pinched it between ring finger and thumb. He held it an arm's length from him; that, I was happy to see. The tuber swung my way. "Daddy," he said, clearly and distinctly. I accepted the butt from him. We moved on. "Thanks, boyo," I said. Pretty soon he learned another word: "Mom." Which he also directed at me. When he referred to Natalie, in those days, you know what he called her? "Dad."

I was learning the zen of parenting. It was a challenge I managed to meet only occasionally. Being in "the moment." Which strikes me as a misnomer. The state isn't a function of time; it's a function of place, of residing in the spot where you're existing rather than whatever netherworld your mind goes when you're talking on a cell phone or checking emails or day-dreaming about how much work you have to complete the next morning. Myron could sense it, when I wasn't there. The challenge was to avoid getting bored.

Kids have adventures walking down the street for the first time that day. Of course they do. Everything's a first for them. Their first cigarette butt in a sewer grate. Their first sewer grate. Their first crossing of the street in September, their first orange leaf in the gutter. I'm old and I'm jaded by my thirty-four years on the earth so walking to the store is boring as fuck to me. To me. But to Myron, it's the first time we've headed to the store between the hours of nine and ten, in September. In like, ever. It's a fresh experience, and it deserves to be savoured.

The trick is to prevent your mind from wandering. But Christ, how do you do that? The Mercedes logo on the convertible at the corner's used car lot sends me thinking, I don't own a Mercedes yet, hell, we don't even own a car, which segues to thoughts about how at thirty-four I still haven't published a book, Christ, what if something fucks up with this book, am I working hard enough on it, maybe I should be back at my desk, what am I doing taking Myron to the store, I should be back at my desk.

Having your work done helps.

Having a good night's sleep helps.

Not having much to worry about helps.

But did I mention I was learning to parent a toddler? None of that was possible! I was a big fucking *ball* of worry! And yet, I was supposed to tail my year-old boy who takes, literally, I've timed him, at his own pace he takes an *hour* to get from our house to the corner, a span of less than a dozen houses! And my mind is supposed to stay focused on him? It's impossible! Maybe. But that's what makes kids so amazing. If you're there for them, if you're inhabiting the same moment they are, then you're experiencing their novelty. If you can manage the zen of parenting then your existence too gets renewed. Parenting as a form of reincarnation because you're experiencing the novelty of life along with your kid.

The closest I approached the zen of parenting was at Myron's one-year birthday. We'd attended a few one-year birthday parties by that point. I found the most extravagant productions to be somewhat distasteful—too naked a declaration by the parents to all the other parents in their lives, we're the parents of a toddler, and yet still so together that we can pull off a production like this one. The kid dwarfed by the candles, bewildered by the fuss.

So we didn't have a one-year party. We just spent the day doing stuff he liked. He liked hanging out with us; he was happiest when it was the three of us together. We ended up going apple-picking. We invited no one else. The place we chose was a farm on the Niagara Escarpment, maybe an hour's drive away—we'd rented a car for the occasion. The rest of the city seemed still to be slumbering as we headed north toward the 401. At one point something drew our attention to the back seat, and then Myron did it again: out of nowhere, he clapped. Perhaps it was the rare time in a car; perhaps he just picked up on our excitement. We were one of the first families there. We obtained our bushel and eyed the fenced area where a slide and some other playground structures beckoned. First was the hayride out to the orchard. Autumn's chill had us all in sweatshirts. The absence of sound was a sound in itself. Once the tractor putt-putted off we felt solitary in a manner we could never achieve in the city. The green seemed custom-designed for this occasion. There was a quality to the light, that day, like it was doing its best. Natalie set Myron down to walk. I picked a couple apples, mostly to show Myron how to do it. The trees were more like bushes; they were low, and pyramidal. You found an apple, walked a bit, found another. Myron ended up on a tree's far side. He stepped out, caught my eye, smiled, then stepped back behind.

"Mom!" I shouted to Natalie. "Have you seen Myron?"

Natalie caught my expression. "No," she said. "But I sure do miss him."

And then it was gone, the zen was gone, of course it was gone, my boy was out of view. I had the sense that basically the entire universe was conspiring to kill my boy. Frequently, it seemed, my boy was conspiring with the universe to kill *himself*. Suicide seemed his default setting. He was a sidewalk-strolling road stepper. A pot of boiling water reacher and an in-bath submerger. Christ! You want a sense of the fragility of human life? Have a kid. It's cars. It's how easily you drop him. It's the spectre of strangulation by every electrical cord. *You* try to be present for your son, for his precious coos and premier noticings, when you're visualizing him and his chest cavity being pierced by your wedding present Henkel. Kind of like the way calculus approximates a curve, the zen of parenting—perhaps it's better to consider that state as an ideal, something not quite achievable but worth aspiring to anyway.

NO ONE HAS ever provided me with a gift like the one Natalie gave me when she returned to work. When my boy woke in the night, apoplectic to an extent I hadn't seen since the colic days, it was me who rocked him in bed, and then, when that didn't work, paced from back of the house to the front and finally calmed him down with a warmed-up bottle of milk. It was me he nudged in the morning with the request to go downstairs, and me who convinced him to sleep another half hour, at least until six. I learned what he liked for breakfast; I learned what he didn't like for lunch.

I don't think he thought of me as his dad. Or: "Dad" was a concept that meant something different to him than it did to you and me. Rather than disciplinarian or parent, rather than influencer or *consigliore*, I was instead a friend, a companion, an accomplice, and a partner-in-crime. Our relationship was more Bert and Ernie than parent and child. Usually I was the straight man, Myron, the cut-up. The same dynamic that existed between my dad and me.

On weekends, as Natalie slept off her night shifts, Myron and I went for walks. Inclement weather forced us into the stores—to the Eaton Centre to check out the fountain. To Mountain Equipment Co-op, where you could play in the tent display if you removed your shoes. To the Indigo bookstore at Bay and Bloor, where you could spend hours on the Thomas the Train display tucked away on the lowest level. The local coffee shop learned to start the hot chocolate when they spied us coming their way—light on the cocoa, easy on the milk-steaming. I developed a list of adequate diaper-changing stations downtown and kept them in mind when I caught that distinctive smell. He got a kick out of streetcars. Sometimes we went for subway rides, just for fun. One day, I set Myron next to me on the Yonge line, in his seat, and he turned around and got up on his knees and raised himself into a standing position to get a good look at the two Goth teens behind us—and he giggled.

My boy, getting a kick out of the subway freaks.

And I thought, Shit, I'm actually—we're actually doing this, it's working, actually, maybe you'll pull this off.

Myron slept in our bed. We had discussed moving him to his crib. These discussions ceased once Natalie returned to work. I read Myron stories until he fell asleep next to me, and then I left him there. I liked the idea of him next to me. He was warm. He was good company. And I sensed he liked having me in there with him. We slept well together. Sometimes he woke up and he cried and all it took was my extended arm to remind him of my presence. Sometimes I woke up and again, all it took was an extended arm to remind me of *his* presence, and I returned to sleep. My kid was okay.

The first few moments after he slept, the fragility of his lips, the smooth of his cheeks. He still slept the way he came out, with a fist held tight against a cheek, as though he was prepared in slumber to defend himself against whatever the world threw at him. That anyone would allow themselves to be so unprotected in my presence . . . it humbled me. It was here that I realized to what extent he assumed his father capable of the act of protection. His calm was absolute. Such rest could be possible only in the presence of someone in whom he had absolute confidence. That someone was me. He had absolute faith in me.

AND I FUCKED IT UP. During Natalie's year off, when I was the only "working" parent, I had been guilty of thinking the following thoughts: "What does she do all day?" "The laundry's not done again?" "Why don't I have any clean underwear?" How many times, that year, did I return from a day of writing at the library, exhausted from the mental exertion required to, say, spew out 3,000 words of text. I came home, barely able to string two words together. I was cranky. "Can you handle bath time tonight?" I said more than once. Little did I realize that when I was watching Myron, such days at the library would seem like a vacation! The ongoing slog of verbiage was nothing compared to the mental exertion required to care for another human being. Days with the kid, to an outsider, to my working-parent self, they seemed pretty easy. It's make breakfast, make lunch, naptime, make dinner, bath time, story, and then bed again. In between you fill gaps with excursions, with playtime. How tough could it be?

What I didn't anticipate was how difficult it was to anticipate the needs of another human being. To consider his limitations, to consider his frailties. And then, on top of that, was the cumulative toll of that consideration. I literally could not bear doing it for more than twenty-four hours at a stretch. I needed an hour, even thirty minutes, to go off, by myself. Not while the kid was sleeping—that didn't count. Even when the kid was sleeping, I had to be ready for him not to be sleeping. That, still, was exhausting. I needed the time to stand in the corner and flibber my lips with my finger. I just needed time away, caring for no one but myself. Childcare was a stress like nothing I've ever experienced, and it's important to realize that I didn't experience it until my wife went back to work.

It helped my marriage. It helped me realize what she'd been through, the previous year. It helped me realize how maddening I must have been, my supposedly private displeasure over the mess that bloomed across our house. It's not something you can realize when you take the kids for an afternoon, an evening, or even a weekend—although a weekend provides a taste. I think a full-on inversion is necessary. To understand the cumulative exhaustion that builds when you fill the spare moments with cleaning, when naps are your only chance to get the laundry done, and if you don't it means your wife's scrubs aren't laundered for the next night shift, and when he gets up early you meet his sleepy face like a personal rebuke.

Straight up: it nearly destroyed my marriage, too.

Despite my repeated vows never to do the stuff while watching Myron, I did it. What to chalk it up to? The pressure of fatherhood? The flight from its responsibilities? The paradox I had in my head, between father and man? I don't care how fucked up you were, Shulgan, it's inexcusable. It happened after a string of Natalie's twelve-hour shifts. She worked two nights at a time and then three nights at a time and then two nights. Two nights on, two nights off, three nights on, three nights off. And yeah, I said I was falling in love with my boy. And I was. I was.

And yet, one night in early October. My sister and her boyfriend offered to babysit until 10 p.m. while I went out on a boozy dinner with friends. And on my way home, I *walked*. My return route passed one of the city's sketchiest crossroads. I could have detoured around Queen and Bathurst. I didn't. This was before they installed the security cameras. This was before the Starbucks took the northeast corner. People who knew how to get it, they hung out on the steps there. On the north side. The stone steps. So even if I took the south side sidewalk it would have been fine. I didn't. The details of the actual buy? I can't remember the specifics. Usually one of the drunks would lurch off the stone steps after my request. They'd take my money, I'd walk around the block and I'd get the drugs on a side street—usually, in the alley just south of Queen, or the bit of Richmond just west of Bathurst.

The vials for the pipe I bought in the Asian market just west of the stone steps. Once the vials were on the counter I asked whether they carried steel wool, because by this point I'd thrown out the cable wire I cannibalized for the pipe screening. The Asian clerk, who was in his 50s, directed me midway down the west-side aisle. I tossed a lighter on the counter, too. And the ancient Asian looked down at the steel wool, the two ginseng vials, and the lighter. And his face twisted. "You're disgusting," he said.

He still took my money. I made my purchase. But—that seems a bit much, doesn't it? Am I misremembering this? It *happened*. The Asian clerk at this corner store called me disgusting as I was buying the materials to make a crack pipe. That the guy knew why I was buying what I was buying, that surprised me. I was too shocked to defend myself. Too shocked to ask why he sold the ginseng vials in the first place. I mean, really, did anyone buy those things to actually drink the ginseng syrup? Surely their main purpose was to be constructed into crack pipes? So he bore some culpability here. If he really disliked the effects of crack on his intersection, he could limit it by not selling a pipe's raw materials. Also shocking was the extent he had me pegged. That his accusation matched so perfectly what *I* was feeling. I mean, clearly: I *was* disgusting. And that's what makes me wonder whether I'm misremembering this bit. It's a little too perfect.

Anyway, when I arrived home at ten to ten, my sister and Isaac were midway through an episode of *Arrested Development*, as I recall, and I feigned sleepiness to prompt them to leave without watching the rest of it. Stretching, yawning, that sort of thing. We talked about how Myron had been at bedtime. He was great. He was always great. They removed the DVD and took it next door, to their apartment. And they were gone.

The baby monitor whispered from the coffee table. I left it where it was to go up and check on Myron. He'd kicked off the duvet and snuggled himself at right angles to how you'd normally sleep on the bed, to get his back up and into the pillows. That's how we slept together; he snuggled his back into the crook of my arm. It was how we kept each other warm.

I almost threw out the rocks. Well, no. There was an impulse to throw them out. But this would be the last time; there had to be a last time. From the upstairs bedroom I went to the basement, stopping only for the baby monitor. I went back upstairs because I needed the scissors to cut a little hairball from the steel wool. I grabbed a butcher's knife to cut up three equal chunks of the $20 rock. I went back downstairs. The baby monitor shushed as I exhaled the white smoke. The second rock went some minutes later. And the third rock, my last rock, the one I promised myself would be my last one ever, because I missed it, right, that was why I had to get up to this, I missed it, this was my last time, the third rock was my last rock. And then: I couldn't find it. I looked in the folded cuffs of my jeans. Everywhere around the desk in my basement office. I went around the kitchen. The counter, the utensil drawer, the stove, the sink? *Nothing.* I was on my hands and knees going over the floor when Myron cooed. I heard it through the monitor. I froze. Then silence. I returned to my search.

More. Getting more would entail leaving Myron in the house alone. But how long would it take me? I'd take my bike. Twenty minutes? What were the chances that he'd wake during that twenty minutes? If it went well, if I found someone immediately, it wouldn't even take twenty minutes. More like fifteen. Seven minutes to ride my bike to Queen and Bathurst, one minute for the deal, seven minutes for the return trip.

I peeked out the front curtains. Traversing the house in a moment or two, I peeked out the back. Moments later I was peering through the front door again. What was I looking for? I have no idea. Crack breeds a paranoia and these habitual perimeter verifications were a symptom. Before I broke the taboo of not smoking the stuff in my house, I would wander neighbourhoods conducting crazier and crazier rounds of these perimeter verifications. It is a fact that it's difficult for someone in the grip of a crack high to find settings that seem secure enough to smoke crack. How long does it take to fire up a rock? Less than a minute, certainly. At first it seems fine to do that on the street, hiding with a cupped palm, perhaps in the lee of a telephone pole. As the stuff takes hold, the over-the-shoulder lookbacks grow more frequent and the residual unease drives the smoker off the open street. Alleys and their niches will work for a time and then the risk of the sudden car prompts a burst from the city block interior space to something else. Sometimes I crouch in the shadows that limn midnight schools and various institutions of the sort. Places where people don't go at night. Baseball diamond dugouts. Park playgrounds work okay until the uncomfortable playdate when my sober self goes down a slide with Myron and, damn, déjà vu, I realized I'd been in the same setting in a different state. One of my all-time favourite places to smoke crack I discovered by accident after one of the few purchases I made in Parkdale, where for some reason the vic percentage is much higher than other troubled locales. I hopped a fence a few blocks south of Queen and found myself in the brush above the landscaped slopes visible from the Gardiner Expressway, where Canada's blue-chip corporations buy landscaped advertising—company logos depicted in white crushed stone that contrasts nicely against the deep green yew hedges and lawns. These slopes were spied by the millions of commuters who drive that stretch of highway each week. And despite the extreme visibility, it felt safe because it was a tough place to get to on foot. Yeah, I lasted there for a good twenty minutes before an elaborate conspiracy theory got to me, that I was being watched, that some cop had seen me scale the fence and now dozens of officers crept toward me in the surrounding vegetation. And I was off again.

This time, crack's paranoia yielded a comparatively more productive result. What if Myron woke up? What if his crying woke up my sister next door? What if my sister came over— she had a key—and, not finding me, ended up calling Natalie? And about that twenty minutes . . . Sure, but it could take a lot longer. And wasn't smoking more of the stuff just delaying the nasty comedown I'd already started? I was still deliberating when the monitor squawked. When my boy's innocent sleep cry travelled from his mouth, to the bedroom base station and then through the ether to the partner device clipped to my belt—well, then I decided. I *couldn't* leave my boy. I couldn't leave *my boy*. I would choose my boy over crack.

Oh, you're so laudable Shulgan. Good for fucking you. Yeah, well. Life features its share of decisions that can project the rest of your years in a future direction. Choice of university, choice of career, decision to get married, that sort of thing. And whether to leave your boy alone while you go out into the night to purchase crack. Many of my choices tonight had been wrong, but at least I ended the night with a right one. Small solace, that. Until that moment I justified it to myself, I wasn't hurting anyone but myself. Crack was something that only happened late, in the dead moments, the zombie hours, when no one was around to see. How bad could I be hurting anybody, if nobody knew they were being hurt? How much was I risking, if no one knew the risks I was taking?

I flipped through some late-night television as I drank a few more beers, to cushion the comedown. Some hours later I went up the stairs. My boy was sleeping over on his mother's side. The monitor on my belt clunked against the wall when I hung my jeans on their hook in the corner. My pajamas were in their usual space below my pillow. I switched off the base station and switched on my book light. Myron stirred, I extended a hand to calm him and soon he was wiggling his back deeper into my ribs, to share the warmth provided by his father, his hero.

The next morning, Natalie came home around 8 a.m. Myron and I were just coming down the stairs as she walked through the door. With autumn's cold on her cheeks she kissed hungover me trying not to act hungover. Following Natalie into the kitchen, I went through the checklist to ensure I'd left behind no telltale signs. I'd flushed the pipe into the downstairs toilet. Had I returned the scissors to the drawer? She was stashing one of those plastic envelopes of breast milk into the fridge when I saw it. Right there on the kitchen table: the third rock. Right there, right out in the open. How had I not seen it the previous night? I couldn't explain it. I still can't. My stomach sank to geologic depths. I scooped it up in my hand while Natalie's back was turned. "Just gonna empty the garbage," I muttered, then stepped out the back to bring the bag to the shed in the yard and while I was out there I stepped into the alley and dropped the rock in to the sewer. Back in the kitchen with Natalie, I asked, "How was your shift?"

9

THE OLD MAN AND THE SEA

"HONEY!"

A month later. I was downstairs in the dining room, writing. Myron was at it with the Lego, at my feet.

"HONEY!"

Natalie was upstairs. Normally a yell of such urgency meant something was wrong with Myron. I'd respond by sprinting up the stairs. But my boy was with me. I scooped him up anyway and sprinted up the stairs. Natalie was in the bathroom. In her hand she held the wand from a pregnancy test.

She looked up at me and beamed. "We did it."

I sat down, cross-legged on the bathroom tile and grasped Myron's small hands in mine. "Boyo, you're going to have a brother."

"Or a sister," Natalie said.

"Right, or a sister. You're going to have a—sibling."

He just looked at us. I think I would have done the same. It's hard to get excited about a word as antiseptic as "sibling."

"Someone to play with," Natalie said. "A friend."

"How accurate are these tests?" I said.

Natalie shrugged. "Accurate enough."

I looked at the box. There was a figure, I don't recall exactly what. There was also a little diagram that detailed the positive and negative readings associated with the stick readout. On the box the pregnant reading was two lines. I looked at the stick. I could see only one line. I looked back at the box. Two lines. The stick: one line. I almost didn't say anything. My wife is the uber-knower-of-all-things about babies in our relationship. I just go along with her edicts: no peanut butter until after a year old, turn the car seat around at the same age, cut up blueberries because they're a choking hazard. But something moved me to speak.

"I only see one line," I said, handing the wand back.

"Yeah, one line, that's right," Natalie said, taking it. She picked up the test box. She read the same text I just had. She glanced back at the wand.

"Oh, crap."

OK, so false alarm. And then, four weeks later, Natalie once again summoned me upstairs with a shout. And that time? She was right.

THAT WAS THE END of November, and I managed to keep things together through Christmas, probably because January represented an opportunity to let loose, thanks to my friend Kenny's stag in Key West over the Martin Luther King Jr. holiday weekend. The stag hovered in future like an oasis to a thirsty desert wanderer. It was kind of a big deal. The groom was a Wharton MBA, and professional men from all over the United States and Canada were convening at Florida's tip. Boston, Dallas, New York, Toronto, we were from all over the place and we were getting together for a weekend of spearfishing and debauch: we were getting together to be men. I endured the minor humiliations that parenting threw at me every day—the accidental facial feces smear, the meal's third consecutive orange juice spill—because I knew it was coming. I could endure *this* until *that*.

The mystical complications of Air Miles meant it made more sense for my half of the Toronto contingent to fly into Miami airport. We picked up an SUV and some booze and by 8 p.m. we were cruising the US-1 along the causeways that linked each of the Florida Keys. It was dark, we could barely see the sea, most times, but we could smell it; despite the highway speed we kept the windows rolled down and the warm wind in our faces. The sea smelled like freedom. Our SUV rolled into the Truman Hotel, an upscale motor lodge just off the Key West strip. What with all the male reunification rituals, the fist bumps and the handshakes that turned into palm clasps that evolved into snapping disengagements, which concluded in shoulder bumps that became back-slapping hugs, it was 1 a.m. before we headed to a bar.

Things grew sloppy fast. Crack, of course, was something I hoped to be able to do on this trip. But the sloppy evening's sloppiness made it difficult. The cargo-shorted, flip-flop-shod, T-shirt-topped ranks of my confreres in the stag, as well as the city's thousands of other revellers, were too busy getting wasted on alcohol to be busy with drugs, it seemed at first. The pull was there, but so was the camaraderie of being out with a group of guys I hadn't seen together since the last stag, the previous year. Around 3 a.m. the membership began to drop off. "Where's so-and-so?" someone would say to answering shrugs until there came the moment I returned to the bathroom to discover I couldn't find anyone in our group. The walk home seemed to take forever. Perhaps I would be good tonight; perhaps I would avoid smoking crack. But there were so many questions to answer: would the stuff be different down here in the Keys, with its proximity to Colombia and Mexico? Would you be able to get *more*?

A set of stairs on the main strip seemed to have attracted a share of layabouts, and I nodded at one, who seemed receptive, so I stepped in and asked, "You know where I could find some blow?" Blow, in my mind being a more socially acceptable drug to do than crack. The guy didn't hit me, or accuse me of attempting to sully his Caribbean oasis; he only nodded further down the strip. The second person I asked just nodded, looked around, and gestured for me to follow him down the cross street. How did I come to understand the illicit transaction I expected was not the illicit transaction he sought to provide? So many things were similar about them—the taboo nature, the furtive quality. But something about his manner was off. Drug dealers often were anxious, but this guy's anxiety seemed a different breed: he kept looking back at me as he led me toward the palm-shaded cottages off the main strip. There was something hopeful about these looks. Rarely had I ever seen a crack dealer wear a polo shirt. Not only did this guy wear a polo shirt; his was tucked in.

I gestured for him to stop. I leaned in close.

"It's cocaine, yeah?" I asked.

He frowned. "Blowjob," he said.

I don't know who was more disappointed. Christ. Maybe he also had a wife and kids back home. While still digesting the parallels I arrived at my hotel and opted for a few hours sleep before the 8 a.m. wake-up call.

NEXT MORNING, maybe twenty minutes toward Miami along US-1, we stopped at an outfitter's and rented equipment for a day of spearfishing. "Speargun" makes the device sound more elaborate than it actually is. It's basically a hack on a slingshot, one that uses thick elastic bands to fire aluminum rods tipped with sharpened points instead of slingshot pebbles. A pair of 150-horsepower Mercury outboards pushed the guide's Boston Whaler out into the reefs that lined the Key's Caribbean side. We stopped after a half-hour in fourteen feet of water.

Wetsuit on, I slipped off the back of the boat and wiggled into my extra-long flippers. The weight belt pulled against my hips. I spat in my facemask, inserted the rubber snorkel and grasped the speargun by its pistol grip. Going under submerged me in a world of light and silence and only the occasional fish. A few kicks put me out of range of the other spearguns; I didn't want an aluminum shaft in the ribs. For some moments I just floated ten feet down. Black fish, long fish, skinny fish, fat. Fish that disappeared when they turned one way, turned another and became wide as sails. A three-foot swell up on the surface churned up sand. Visibility was maybe thirty feet in this world of silence. I had the sensation of flight. Every few seconds I twisted to get a look behind me. Later that same winter I read Stephen King's *Duma Key*, which derives its power from the sense that the water past the Keys hosts forces we don't fully comprehend. It was a feeling I knew well.

Hunting, fishing. Things I've considered pursuing as hobbies. It sounded cool, the business of hiking around woods with a rifle in hand. I knew guys who did it. I'd been invited before on hunting trips, which prompted debates with my vegetarian wife over the ethics involved; each time, something came up to prevent me from going. My general sense went something like this: If I was going to spend my life eating meat, then I should probably kill something myself, at some point. My duty as a carnivore. The logic was similar to why I watched my son's circumcision—I had a sense I should witness the carnage my decisions wrought.

Mice don't count. Qualifying as killing something required direct action. It had to be a short causal linkage. You pulled the trigger, the thing died. The speargun kicked back after the finger twitch. My spear glanced off a rock. I surfaced to reset the elastics. Another deep breath. A few ankle pumps and I came two spearlengths away from a three-footer. Wait a second, did the thing have teeth? If I shot at it, and missed, if my spear glanced off it and hit a rock instead, would it retaliate? *I* would have, if I was minding my own business and some hungover Canadian fuck tried to spear me in the ass. I headed off in search of something less threatening. Intent on something in the coral was a trim silver blunt-nosed bullet. The spear went straight to where I'd aimed, but by that point the fish had turned sideways, offering a target of only two or three inches. Impossible. A breath and I found him turning wide-side my way. When his length was exactly perpendicular to me, I fired, and the spear went through just forward of the pectoral fin. The fish wriggled. The cord jerked. A barb kept the speartip from slithering out. I broke the surface with the fish held aloft.

"Oh, that's a big one," I heard someone say in the Whaler. "Who is that?"

"It's Shulgan," I said, feeling the thrill of conquest. A dirty cooler served as the fish locker. When I slung in my catch, blood smeared against the grey liner. Already the scales exchanged silver for yellow. He thumped against the cooler's side. I thumped down the lid. Noise drew me to the Whaler's stern. One friend was treading water just off the swim ladder. The noise came again and he spat the little that was left of his breakfast in the Caribbean. "Ah, tequila," he managed. I offered another friend my speargun, because there weren't enough to go around, and he shook his head and held his own stomach. "Not feeling so great myself," he said.

My second trip out I allowed thought to distract me. Fish, name unknown, darted in and out of crevasses a little out of spear range. A kick or two brought me closer. It was remarkable, the speed with which the creature moved. He was in one crevice, then a flick of the fin and he was six or seven feet away, investigating a fresh crevice. These fish combined alien features with such grace. The thought came unbidden: why would you want to kill one? I tried to concentrate on aiming, but then a bit of coral reminded me of a scene from *Finding Nemo*. No! Twelve feet down off the Florida Keys and some Pixar flick is fucking with my masculine instincts. And then, how could you be in wilderness anywhere around Miami without considering Carl Hiaasen's eco-satires? Hadn't this been Manhattan for fish, back when it was Hemingway's 'hood? Where were they now? There weren't any crowds in this aquatic downtown. Manhattan? Pshaw—this was the fish version of downtown Detroit. This was *deserted*. And hey, wait a second—was that my fault? And the fault of other tourist spearfishers like me?

Some hours later the guide filleted my catch and the handful of others we'd caught, and set them out raw with some wasabi and soy sauce. This was in the hotel's parking lot. The group of us gathered around the back of the suv, beers in hand and forcing out observations about the special flavour of food you'd killed yourself. Shouldn't this have been a glorious moment? The thrill of the hunt, the glory of the kill, all that? Instead, at least in my case, guilt made rubber of the fish flesh.

BE A MAN. That's what a ritual like a stag was designed to permit a participant to do. The ostensible purpose was to provide the groom with one last hurrah, which meant what, exactly? One last chance to exercise his freedom as a single, unattached male? Naw, not really. At least in my crowd, stags are more about hanging around with guys than pulling girls. And they have surprisingly little to do with the groom. Many of the participants are guys like me, guys who've been married for years, and we see these party getaways as opportunities to indulge a side of ourselves that otherwise isn't, because most of the time we're concentrating on fulfilling responsibilities to wives and children, careers, and whatever else.

We're going away *to be men*. It makes us sound like a bunch of twats, putting it like that. For some reason, talking about masculinity is inherently unmasculine. Well, so be it. Look, the fact is, that's why we were in Key West. But how were we supposed to do that, again? Were there any ways left? Reckless stuff, stuff like hunting exotic game, or racing dune buggies over enormous sand hills—these outlets may have been permissible fifty years ago. But the planet had only three billion people in 1960. Our tired orb supports more than twice that figure today, and it takes work to find an expression of masculinity that remains sustainable in an environment that's so fucking *crowded*. The fact is, the spearfishing had left me feeling unfulfilled and kind of frustrated, and with an intense desire to go out and get really, really wasted. Yeah, if spearfishing didn't work, I would try another way—apparently, one of the few ways I had left.

A couple hours later I stood in the parking lot of a strip mall convenience store just off Key West's main drag. A cop stood before me. He wanted to know whether I asked a guy across the street whether he had any drugs.

"No sir," I said. "I'm just a good Canadian boy."

He let me go. I walked off. Soon the evening's third and fourth rocks were rattling against the change in my pocket. The night had begun the way so many others had. Drinks, shots, things got blurry. It was simple enough to flee the other guys. I just walked through the door. Some dude on a bike told me to try the intersection of Duval and Olivia, coincidentally mere blocks from my hotel, and the first shifty-looking character I tried exchanged a rock for a $20. And that's pretty much what I did that night in Key West. I walked and I smoked crack. I'll spare you the specifics. You probably get the drill by now, anyhow. I walked so much and smoked so much crack that my one foot became one large blister. The big difference from home was that here in Key West there wasn't any reason to stop. The sun rose. I was still smoking crack. My heart speed-bagged against my ribs. I thought, if I keep smoking crack I am going to have a heart attack. I kept smoking crack. I thought: you have to stop smoking crack. I kept smoking crack. You are going to die if you take another hit. I took another hit. This was the point, I realized: I was no longer in the driver's seat. I wasn't controlling things here, anymore. Crack was controlling things. I could hear early risers on the walkway outside my hotel room. My rocks gone, I snuck out to Duval and Olivia and the guy I'd bought from all night was gone. Probably gone to bed. Fuck. I flushed my pipe down the toilet and lay on my bed. I paced back and forth in the room, bathroom door to exterior door and back. I turned on CNN. It was too depressing. I read my book—Denis Johnson's *Tree of Smoke*. It was too depressing.

At some point my roommate stumbled in from parts unknown. I pretended to be asleep. I lasted another hour of tossing and turning. I got up. I limped outside. I limped down the stairs.

Have you ever been homesick? There was a period in my pre-teens I was homesick every time I slept away from home; after a couple of times, I just quit sleeping away from home. The one I remember most happened at a camp in Muskoka, north of Toronto. It was the summer of Dire Straits' "Money for Nothing." I was twelve—way too old to be homesick. The counsellors blared Sting's prelude from their boom boxes. Walking from the fetid woodshed that constituted our cabin, I went and found my brother and pulled him with me. We picked our way over roots. We sat on a pine stump that had a view of the lake. "Why are you crying?" the nine-year-old asked. I hugged him. His little arms around my chest. You know, back then, I didn't understand why I felt so bad.

People who don't get it denigrate homesickness as simple wussiness. In fact, it's a more complex emotion. It stems, I think, from the disconnect between identity and environment. It's the fear of the unmoored self, the fear that different surroundings will knock the you that you know into a you that you don't. I craved my parents because they tethered me to me. My brother represented a connection to them. That's why his presence, even his nine-year-old presence, made me feel better.

Later that morning, on the balcony overlooking this Key West motor hotel parking lot, I had an encounter with my brother very like the one that had happened twenty-three years before. A tweaked and wired me emerged from my darkened hotel room. At the time, I blamed my insomnia on general partying, but the truth was, it was the $300 of crack I'd smoked that night. I tried to mask the thickness in my voice. I scuttled my fingertips up into my palms, to hide the burns on my thumb and forefinger.

"How you doin'?" Mark asked.

"Great," I said. "How you doin'?"

I got the same response.

Mark possessed a gene I lacked, a regulator that governed him.

"Oooh," I said, gulping air in quick hiccups not unlike the gill motion of the fish I'd speared. "I feel like shit…I don't know if I can last another night…I miss Natalie. I miss Myron."

He didn't say anything. He just gave me a hug.

I went in and did a search on my laptop for earlier flights. The airline operator named an ungodly flight change fee. Which I considered. Natalie answered when I called. I stood on the balcony of the Truman Hotel with my cell phone pressed against my ear, overlooking the parking lot macadam heating up in the Caribbean sun. She'd just had breakfast. She was taking Myron to indoor playtime in the gym at the Trinity-Bellwoods community centre. It was a trip we'd made frequently together and I wanted to be pushing the stroller alongside her. The solace of my wonderful son, my perfect child. I'd so ached for the liberation this stag represented, and now that I was without responsibility I wondered why? What was I doing away from my family? Why had I ever wanted to leave? The debauch I'd once found so thrilling had twisted into something else. A thousand miles away Natalie made sympathetic sounds into our cordless. I spun my despondent mood as the result of simple separation. I realized later the sympathy she offered saw through my hypocrisy. She figured her husband's down-in-the-dumps had a pharmaceutical origin. She understood that the man she married was fucked up and broken and the sympathy she offered came as the result of that. In a way I didn't yet comprehend, Natalie saw I was trapped in Key West with the Chris I didn't know—one I didn't even *like*.

A Denny's peddled its all-day breakfasts on the corner of Duval and Truman. I limped up there with some of the other boys. "Big appetite, huh fellas?" swished our waiter afterward as he cleared a tableful of mostly untouched omelettes. We were a half-dozen slack jaws. Another of our mighty stags rested his head on the table formica. The lone American among us returned from a trip to the bathroom, eyes watering, wiping his mouth with the back of his hand. He said, "I feel much better now." On our way out we passed other tables of guys our age: cargo-shorted gladiators still recovering from the previous evening's Battle of Sparta.

It was a snatch of this other table's dialogue that did it. One of them was talking about his son. Huh, I thought. That guy's a father, too. Then I realized each of the other five hangover zombies at *my* table also were fathers. And that prompted a related epiphany. Oh, debauch. It was the two-four and the sixty-ouncer, the scotch tumbler and the shot glass. It was white lines and ecstasy pills and night clubs and dance caves. What I saw at the Denny's in Key West was what a cliché that made me. It was there I realized there was nothing exceptional about being a fucked-up father. Everybody else, in their own ways, perhaps. But still: Like me, these other guys were rebelling against fatherhood. Was it still rebellion when everyone else was doing it too?

THAT WASN'T ALL. It wasn't *just* that. The following month I went in for a physical and discovered my blood pressure was so high my doctor wanted to put me on medication. And something called my ketones—they were up. "How much do you drink?" he asked.

I pressed my palms into the examination table's paper cover. "Not much," I said. "Maybe a case of beer a week? More, if I go out and, like, actually party."

"Party," he frowned. "What's that entail?"

"A little cocaine," I shrugged. "Sometimes a lot of cocaine. Crack."

His eyes flicked again over the results of my blood test. I felt I could be honest with my GP. His office was downtown, just south of Toronto's gay enclave. Plenty of his patients used plenty more recreational drugs than I did. So I was a little taken aback with his reaction.

"You've got to stop," he said flatly. "These levels are un-usual for someone your age. They could lead to some serious trouble."

And this: Sunday morning and we were late for a brunch date. Mittens and hats and where the fuck is Myron's balaclava, getting on his boots and my boots and his snowsuit and my coat and where are my gloves, where the fuck are my gloves and there they were, stuffed into my coat pockets and we were almost all set when Natalie did her little mental checklist of what we had—diaper bag, Myron is covered, snack, drink, and then we realized, we forgot the pacifier.

If there was one thing we couldn't leave the house without, it was that. Eyes unfocused while we considered possibilities. I checked my pockets, Nater checked hers, we checked the little wicker thing where we kept the hats and mitts.

Myron and I sprinted up the stairs, well, he was in my arms, and I sprinted down the hall to our bedroom at the other end of the house, and there it was, the little clear pacifier—and by the way, whoever invented a clear pacifier, don't you want to make the thing *easier* to find? Rather than completely fucking invisible?

"It's 8:40!" Natalie shouted up the stairs, and I ran down the hallway with Myron giggling in my arms—by this point the boy was an expert Daddy-rider, which is probably a talent that requires skill like horseback riding; he moved in sync with me—I rounded the banister and stepped down the first stair and caught a toe.

Momentum, cursed momentum, carried me forward. I arched my back, I threw my weight rearward, away from open space and the twelve-foot vertical fall before me. My arms spread. No: *I* spread my arms. One hand hit the wall on the right; the left cranked into the stair railing. My hands now were at waist level. Myron fell. He was about the level of my waist when I grasped what I'd done. I caught his neck. I pressed his head to my thigh. Fucking momentum. His head slid away. He fell backward. He was horizontal and his face wore astonishment. He landed at the stairway's midpoint, head lower than

feet and flat on his back. He bounced. He bounced into a backward somersault.

My little boy crumpled at the bottom of the stairs.

Natalie got to him first. She scooped him up. She just held
him to her for the first moments. I stood awkward over them.
He was in her arms, face red, mouth open, totally silent. She
carried him to the couch and it wasn't until all of us were on
the cushions that the first wail arrived. By that time it was a
relief. I had been wondering whether somehow the fall had
removed his power of speech. Blood trickled from his mouth.
Scarlet skin joined left eyebrow to hairline. I ran my finger over
it. It formed a ridge. And a lump appeared, volcano-like, at the
back of his head.

The weekend's rental car sat in the lot across the street. I
sprinted for it. Natalie held him in the back seat as we drove.
The city slept under the recent snowfall. Myron was quiet
when we pulled into the Hospital for Sick Children's emergency
driveway.

All I could think was fractured skull.

They called his name within minutes.

"How'd he fall down the stairs?" asked the admitting
nurse.

"I dropped him."

She looked at me. Her focus took in my red eyes, my tear-
swollen face. Her tone came softer. "It happens."

Myron was quiet by this time. He peeked out from Natalie's arms long enough to accept a nurse's offer of stickers. A
scab marked his upper lip. A fat lip bloomed out from under
the soother. Both Natalie and I kept a hand on him, as though
our touch was keeping him healthy. The nurse did her stuff.
Stethoscope, blood pressure cuff, temperature. The doctor's

examination: the pupils, the abdominal palpitations—everything seemed okay. Perhaps he had a minor concussion, the doctor said. Perhaps, not even that. Kids were pretty resilient.

Round trip, the hospital visit took 90 minutes, and through it all something new hunkered in my chest cavity. It stayed there even after we walked through the front door. In lieu of our long-cancelled brunch, we toasted bagels. Until now, Natalie had done all the morning's consoling. I'd wanted to hold my boy, but hadn't felt I deserved the solace. And what if he rejected my entreaties? I didn't know whether I could handle that. So Natalie'd given the hugs, she'd held him while the doctor did the examination. She transported him from car seat to house. Now Natalie took Myron upstairs for a nap. I followed behind. On the bed we formed parentheses around him. Then, without prompting, he climbed on top of me. He set his head down on my chest, so we were belly to belly. The sound of his breathing. Only as he drifted off did I realize he forgave me.

This would have been easy to explain had I been hungover when it happened. Had I been out late smoking crack the previous night. Drinking, at least. Were there some connection between my caught toe and the rest of it. There was not. The previous evening Natalie and I had watched a movie. We turned in by 11. Still, as days passed, as my boy showed no lingering effects of his fall, this incident became associated in my mind with all the other betrayals represented by the drinking and the drugs. It was yet another sign of the way I was failing my son.

It's simple what happened: I dropped my son. Faced with the choice of saving myself or my boy—because when I caught my toe on the top stair, I could have saved my boy. I could have rolled forward, and twisted, so my boy was above me as we both fell, so I landed below him, first, cushioning his impact.

Instead, when I caught my toe on that first step, I let go of him and arrested my own fall. Until something tests you, it's easy to move with the swagger and voice of a hero. Except hero isn't something that just comes. It's something you have to work at. To be heroic when you're needed, you have to be a hero when you aren't.

AND STILL. And yet. How was I still? My god, Shulgan: how were you *still*? It was late April and there was a launch at one of the Ossington bars. The keffiyeh to blazer ratio was maybe one to one. It took me about ten seconds after I entered the bar to register a feeling of old and out of place. Possibly, I was the only parent in there. My friend Josh Ostroff was DJing. I went to the bar's back room, and I sat there watching him. He wasn't even spinning vinyl. He just stared at his computer. Every so often he looked at his iPod. It was the most boring thing ever.

"Shulgan! Sorry, I haven't seen you for, shit, like, ever. Where have you been?"

Not Ostroff—one of Ostroff's friends.

"Writing a book. Having a kid."

"Which one?"

"Both."

"A kid! What's the sex?"

"What?"

"The gender? Like, is it boy or girl? Your baby?"

"The one who's not born yet is a girl." It was pretty loud. I'm pretty sure he didn't hear. "And then the other one, he's not really a baby—he's nineteen months. He's walking."

"He. Boy. Your baby's a him?"

"Right. Myron."

"*What's* his name?"

"*Myron.*"

"Ah, okay," he nodded, clearly not hearing now. "And how's that going for you?"

His tone suggested we were discussing a cranky pet, maybe something with three legs we both understood really should be put down. Each successive sentence of mine might as well have included a request to look bored—requests with which he complied. I invented an urgent need to use a urinal. Soon the washroom mirror was providing roughly the same amount of companionship.

Was it Kaplan's arrival that made the night a big night? I'd argue not. I'd argue the moment it became a big night was the moment I discovered I had the freedom to have a night out. Nights out were a precious commodity now. *Every* night I was out was a big night out. Kaplan and I cabbed our way to the Little Italy bar where you buy blow in the basement office. If they liked the look of you, that is. This time, they didn't.

We discussed options on the sidewalk outside. It occurred to me that I lived just a few blocks away. There was a pull toward my bed. To my life as a father. I stuffed down that feeling. Who knew the next time I'd get a night out? Brainstorming over coke-procurement strategies ensued and something in there knocked loose in Kaplan a number that might work. He called it. We caught a cab to the Drake Hotel, met the guy on the rooftop patio and seconds later I was figuring out how to manipulate my swollen-seeming fingers into snapping open the baggie in one of the hotel bar's gloriously private bathroom stalls. I resorted to using my teeth. That worked. I fished out my house key and dug a tip into the little bit of powder. I plugged my one nostril and sucked with the other.

All Systems Go.

After that the night just became about cocaine, as every night with cocaine does. It was conversational interludes between trips to the bathroom. Somewhere in there came a call from my wife.

"Where are you?"

"The Drake. I'll be home soon."

"You said you'd be home at 11."

"I'll be home soon."

The setting changed. Last call kicked us out of the Drake and we headed to a weeknight-only after-hours club on Queen Street. At some point fatigue surmounted my desire to do any more cocaine. I walked home. I crawled into my side of the king size. Four a.m. Over on her side of the bed my wife didn't move. And I stared at the ceiling for maybe another hour until my exhaustion overcame the coke. I slept.

FIRST AWARENESS: A bang. The bedroom door against the bedroom wall. Myron sprinted, launched himself toward me and faceplanted against my knees. "Daddy!" and "Daddy" and: "*Daddy!*" Look, type can't capture the varieties of intonation. He crawled from knee to hip and sat on my chest.

Myron had only a handful of words, with Mommy and Daddy the ones he used most, and yet in those two words there were thousands of words. "Daddy" said one way could mean take me out of my high chair. "Daddy" with a different inflection meant, "Check out this cool thing I'm doing." He had dozens, hundreds, maybe a thousand variations in those syllables topped with the twin hard consonants. One of those *Daddys* was a display of delight. There was a request to tickle him

more. There was a "Daddy" leavened with a pinch of rebuke—
"Daddy," he might be saying. "You're so silly."

"Hey buddy," I said. He fit the top of his head into the
curve under my chin. He just stayed there, content. I closed my
eyes.

"I'm just getting my wallet," Natalie said, retrieving it from
the top of the dresser.

Once their departure was marked with the front door slam
I slid to the bed edge, steeled myself for standing and made it
to the hook on the wall without any significant leakage of spi-
nal fluid. Cigarette smoke sloughed off denim. I peeled off my
jeans and slung them atop the laundry pile. I pulled on a T-shirt
and went downstairs to make some coffee.

My phone was on the kitchen table, six messages heavier
than the last time I cleared my voice mail. One was from an
insurance broker calling to inform us everything was set for a
car we were planning on buying. The next five were from Natalie, who had apparently called every hour, on the hour, that I
stayed out past the time I had promised to be home the night
before.

With *The New York Times* for company I went out and sat
on my front steps to sip my coffee. The caffeine cut the raw-
husk feeling coke always left me with. Natalie pulled up onto
the sidewalk before our house. We dispatched the grocery bags
with a fireman's relay.

Myron and I flopped on the grass of our postage stamp front
yard. I took off my shoes and socks to enjoy the grass, and helped
Myron off with his. The tickle of the grass on his feet made
him giggle and soon we were wrestling among the blades.

He went over to the other side of the fence, where my sister's
garden was freshly tilled soil. A bit of fun involved cupping

hands and dumping dirt on the sidewalk. Next was a diverting game that involved circumnavigating an ornamental evergreen. Vasco de Gama picked his barefooted way through the topsoil. We made it to the next lot down, where the letters M and D were arranged in the cement path, a custom mosaic done, I'd imagined, by some long-ago neighbour. Myron scrunched his toes on the concrete. He touched an arm of the "M."

"Em," I said.

"Em," he said.

It must have been a remarkable variety of textures, and I could see him cataloguing each one—the pebbled nub of the path cement, the sandy dryness of the top soil, the grains between his toes. I caught movement in my sister's garden. It was a grey tomcat, setting itself up, arching its back, its face, tensing into posed concentration. I recognized that expression. I saw it on Myron each morning, maybe a quarter hour after his oatmeal. Except this cat wasn't wearing a diaper. And it was perched in my sister's garden. Where my son played in his bare feet. This creature was fouling where my son put his feet. I shouted: *Hey!* I picked up the nearest object available—my hightop Adidas. I flung it. A direct hit. The thing scampered off across the street, into the schoolyard. I looked around, to see if anyone had seen, and when I turned back, Myron had his shoe, his little brown DC skate shoe, held aloft, baseball-style, and he flung it toward Julie's yard, where the cat had been.

I said, "Myron, you are not to throw shoes at cats."

He said, "Cats."

He threw his other shoe.

My boy was imitating me. This was a point when Myron was learning and changing and growing and just in general *becoming*—going from a baby to a person. I'd started picking up on other imitations. That was what his learning process was, right now: imitating. Speech tics. Shaving. Typing on my laptop, typing on my typewriter. He was learning to become a person, a little boy, one who spoke and who processed and who thought, and he was learning how to do much of this stuff through me.

"What do you think that stuff does to your blood pressure?"

After lunch, Natalie, our first opportunity to talk. Myron was upstairs having his mid-afternoon nap. Natalie was on the couch, perched on the seat edge. I was on a chair facing her, my crossed legs indicating a relaxed state I didn't feel.

This referring to "that stuff"—this was new. Finally, apparently, Natalie had had enough.

"I worry about that."

"I do too. Not for your sake. Don't you want to see Myron grow up? That stuff might not kill you now, but with you hitting 150 over 90, relaxed, you might be forty-five, you might be fifty, and it's coronary care. If you make it. It's stroke."

Myron would be sixteen when I turned fifty.

"What goes through your mind? What is it that you are thinking when you make the decision that it's a good idea to blow however much money you blow on this stuff?"

"I *know*."

"You talk about how much you love Myron. And I believe it. Anybody can see it, how much you love him. That little boy has a best friend and a partner and a hero and it's you and I think you feel the same way about him, all of that, you can see it in the way you—you—the way you're always the first one to him when he cries at night. How absent-minded you are and still you always remember to bring the baby monitor downstairs with you. How impatient you are and still you take twenty minutes to get to 7-11 because you wait for him to do his exploring. Chris, I see how much you love him. And what I can't understand is how there's still a moment on these nights when you give yourself permission to buy the cocaine, to stay out until 4 a.m., knowing that you have this guy, this kid, who is going to be wanting to wake up with you in an hour or two."

"You love this," I said. "Now that it's all out in the open. You can spend the next year beating up on me."

"You're just crashing. You were all strung out and now you're coming down and you're taking it out on me. You'll be depressed for a day or two and then it'll all be the same and two weeks later you'll be out again all night."

My nocturnal failures made the house too crowded for Natalie and I. Once Myron woke up I took him to Robarts Library, where we made our way to the tenth floor to survey the stacks. I was looking for books related to a book idea I'd had. This was something of an audit; I was surfing through bibliographies to attempt to learn whether anyone had done the book I wanted to do. (And, I discovered, somebody had.)

Myron occupied himself with pulling hardcovers from the bottom shelf while little bits of the previous evening got between me and the book spines. I followed the absurd impulse to taste the tip of my house key. Here was the tool that secured my family from the outside world. Even this I'd sullied with cocaine's bitter powder. All at once I felt exhausted. This was the third time this month with the stuff and there remained a week before the calendar flipped. With Myron on my lap I sat at a catalogue terminal and typed in *Rabbit, Run*, then led my boy to the proper place in the stacks. When I first read it in my twenties the book was a slog. How could Updike expect anyone to identify with his asshole protagonist? But *I* did, now. Now the opening pages seemed a thing of exquisite beauty: the day in early spring, the young father joins the kids in their basketball game and then, pages later, leaves behind the connections to wife, fetus, and toddler that prevent him from ever returning to those afternoons of net and leather and wood. How strange to realize an affinity with the literary character who'd originally repulsed. I considered running from Myron and my own pregnant wife: "Harry's boy is being fed, this home is happier than his, he glides a pace backward over the cement and rewalks the silent strip of grass . . . He cuts up Joseph Street, runs a block, strides another, and comes within sight of his car, its grid grinning at him." Where to go? Whistler? Mexico? Moss Park? All those years of Shakespeare and Dickens and yet I've never been to London.

The thought occurs, that these evenings of cocaine and lager have formed my own versions of Rabbit's flight. Those T-shirts worn by the offspring of hipster parents: "I make Mommy drink." My own version: "I make Daddy smoke crack." Was that it? Just another fucked-up father torn between fun and responsibility, between family man and swingin' man.

Think it through, Shulgan: last night you and Kaplan got your little baggies around midnight. And what did you do with the four hours that ensued? You stood in graffitied cubicles floored in piss and errant scraps of TP and you thumbed open the Ziploc seal and dug with the house key and hoped some bouncer's head didn't pop over the stall's upper rim. You stood and looked around at people who were every bit as fucked up as you. Was there witty repartee? Sparkling bon mots you could scrawl in your notebook to regurgitate on the page? Yeah right. You were so fucked up you couldn't talk.

That four hours cost you time with your boy. So in the light of day, on Robart's tenth floor, how does that trade-off sound? In the cold light of day, you fuck, which would you rather have: Four beer-smeared hours spent so wired you can't get out a coherent thought, or time with a kid whose laughter is quicksilver happiness and who regards you as supreme being number one?

Myron looked up. "Da-dee," he said, and returned to his mess.

Deciphering *that* "dad" was simple: "Hi," it said. And I thought of the day's first "Daddy," when he burst into the bedroom. You know what it meant? Daddy—you're my hero. When was I going to start acting like it?

AND FINALLY: the look. I've puzzled out why it meant so much, why it gave me the shock it did, and I think it involves the dissolution of the fiction I'd maintained, of separation, of different spheres. It was a night out like any other night out. By now, you get the idea. The characters included Greg Goldberg, a Montreal writer in town for the night, and a few media types he knew better than I did—a writer who'd made his name in the 'zine scene, and a CBC radio host and his attractive girlfriend.

'Zine boy, Goldberg, and I ended up at a terrible little strip bar, Baby Dolls, on Ossington's hipster stretch. Once we settled into our vinyl banquette, the 'zine guy blanched. He gave a little wave to the girl onstage, who teetered over after the song's conclusion. Was she in one of his writing classes? Naw, it became apparent they were old friends. Or something. The way I understood it, years before, the stripper had a 'zine, quite a good one, and in fact she made some reference to her job at the strip bar doubling as research for something, possibly a grad school dissertation.

With a glance toward the bar, she slagged her manager and said she'd have to be going, she was supposed to be making the rounds, working the room, soliciting lap dances—the manager didn't like her talking to non-paying friends. We got the hint. Each one of us followed her in sequence to a banquette at the back, where she dutifully did her thing. Certainly, during my turn, I would have asked whether she had any drugs, or, did she know where to get some. She brushed off my request, and despite the proximity of our respective groins, what followed was small talk as deadly as what occurred at any corporate networking mixer. I went analytical to fend off the clichés: I didn't understand people who spent money on lap dances, I said, cleverly, you know, because I was currently in the midst of spending money on a lap dance. Was it just supposed to be foreplay, for a wank to be had later? The $20 could pay for a month's membership to a porn site of one's choosing. "Yeah, but this is real," she breathed into my ear. "What's real about it?" I wondered. "This look of sexual ecstasy you're wearing— is that real?"

She interpreted my disaffection for a challenge; she grasped my neck, my shoulder and at one point, my bum. This, while staring intently into my eyes and grimacing or bearing other expressions of apparent discomfort. Her choreography seemed the lead-up to a really painful Vulcan mind meld. Perhaps sensing things weren't going well, she became more enthusiastic during the song's final bits. Now the Vulcan mind meld was paired with repeated slow-motion knees to my groin. She suggested she'd try harder during another dance—if I paid her another $20. But by this point my testicles felt a bit like mashed potatoes. They'd suffered enough. Besides, two songs wasted $40. I had to save the rest of my money, as I wanted to waste it on drugs.

Existing the next morning in a haze of headache and self-loathing, I took Myron for a walk. We played on the forklift by the corner grocery until the grocer caught me doing my best imitation of a diesel engine. The Scooter Gollum pinched Myron's cheek. We wandered into the park, played soccer, and wrestled on the grass. I noticed Myron noticing—what? I turned and saw a hipster and her purse. She recognized me; I recognized her. It was the stripper I'd met just a few hours before. She looked at Myron, and at me, and the look she threw my way was all indictment and accusation. Here was my guilt's apex. Here was my boy's hero made for the cretin he was. Here was me failing my son. She stalked off on the park path and I stayed there as my two separate lives short-circuited. Her glance said *scumbag*. Her glance said *hypocrite*. Family man, swingin' man. Her glance said *choose, motherfucker, you can't have it both ways*, and finally, finally, I did.

-10-

FIFTY-TWO PICKUP

"What would you like to drink?" I asked Natalie, and she said her usual, water. Glass rattled with the heavy door's swing. Five brown bottles beckoned. My hand went to the apple juice. Myron got his usual cocktail, half Brita water, half apple juice. I made the same thing for myself.

"No beer?"

"Naw."

Natalie's raised eyebrows asked for an explanation.

I shrugged. "Not tonight."

Dinner. The interim hours were pretty low-key. They always were, these evenings after. Natalie gathered her scrubs and slopped some pasta leftovers in a Tupperware container for her late-night lunch break. Myron and I followed her to the front door for a round of goodbye kisses. Natalie's lips seemed softer, although I didn't know exactly what she was trying to convey. Once she was two houses down the street Myron and I walked out to the sidewalk. Only once Natalie turned the corner onto Dundas did Myron, somewhat confused by the timing of this goodbye thing, start flapping his hand in the air.

"Bye bye," he said. "Mom!"

Soon we were both of us dressed in nightclothes, snuggled under a duvet and backed up against a berm of pillows, working our way through the poems of Dennis Lee's *Alligator Pie*. By the time Billy Batter baked his butter, my boy was out.

It was 8 p.m. Twenty-four hours before this my third beer was greasing my system. All the manifestations of this weird drug problem I had included one common denominator: alcohol. If I was out late and everybody else was asleep and it was only me walking homeward solo—I was okay. I would go home, and go to sleep. But if I was out late and everybody else was asleep and it was only me walking solo homeward, *and* I was wasted—then perhaps I would zip off in search of a certain species of urban sapper, with the furtive look and the cellophane twists that held the pocket rocks.

I USED TO QUIT drinking all the time. I went through a phase, I heard about the power of the public disavowal, and so I spread my quitting around, I told the people who most cared about me, and I told them often enough that such promises lost their zip. This time, I kept it to myself. I didn't even acknowledge to myself I'd quit drinking. I was taking a break, maybe for a month. And you know what? There's power in public utterances, but there's something also in the secret vow. Silence has a potency all its own.

Most of May I stayed in. When things came up I made excuses, work was insane, Natalie had something going on so I had to watch Myron. Those five beer bottles stayed on the fridge door, unmentioned. I spent a lot of evenings lying in bed with Myron next to me. He slept; I stayed up, restless and zipping through novels like I hadn't done for years.

Did I notice any changes, once my abstinence began? Sure, but they were subtle. Around this period Myron was really into playing outside with me. I'd get home, and after the bit where he tackled my shins he got into this routine where he'd point out the front door.

"Okay, okay, let's go outside, buddy."

The two of us on the lawn rolling around on the grass. We had this thing we'd do, where I'd fall on my back and he'd get on top of me and I'd pretend he had me pinned, and then I'd roll over on him, my weight on my elbows, tickling his chest with my chin, and he'd giggle. "Daddy," he'd say. Two or three weeks into this drink recess, I noticed something about Myron's Daddys. They hurt less.

One afternoon, as my one-month anniversary without drinking approached, Natalie returned from a play date with the wives of some guys I'd gone to university with. "What did you talk about?" I asked.

"Kenny's reception was a big one," Natalie said, taking off her shoes by the door. Kenny was the cause of the Key West stag. His wedding was a family-only affair staged in the Caribbean. Now he and his wife were throwing a Toronto celebration for the friends in his old home base. "Oh, and your book launch, everyone's excited for the parties for that."

"Did anyone ask whether I was still not drinking?"

"No, nobody."

"Oh."

Something in my tone made her look at me.

"*I* haven't had a drink for seven months."

"You're *pregnant*."

"They've all been pregnant, too. None of them think it's a big deal."

Some part of me expected that spring to be bliss between Natalie and I. I had removed my marriage's single biggest problem, and I wanted some gratitude for it, despite never having fully acknowledged the problem in the first place. Not laudable, possibly not even rational, but there it was. Natalie didn't offer any plaudits. She wasn't so certain those problems were behind me. How was this break different from all my other attempts? Plus, I was conducting brief experiments in disclosure. For example, I was craving crack. This happened after any significant use. Nothing new there. The cravings tended to manifest themselves in an overall feeling of internal unreliability—in a quality of sketchiness, as though there was the possibility, however faint, that I might suddenly drop everything and sprint toward a crack purchase. The big difference with these cravings? I caught myself alluding to them in conversation with Natalie. At one point in early May, heading into a weekend of her night shifts, Natalie offered to ask about a babysitter, maybe I wanted some time to myself, maybe go see a movie? I shook my head. "I think I'd better just stay close to home," I said. "I'm feeling a bit sketchy." I certainly didn't use the word "craving." Not yet.

Some part of me expected that spring to be bliss. Dude: are you an *idiot*? These little hints I was dropping about past drug problems were bound to create some friction. Natalie could figure out that the presence of sketch implied problems more severe than dabbling in powdered cocaine. My use of the word "sketch" was a carryover from the first round of problems. If I felt sketchy then I had been using crack. My hints put her in a strange position. Armed with these tacit confirmations, she felt angry with me for allowing a drug problem to bloom again, for allowing myself to get into trouble with something I should never have done in the first place. But she couldn't act on this anger. Acting on it would force her to confront that drugs had become a problem in her nuclear family, and something about her past history prevented her from admitting that. Rather than arguing about drugs, we argued about other stuff. It seemed every day involved f-bombs. There was, for example, the question of orange juice. Wandering our house I started noticing half-drunk cups all over the place—of water, sometimes, but mostly of orange juice. Every day as I was tidying up from breakfast I would find a glass containing maybe an inch of Grade A Tropicana.

"Look at this," I demanded, thrusting the quarter-full glass toward my wife, who was, at that moment, changing Myron's diaper. "Can't you just finish it? Or pour yourself less?"

But no. Even if she poured herself a smaller portion, she always left those final dregs. It came down to saliva. She's squeamish about the stuff. Natalie would never, ever, under any circumstances, drink someone else's drink. No matter how careful one is, a certain amount of backwash happens in every swallow, and she doesn't want to drink someone else's saliva. In fact, she is *so* crazy about saliva that even her *own* creeps her out. Hence, those last few centimeters in the bottom of the cup. By the end, Nater figures, there's too much of her own saliva in it. So she doesn't drink it. It stays there, on the kitchen table, for me to find.

That May, this practice was driving me *crazy*. One morning I found a glass of Florida's finest in our bathroom. I made a sound meant to symbolize my internal frustration (*arghbuble*) and stalked downstairs to point it out to Natalie. At some point, Natalie yelled toward my back. "That never used to bother you," she said. "When did you become such a *dick?*"

Some minutes later, Natalie came up the stairs and into Myron's room, where Myron and I played cars.

"Whew," she said, leaning over, her palms on her knees.

I stopped my Matchbox racer.

"What's wrong?"

"Coming up the stairs—I'm having one of those blood pressure episodes."

"You want me to go down to the kitchen and get you a glass of water?"

Water being a thing with us. I'd read somewhere that water helped the body regulate blood pressure, and I'd got it in my head my pregnant wife wasn't drinking enough of the stuff.

"No, I'm going to lie down."

"That's good," I said in this sarcastic tone I use when I'm in all-out jerk mode. "Treat the symptom rather than the underlying problem that's causing the symptom. Smart."

She stopped halfway down the hall and swivelled that belly around so it faced me.

"I don't even *like* you anymore."

When I went into the bedroom, Natalie was on the bed, reading.

"I'm just telling you what I think."

"You've become so self-righteous."

"Huh," I said. "Tables are turned."

"Oh Chris. Look, *do* something with all this nervous energy. Go for a run."

It wasn't a bad idea. Just to show her, I didn't do it immediately. Instead, I went downstairs and made peanut butter sandwiches with the crusts cut off for Myron and paced back and forth in the kitchen while he ate. The pre-nap story was the latest Munsch favourite, *Stephanie's Ponytail*, and after it Myron wanted to go downstairs for a glass of chocolate milk.

"OK," I said. "But first let's count to 100."

He fell asleep in the high thirties. I pulled my arm from underneath his head and headed into the basement. My running shoes were under my winter boots. The first pair of running shorts I pulled on were too tight so I opted instead for my soccer shorts and a T-shirt. Natalie passed me in the hallway as I was tying my laces and I kept my eyes on the shoes instead of looking at her. And then I kept my eyes on the concrete as I ran the first couple of blocks. It felt like everyone I saw knew this was my first run in—shit, I don't know. It felt like years. Out on the road I had a conversation with some hyperobjective otherness, who, in this case, was informing me that, hey, Shulgan, you *had* become a dick. And when did *that* happen, exactly?

It would take me a lot of runs to work that one out. During our decade together we'd developed a cycle. I stayed out too late, weathered the hangover, and then spent the following days making up for it. Guilt-ridden me would go out of my way to be nice, to ignore the invariable irritants, to be helpful around the house. The cycle became especially pronounced when it was complemented by drugs. So when I *quit*, the cycle evened out. Rather than being an enormous jerk one night every couple of weeks, I became a bit of a jerk, all the time. I was faster to criticize and slower to forgive. Our fights stretched on for days. I wondered, is it possible the drugs and the drinking had made me a good husband? Had they actually been helping my marriage?

Before, our marriage had been messed up, but things went more smoothly. They worked. Now, the marriage was less messed up, and it wasn't working. I considered making a sacrifice. Like an errant Sir Galahad: "Maybe I should go back to drinking," I said. "You know, for the good of the marriage."

"You do what you need to do," Natalie said.

"Kidding," I said.

I began to run every day. At first I just ran to get rid of the nervous energy. The running opened me up to these odd conversations with myself and eventually I was running because I found it therapeutic; *because* it opened me up to these meditative bouts with myself. Out along the paths that formed a frontier between Lake Ontario and Toronto I thought about starting drinking and quitting drinking and taking drugs and what it meant to stop. The idea, at first, was to take a break. A month, yeah, and then I wondered: could I do two? It was a recess, a lacuna, a hiatus in an overall much-starred career, and afterward I could go back to it, I could drink a bit, and then I'd control the drugs. But this otherness I talked to on my runs suggested the ban's extension, and I listened.

Life improved. My first book launched to good reviews. Which was more of a relief than anything else. I'd put the whole of my heart into that thing. And once it was out, I just thought, well, at least I didn't fuck that one up. Then Natalie's dad bought us a car—a Volkswagen Jetta wagon, a sensible but sporty gas-sipper. For years we'd relied on rentals and borrowings, but with us set to have two children, ambulating about the city was about to grow a hell of a lot more difficult, and then pow, suddenly we had a set of wheels. It was a generous thing for him to have done, and it changed our lives in a subtle but significant way.

The same week the car arrived I had a social engagement I couldn't avoid: Kenny's return to Toronto. I drove over in the new car with my sister's boyfriend, Isaac. We didn't really need to *drive* over; the bar where everyone was meeting was a ten-minute walk from my house. But the car was only two days old. We drove the thing every chance we got. I almost drove it to get to my sister's place, next door. We *invented* reasons to drive it. So regardless of how close this bar was, the car was my chosen choice of transportation.

We parked down the block and as we approached the bar I could see them lined up, old friends and family gathered around a series of pushed-together bar tables set on Queen West just on the opposite side of a wrought-iron fence. There was an impulse to flee, and I probably would have turned back had Isaac not been with me. I didn't want to do this; I felt exposed and alone and I just wanted to be reading a book in bed next to my sleeping son. The table reorganized itself to accept our additional pair. I was just sitting down as the waitress fixed her gaze on me to take my order. I guess I panicked. I blurted out the first non-alcoholic mixed drink that came to mind.

"A Shirley *Temple?*" echoed one of my friends.

I shrugged. It did sound silly. I made a note: next time, order a Club Soda.

"Not drinking, Shulgan?"

"I'm on the wagon for a little while."

"But Kenny's in town."

I looked at Kenny. I shrugged.

At this point in the night, no one made a big deal about it. The culture of the alcohol recess was familiar to this crew, some of whom made it an annual thing—one took off the month of January, another February, another guy we knew did October. Even gladiators needed to take a break from battle. It helped keep the ferocity up, the rest of the time.

"How long's it been?" somebody asked, and the span I supplied—six weeks—earned some raised eyebrows. "Sheesh," I heard. "Congratulations." The camaraderie of the beer mug developed around me. The tabletop disappeared under pitchers of beer and pint glasses. And there was me, sipping soft drink and grenadine and playing with my little umbrella.

I found myself taking little sips of water. I invented excuses to get up and take a walk around. I went to the bathroom about a dozen times. It's a small separation, your choice of drink. On some level, who cares whether fermented liquid passes whose lips? The thing about drinking is, it's a team sport. The shared rounds, the mutual grimaces. And I'm not playing. I've left the team. This small thing is just enough to introduce some stand-apartness from the rest of the group. And if not drinking separates me from *this* group—this group that includes my brother and sister, my cousin Kate, my boy Eric (known since kindergarten), Fraser (since grade ten) and three of my university housemates . . . If a little thing like not drinking separates me from *this* group—then I'm fucked with everybody else.

And I see this. I see this as the beer tally increases and my inability to make conversation grows. There's a store of standard, catch-up kind of questions. What are you doing now that the book is done? (Not much.) What's the next book about? (Not sure.) Before, once the store was exhausted, I was pretty good at inventing topics for conversation. Dredging up life experiences and spinning amusingly self-deprecating stories from the disturbed muck.

Not drinking seemed to have robbed me of that talent. Not drinking, the only thing I can think about is not drinking. I blame other people for this. The stupid fucks won't let me forget I'm not drinking. They keep bringing it up. And then if *they* don't bring it up, *I'll* figure out a way to work it into the conversation. I'm a master at it, at working not drinking into the conversation while seeming to not want to talk about it. Any number of conversation topics can be manipulated by me to wind back to my abstinence.

My cell phone buzzed and a minute later I roped Isaac into an exit. This was the night of the National Magazine Awards and my friend Greg Goldberg, the Montreal writer, was in town for the ceremony. He'd won his first NMA. Isaac and I headed to the afterparty to offer congratulations. "Grab a drink, Shulgan," said Goldberg when we got there. I muttered something about this break I was on.

"No, seriously, grab yourself a drink."

Goldberg grabbed my shirt collar and sort of shoved me toward the table where the drinks were. With that momentum as my initial push I sidled my way through the suits and party dresses and grabbed a Coke for me and a beer for Isaac.

"You're *seriously* not drinking?" Goldberg again. "You're such an asshole, just have a drink."

I reminded Goldberg of the last time we'd seen each other, how drunk we got, and how it had taken us, like, three hours to find cocaine—because it was a *Monday*. "So," I said, "Too many nights like that."

Goldberg was so taken aback his chin snuck into his Adam's apple. "Shulgan, don't be ridiculous," he said. He pushed a beer toward me. "Shulgan, this is my friend, Giancarlo. Giancarlo, this is my pussy friend Shulgan, who is about to have a beer."

It was unbelievable. Not how wasted Goldberg was—he'd just won a National Magazine Award, he was celebrating, had I been drinking I would have been just as wasted as he was. But come on: was I in a *Degrassi* episode? The whole situation was just so ABC *After-School Special*. And dude didn't stop. "At least make yourself useful," he said. He shoved a $20 bill into my shirt's breast pocket. "Go get 'em, Tiger."

"Dude," I said. "Even in Montreal it's not that cheap."

"You can get little ones for $20."

"In Montreal, maybe. Here the smallest is $40."

With a facial expression that suggested he was moving some large, heavy object, Goldberg rummaged through his suit pockets until he found a second $20. The bills hovered in the air. It was appealing—a quest to give this dud of a night some purpose. For whatever reason, my reluctance set him off. "Don't be an asshole!" he said. He kind of grabbed me and kneed me in the groin. An editor I knew got between Goldberg and me. "Take it easy, Greg," the editor said.

"*I'll* take the money." This was Isaac. Greg gave it to him. We left a few minutes later and walked to where I parked the car. As I reversed the Jetta, the new Jetta, the days-old gleaming Jetta, I scraped the front quarter panel along a yellow parking barrier. Both Isaac and I got out to eye the damage. It wasn't much—a few paint smears. Some scratches. But still. "That sucks," Isaac said.

"I'm not going to find anything," I said. "What Goldberg wanted, I mean."

"Me neither."

"We should probably return that money."

"No way," Isaac said. "That's an asshole tax."

It was 1 a.m. when I returned home. I roamed my main floor feeling edgy and lonely. Amputating a diseased part of your life is an amputation all the same. I missed the partying my partying friends were up to.

THE NEXT MORNING I woke up at 6 a.m. and eyed a crack in the wall's plaster. It started—well, I don't exactly know where it started. Somewhere below where the mattress met the bed. It zig-zagged along the window's vertical edge and then it stopped precisely where the wall met the ceiling. I knew this crack. It's what I stared at every time I woke up before anyone else.

Crack crack crack.

Call it a rip. A zigzag. A jagged plastergap zed. Anything but that dreaded word, with its rare power to provoke a flinch on my part. Every utterance of that word, in this period, was italicized. Its presence in any sentence is highlighted to such an extent I even started to notice the real-world, rebus forms of the word—wiggly breaks in concrete sidewalks had me stepping carefully, for example. An editor friend of mine, oblivious to my difficulties, used *crackhead* as a synonym for idiot. "What are you, on crack?" he asked when I suggested a wording change he didn't like. And the coffee shop around the corner, Ella's Uncle, has these snacks they call crack cookies, so-called because they're so crammed with chocolate chips and toffee they're addictive, and each time I ordered one I performed little word games to avoid mentioning that awful syllable. "That one," I said. "Right there."

And hey, wait a second, why haven't I fixed this *crack* in the wall? Who has the time to fix everything in their houses?

Houses decay. That's what the damn things do and damn it's tough to keep those fuckers up. But now I'll have a lot more time. I'll have my nights free, for example. Maybe I'll patch up that—that line. Maybe I'll patch up all the zagged zigs in my life.

I rolled out of bed and achieved the vertical plane without waking either Nater or Myron. Down the stairs and out the door to the Jetta and the front quarter-panel I'd scratched the previous evening. Christ, the irony, that the first damage to this fresh helping of transportation would happen when I'm *sober*.

With a moistened bit of my T-shirt I rubbed against the yellow paint. Dolphin squeaks. The car rocked with the pressure. Once the shirt dried I brought the fabric to my mouth to wet it again. My haunches hurt. My tricep ached. I changed position.

Perhaps I would always be a fuck up. Perhaps it wasn't the drugs and the drinking that did it; perhaps it was just me being me.

One stripe off.

When did my thing become getting fucked up? When did my life's pursuit become evading my life?

Why'd I ever *start*?

Someone called my name. I stood. Blood returned to my legs. I flung my hand away a few times to shake out the stiffness. Road grime and paint smeared across my T-shirt. Most of the yellow was off the car. What remained was just a few black streaks.

Myron's silhouette showed through the screen door. A sleepy Natalie opened the entryway and he stood on the porch to make himself taller, the better to reach my embrace.

"What's up?" Natalie asked, an eye at the car.

How tight I wanted to squeeze my boy would have suffo-
cated the tyke. Your child's embrace as just another altered
state. You've made it this far and still he loves you. Now's your
chance, motherfucker, to live up to his love.

I explained about the car. Natalie got in close to the
quarter-panel. Her mouth pressed tight. "Hey, come on, don't
be like that," I said. I pulled her in for a hug and she stayed
rigid. She sniffed.

I heard it, and knew what was going on.

"I *didn't* drink last night," I said. "I didn't. Not a drop. Of
alcohol, I mean."

She stepped back and looked me over.

"I don't know when I'll be able to trust you."

"I know. I'll wait."

"Maybe not ever."

"It's okay. It'll be okay."

She sighed. She looked at the car, where Myron was rubbing
the paint. "Something like that was bound to happen some-
time," she said. I picked up Myron and we crossed the road,
Natalie holding my hand, my boy on my arm.

SATURDAY NIGHT AND SUNDAY MORNING

Sometimes when I'm running, I consider whether I need to quit the drinking and drugs. Was I that bad? I mean, I was keeping it together. I had a son and a beautiful wife who was a great mom. "You're *still* not drinking?" my friend Ostroff asked me, seven or eight weeks into this thing. "I don't think you have to *totally* stop drinking. Just, don't drink so much, when you *do* drink."

I do wonder whether I can ease myself back into it, so I'm not cutting myself off from *all* the fun. I consider easing this total ban. Perhaps one day in the future when I'm offered wine at a friend's party, I can put up my hand to decline, then explain, "Sorry, I don't drink...*in Toronto.*" So that, you know, on trips to New York, on trips to Los Angeles, I could have a beer or two. Or if that doesn't work, extend the ban's range: "I don't drink...in Canada. In *North America.* On *Planet Earth.*"

I don't drink . . . on even-dated days.

On *land*. In *buildings*.

Sorry, I don't drink with *white* people.

I am suspicious of friends who profess not to believe I ever had a problem. My skill at compartmentalization extends to my relationships with my friends. Many don't know about the crack, so my abrupt transition to all-out abstinence strikes some as rash. And for the ones who *did* know about the drug problems, a conflict of interest exists. Many of them reside on the same continuum I did. My conclusion, that *I* have a problem, suggests *they* have a problem. So they deny I ever had a problem. Shit, there are moments when I would argue that we, all of us, our entire society, has a problem with substance abuse. We base the whole of our social lives on the stuff! Which poisons us, impairs our judgment, slurs our speech, and dulls our senses. We stage events called parties that amount to exercises in simultaneous mass consumption. (Of course we do! Have you *seen* it out there?)

Was I *that* bad? Do I *really* have to quit drinking? My capacity for self-delusion causes me to doubt both sides. Before, I believed I was fine. Now, I believe I was not fine. Which was the delusion? In relation to my teetotalling, I've been thinking lately of the nine years I spent believing that I was bald. It started when I was twenty-six. The misapprehension began in the barber's chair. I sat down in the hair salon for my usual monthly appointment, and the stylist got this weird expression on his face. Scissors in one hand, a brush in the other, he leaned in close to get a good look at my dome. When he straightened he was frowning. "You know," he said. "You'd be better off just shaving your head."

To someone who had never thought of thinning hair, this was a shocking declaration. And what a thing to say! I mean,

essentially, he was breaking up with me! My barber was breaking up with me! Back home I spent some time before the mirror
with my chin down around my chest and my eyeballs inclined,
the better to get a good look at my hair's front bits. And I realized he had a point. I could see through them. I could see my
scalp through my hair. You know those twin Vs that some guys
get? It looks sort of cool, actually, right? And then they climb
steadily higher until they're just bald. Well, I wasn't getting
those twin Vs. The entire top of my head was losing density at
the same time. On my twenty-six-year-old scalp, the effect was
profoundly weird.

The next day I shaved my head. Not bald. But pretty close.
You could see little sprigs of hair up there. And as time went on
I accepted the fact my hair was thinning. I went out and bought
one of those Wahl electric clippers that people find in barber-
shops, and every three weeks or so I would drop a couple of oil
drops on the teeth and get to it. This went on for years. It drove
my father crazy. He'd inform me of his belief that I should
grow my hair. Every time I saw him. "There isn't enough up
there for me to grow!" I insisted. "It looks weird!"

"It doesn't look weird. You have a Slavic hairline. I have
one, too."

I didn't really know what he meant by this term, Slavic
hairline. It's irrelevant: my dad was wrong. The genes for my
hair had come from my mother's side, I thought, from the Irish
side, where the men went bald in their twenties. I felt affinities
with bald celebrities, the whole gamut: Michael Stipe, Bruce
Willis, Jason Statham. I even wrote a feature story about my
baldness for a men's magazine.

Around the time I stopped the drinking and the drugs, I
conducted a bit of an experiment with the hair, too—you

know, if you're changing one thing, you might as well change everything. I kept hats on through the awkward stage, where my hair Moncheechee-ed straight out from my scalp. Curiosity was the motivator. After all these years, what was left up there?

A surprising amount, as it turned out. In fact, up there resided pretty much the same amount of hair I had when I was twenty-six. I had been under the impression for nine years that baldness progressed steadily. If my follicles were sparse when I was twenty-six then they must be basically gone by now. In fact, I was wrong. Things had stayed as they were. I discovered something else: what had looked odd when I was twenty-six looked normal today. A twenty-six-year-old dude with thinning hair seems sort of strange. You feel bad for him, and his thinning hair. But at thirty-five, my thinning hair looked normal. My peers had caught up to me.

There were a few double-takes. Opinions were split maybe 70–30 over whether I looked better or worse with hair. I didn't much care. I was enjoying the stuff too much. Serious deliberation went into deciding where to get my first cut. I ended up choosing this old-time barbershop at the intersection of Dundas and Bay, in Toronto, where the men's magazines are stacked on the tables and the air is thick with Barbicide. "How long has it been since your last cut?" asked the barber, trying to gauge how short to cut the stuff.

"Nine years?" I said.

"Geez," he said, eyeing the inch and a half or so length on my scalp. "Slow-growing."

"Shulgan!" cried Chris Nuttall-Smith, the first time he saw me with hair. "Hair plugs? They look great."

"Naw, I just grew it out," I said, and then, thanks to his skeptical look, I added: "Seriously." I'm still not sure whether he believes me. But others do. Others regard my growing my hair as a sign I've finally come to my senses.

"I always knew you weren't bald," said my editor friend Pat, who handled the piece about my trauma about being bald. "I just figured you were crazy."

Natalie and I also talked about this. I was in the shower, shampooing my hair, thinking about how much more shampoo I required now that I actually had hair. Natalie was at the mirror, blow-drying.

I called out across the shower curtain. "Hey, you know how before I would refer to myself as bald?"

She turned off the hairdryer.

"What?"

"You know when I was shaving my head, and I would describe myself as bald, what would you think?"

"I didn't ever think you were bald."

"You thought I was wrong."

"Yes."

"Why didn't you ever tell me?"

Natalie skittered open the shower curtain.

"Are you kidding me? I told you *all the time*. How can you even say that?"

Naked, wet, with my eyes closed to ward off the shampoo, I felt too vulnerable to argue with a fully clothed woman armed with a plugged-in hair dryer. Besides, now that she mentioned it, I did remember her saying that. I reached out and closed the curtain.

"So you thought I was deluding myself."

"Yeah."

"Didn't you think that was weird?"

"Yes! I did."

"But you just accepted it?"

"Right."

"Did you think *I* was weird?"

"You're fairly weird. But I wouldn't say *really* weird."

"Well, what I'm wondering is, am I deluding myself now about anything?"

On the other side of the shower curtain came silence. Then Natalie spoke. "When you wear the same pair of pants for a week in a row and think that's okay? That's deluding yourself."

"No, I was thinking more about this not-drinking thing." I shut off the water, slid open the shower curtain, and retrieved my towel from its hook. "Like, am I deluding myself that I had a problem? Because when I tell people I quit drinking, some of them say they don't think I had a problem."

"Who? Who says that?"

Natalie was leaning against the vanity, arms crossed, hair-dryer holstered into the crook of her opposite elbow, watching me.

"Mike said it. And Ostroff. He said he didn't think I needed to quit altogether. He said I just needed to quit drinking so much, when I *did* drink."

"Well, that's the trick, isn't it?"

"Right. Right. I guess it is."

"Plus, they don't know how bad the drugs were."

"Nope. No they don't."

What's rich about this conversation is that it would be many months before *I* realized how bad the drug problem was. At this point those nights and early mornings remained packed in their boxes, out of view. Many months would elapse before I started unpacking those evenings, and it's a measure of my delusion that I started the unpacking as research into what I thought would be a lighthearted fatherhood memoir. And hey, the *first* draft was. I joke to writer friends that I don't deserve the label "writer." I'm terrible at the writing aspect of this business. Scribbler, scrawler, note-taker, all of these are labels I deserve more than writer. Where I excel is the editing. The mistruths and the clichés exist in my early drafts for me to clear away, revealing the truth beneath. Some of these evenings didn't get unpacked until the sixth or seventh draft. Close friends who didn't know about the drugs, please don't feel betrayed by my duplicity. Or do, but know this: at this point, I was still fooling myself.

ON MY TWO-MONTH anniversary I went for a run with my brother. My brother, the human running machine. Thirty pounds lighter, able to do fifty push-ups at a time and twenty pull-ups. Mark likes to be at work early, so my alarm dinged at 5:30 a.m. Over the two-minute jog to our meeting point I considered the anniversary and the changes wrought by my decision not to drink. Like milk, for example. The stuff had for years sent me hurrying toward the washroom, where unspeakable things transpired. I attributed those unspeakable things to lactose intolerance. For the last fifteen or so years I've limited my milk consumption. Lately I've been having these intense cravings for chocolate milk. And hey: no effects. I've been fine. Somehow, not drinking has made me lactose *tolerant*.

Punctuality: I've become a lot better making it to appointments on time. Losing things. Sunglasses, cell phone, keys, baseball caps, wallets, I left these things littered behind my drunks like a motorboat's wake. Except now I hadn't lost anything for several months. That felt nice—programming in new numbers to your cell phone is a pain I didn't miss.

At precisely 6 a.m., I met the Human Running Machine. The pace was fast. It always was with Mark, and I felt every pound of the thirty I had on him. Around Davenport Road we headed up a series of railroad-tied steps, and as I went over the decaying wood I could feel last night's French Vanilla Häagen-Dazs gurgling and swirling around my insides. What sort of an idiot eats an entire *pint* of ice cream in one sitting?

Conversation topics, cycled through—Mark's kids, my kid, weekend plans, the distance of the last run. At this point we were rocketing along at 7:20 minute per mile, not all that fast for him but something that usually would have had me coughing up blood. Except it wasn't that bad. I sucked in deep draughts of wind, in clean, cough-free gulps. My arms pistoned, my legs scythed, my lungs sailed out and in, everything working as it should. At that moment, I felt like I could have maintained that pace for hours.

Just south of Eglinton we found an entrance to the ravine system that spiderwebs Toronto. Maybe five miles into the run now, and I started talking about the danger that came with getting in shape. No, with having got in shape—the danger that plagued me once I felt like I could run forever. I'd last a couple of weeks at this level, and then my training would taper off.

"You need a goal," my brother said.

My reply came out like this: "Well. Fall marathon. I was. Thinking."

My brother stayed silent. Consequently, I blamed him for the following pledge. Motivated by a need to interrupt our breathing with words, with meaning, I uttered for the first time a possibility I had been keeping to myself.

My pledge concerned the Boston Marathon, North America's oldest marathon. So many people want to run the Boston

that race organizers limit the number of contestants they allow
to enter the race. There are several races around the world that
have this problem. The New York marathon, for example,
which runs a lottery every year to decide which contestants get
into the race. The Boston does something more ingenious,
however. They require you to qualify, to run another marathon
in a fast enough time. The implication is that they're requiring
runners to prove they're *worthy* of running the Boston. All told,
I've run four marathons, and my best time is 3 hours and 32
minutes. It's not a bad time, 3h32mins. If your training schedules get interrupted by hangovers; if you already have a tendency toward schlubbiness, as I do, then 3h32mins is in fact
quite respectable. It's faster than most people are ever able to
run a marathon.

I felt I could do better. If I kept to my training schedule. If
I worked harder than I ever had before.

"I was thinking," I said. "Of trying to qualify. For Boston."

Mark was silent for a few paces. Then: "How much time
do you need to cut off?"

"Seventeen minutes."

More silence, a longer one, this time. If he indicated any
sort of negative opinion about all this, I would have opted for
some other task. But he didn't. Of course he didn't.

"That's possible," he said. "You'll have to train your ass off.
But that's definitely possible."

Well then. Here was another goal to keep me off alcohol—
a goal I could use as an excuse. The fall race, the Toronto Waterfront Marathon, formed a qualifier for Boston. It happened in
late September. And I would stay off the drinking until then.

WE ENTERED THAT weird zone one enters while waiting for a child to be born. By late July, many of my training runs were to be around twenty-five kilometres. Most of them were conducted with me clutching my Blackberry in case Natalie's labour started and I had to dash home. The only time I left the house in this period, other than runs or baby-related medical appointments, were occasions to promote my book. One required an overnight stay in Northern Ontario—a Georgian Bay town called Midland, where I was to read in the early evening, go out to dinner with my hosts, then spend the night at a bed and breakfast the Internet described, inevitably, as charming. Natalie and I fought before I left, thanks perhaps to our mutual anxiety concerning my unsupervised night ahead. On the drive up I told myself my anxiety was ridiculous. This was northern Ontario! A bed and breakfast! Even if I wanted them, drugs would be difficult to procure. Perhaps impossible.

Arriving early, I wandered Midland's commercial stretch and found a hardcover of *The Mysteries of Pittsburgh* for $5 in a used bookstore. My reading went off without serious flubbing. The audience asked great questions, and the organizers were great, as was the restaurant where we dined after. The second I left the restaurant I retrieved my bags from the B+B, left an apologetic note explaining about my ultra-pregnant wife (as though that was the reason I had left, and not my own appetite for destruction), and aimed the car south, toward Toronto. Natalie had Myron snuggled in close to her when I lifted the covers just after 1 a.m. She opened her eyes and lifted her head for a kiss. "How you doin'?" she asked.

"Fine," I said. "I'm doing fine." And this time, it was true.

LABOUR STARTED several days later. Regular contractions elevated the tension for a few hours, then disappeared. We discussed whether Natalie was having a baby. "Are they painful?"

"What do you think?"

"Are they regular?"

"They'll be regular for a while, and then they'll stop."

"Should we call Fariba?"

Our midwife. Jen, our previous midwife, was on maternity
leave.

"I don't know. Give me a minute."

Myron looked from me to Natalie and back to me. And
just like that he was crying.

"He's picking up on our anxiety," Natalie said.

"I should do something with him," I said, my voice raised
to make it audible over what was in general an impressive cry.
"Can I do anything for you?"

"I'm going to lie down."

Myron and I washed the car. I was getting the detergent
out of the broom closet when Myron got agitated again. "Buh-
buh," he said several times in a row, each time more insistently
than the last. He seemed to be pointing to the Pine-Sol. "No
boyo, that's poison." It was only once I had to take a second
trip into the broom closet that I noticed the container next to
the Pine-Sol, a pink plastic bottle of the detergent we used to
blow bubbles. "Buh-buh" he'd said—*bubbles*. He was talking!
He was using words! And I had ignored him! Gaaah!

Natalie came into the kitchen as I was still getting over
that. "I feel like I've barely figured out how to care for our *first*
kid," I said. "I don't know whether I'm ready for a second."

"That's pretty much *exactly* what I don't need to hear right
now," Natalie said.

My labouring wife clutching the counter edge, in mid-contraction. Of course she was right. Gaaah! Awash in the pain of being me, with my seemingly infinite capacity for saying exactly the wrong thing at exactly the wrong time, I wondered whether it was ever possible to go through childbirth without being completely like out of your mind freaked out about the future. Maybe around kid fourteen?

Those contractions turned out to be premature false labour. In fact, the second snapper didn't arrive until two weeks later. We named her Penelope, and she basically rocketed out of Natalie. Ninety minutes of labour ended at 7:51 p.m. on a Saturday night in August. She had none of Myron's coneheadedness; there wasn't time for that. She had hair on her head and somehow she exuded calm. I held her and I felt calm. You know what? I had been prepared to react to her with something like low-level resentment. That's a terrible thing to say about your newborn daughter but it's true. I was slightly peeved at her before she even existed because her entrance onto the scene risked fucking up what was finally settling into a fun and stable family life for Myron and Natalie and I. But all that flowed out of me once I held Penny the first time. The little girl radiated strength. She beamed happiness out of her face and into mine. She was happy, and I was happy. She was a nine-pound eight-ounce offensive tackle home-delivered by midwives without any anesthetic—wait a second. *Nine* and a half pounds? Without anesthetic? At *home?* Dude, my wife is pretty incredible, but I swear: Penny *helped*. As soon as the membranes ruptured my daughter's mutant energy eased out from her and into Natalie, she soothed and cooed and relaxed and her mother swore a fraction of what she had the first time.

Can a little baby have a presence? Penelope Claremont Shulgan owned every room she was in right from the beginning. Her eyes—that's where her superpowers were most apparent. For the first year of her life every person we met commented on her eyes, with their inhumanly blue irises rimmed with the merest hint of black. A look from her could stun someone. "Her eyes . . ." they'd say, apparently made dizzy by my daughter's orbs, and to ease the weirdness I'd crack a joke. "Yeah," I'd say. "She's part husky." Those motherfuckers could zap you dead in an instant but around her family she just uses her powers for the common weal. With time she'll grow into a little cannonball that careens around our house. Everybody says she looks like me. I'm not sure about that—I think there's a fair bit of Natalie in there too. She turned out to be left-handed, like me. She's got my intensity, and my temper. And playing with her is different from playing with Myron. Playing with Myron is like hanging out with my best friend. Playing with Penny is like hanging out with another version of myself.

On her first night she slept a good eight hours—apparently these special stunts wreak a depletion of her energy stores. The next morning I looked out the window. "Nater, check this out," I said, climbing on the bed to pull up the window shade. "A rainbow."

"The sky knows," Natalie said.

And I am not altogether sure that it didn't.

THE MARATHON was eight weeks later. The day before, I broke off from work early in the afternoon and Natalie and I took the kids to Trinity Bellwoods Park. Myron took this little plastic car he likes to push around and nagged me into going on my skateboard. Natalie pushed Penny in the stroller. The park had been recently mown. It was maybe 17 degrees out, zero humidity, the sky a palette of blues. Myron and I kicked a soccer ball up a slight incline. We spread a blanket in the centre of a baseball diamond's outfield. Natalie flopped down on the blanket with Penny alongside her and the latest *Us* magazine in her hands. Myron wanted his shoes off, and his socks, which seemed to me like a good idea. Barefoot, the two of us circumnavigated our little family island, me chasing him, him chasing me. Lured in by our giggles, Natalie came over, grasped Myron by his armpits and twirled so quickly his legs were basically parallel to the ground.

"Again!" Myron said.

She did it again. She did it twice more. And then I grasped him in the same spot, and I did it. Each time he giggled. He locked eyes with his twirler and you could measure the width of his smile by the degrees he rotated, he grew more delighted the longer it was happening. Natalie already was sprawled on the ground. I sprawled on Natalie and Myron sprawled on me and we lay there on the freshly-mown grass and waited for the world to stop spinning.

"Run!" he said, and headed off toward no discernible goal.

Natalie and I watched him run for the sake of running.

"I love you, Chris," Natalie said.

"You love me, Chris?" I said. "You never call me Chris."

"Maybe that's how much I'm loving you right now."

We sat up as Myron came sprinting back. A giggling two-year-old collapsed onto us. I held him up in a fireman's carry. He wriggled around and I helped him climb me so he was sitting on my shoulders.

"Run!" he said, patting my head, and I went off with him using my ears for bridles for an arc through the diamond's outfield. On the return I picked up speed and then headed off into a different direction, came back and went off again. Other people were in the park. Of course there were. We were in downtown Toronto. There were always other people in the park. They were around us as we twirled until we were motion sick. They walked their dogs past us as we bounded. They smoked pot on picnic tables as our sweaters picked up grass stems through steamroller rotations.

And I ignored them. I was able to ignore them. In contrast to years past, the fact that they were watching, it didn't make me feel strange. I didn't feel like I was under surveillance. I didn't feel monitored. I didn't feel other people at all. Playgrounds, parks, sidewalks, anywhere I went with my boy—they felt different, now that I had some self-confidence.

Myron deserves a whole hell of a lot of credit here. Basically the kid seduced me. In a completely paternal sort of way. He seduced me with unadulterated kindness. He seduced me with the way, just as we were about to fall asleep, he picked my nose. And the attention he gave my bedtime stories. The kid was just plain good company. You had to work to get into his good graces, and once you got there, it felt like it meant something. You know, for a moment, crack gives you a feeling of perfect contentment. And once I fell in love with him, Myron did, too. But Myron's feeling lasted longer. And there was no downside to it; in fact, Myron's was self-reinforcing; the more I got it, the easier it was to get. All I had to do was lie down next to him when he was sleeping and there it was, the feeling of peace impervious to external factors like apocalypse and earthquake and whether a world existed outside the closed bedroom door. So long as I could feel his warmth against my ribs everything else was fine.

Who knew that fatherhood was one of those things that becomes easier with practice?

THE EVENING BEFORE the marathon, I stayed up and prepared. I pinned my bib onto my moisture-wicking shirt. I stuffed Power Gels into shorts pockets. My sunglasses, my Garmin GPS stopwatch and my headband all went into a pile where I'd pack them in the morning.

Next morning I woke up before my alarm, a few minutes after five. A bagel, the Sunday *New York Times*. A shower and a shave reincarnated me as a clean, contributing member of society. The race bib whispered as I pulled on my shirt. Mark arrived at 6:25. We went next door to make sure my sister was ready. By that point Myron, Penny, and Natalie were up. "I'm proud of you, whatever your time is," Natalie called out.

Kenny K, in town from New York to run the race, drove the three Shulgan siblings downtown. The car was filled with strategy discussions and target finishing times. We separated with a round of good lucks to head off to our corrals. The girl next to me was looking at her Garmin just as I was eyeing mine. "Do you have a signal?" she asked. I didn't. It didn't matter. I didn't need a signal. I just needed the stopwatch. I took my iPod out of my shorts pocket and was still untangling the earphones as the horn sounded the race start. Maybe a thousand people had to start running before the beginning reached me. I inserted the earphones and found my marathon playlist just as the wave arrived. And I was running.

-12-

RABBIT REDUX

On some level marathons are insane. It is just stupid to do any one thing for three hours at a time. Even pleasurable things work only in moderation. One doesn't eat Häagen-Dazs for three hours straight. Warm showers are nice, but the drizzling sensation on the shoulders gets irritating when you stand under the water for that long. Hell, *sitting* gets tedious after an hour or two. Trying to run for 180-odd consecutive minutes is just willfully dumb. No matter how hard you train, it is going to hurt. The hurt is part of it. The hurt is why I love the marathon.

Other cultures have their own cleansing endurance rituals. Many North American school children know about the Native American sun dance practices that saw braves connect themselves to a tall pole by fixing a cord to a piercing on their chests, aiming to hang back with their weight on the piercing and dancing for hours until they fell into a hallucinatory trance. During the festival of Ashura, some Shia Muslims perform a practice, *zanjeer zani*, that involves being flogged with chains tipped with razor-sharp knives. And in an ordeal remarkably similar to my marathon, on the Feast of Our Lady of Guadalupe, Mexican Catholics struggling with alcoholism have been known to crawl over miles of dirt roads to a certain basilica, where ensuing prayers are supposed to provide them with the will required to avoid drinking for the following year. Yeah, contemporary secular society tends to be appalled by such stunts. And yet we consider normal running for three or four hours at a time.

Here is a way to prove something to yourself in a way that causes pain only to you. That's how so many use the marathon. They train for it because the focus helps them get over a bad boyfriend. It helps them lose some weight or gain some respect, either their own or from others. It's a whole lot of people proving to themselves they can do something that's a whole lot hard. What I love about the marathon is that it is thousands of runners proving these things *together*.

I didn't know what I was proving when the race started. My thoughts just followed my iPod's first song, all synth tones and cacaphonous percussion and Dizzee Rascal throwing out rhymes in his British accent. While I tried to avoid getting stepped on. Did I mention it was still dark? Did I mention we were running through a concrete canyon ribboned by crowds? Armed with clappers and airhorns and all sorts of other noisemakers? The din like New Year's Eve.

And the clearest feeling came into my head. Perhaps it was the adrenalin. Oh shit, of course it was the adrenalin. And the music piped into my brain and the people cheering and being around everyone else they were cheering for and the sense that something I had been anticipating for five months was here, I had made it, I hadn't given up, I'd stuck with my training but more importantly I had stayed off crack and away from alcohol, I was here, the moment was here, I was three hours and change from the answer to a question that had occupied me for months.

But it was more than that. The culmination of five months of training tied in with another of life's waypoints. For years I'd been asking myself, when was I going to start taking myself seriously. When was I going to quit fucking up. It was as I ran this gauntlet of air horns and inflatable clappers that I realized I'd passed that point. The people around me were cheering for a race, but it didn't feel like that to me in the moment. It felt like they were cheering for maturity and adulthood, for self-respect and responsibility. Congratulations, Chris, you made it through, and the moisture that ran off my face was too early in the run to be sweat. What a relief it was to discover that all those people who kept telling me I was better than my fuck-ups—my wife, my brother and sister, my mom and dad—that all those people were right.

At that point, I'd extended past the marathon my vow to stay off drinking and drugs. The current target was a year. Once I wrote an early draft of this book I extended the ban to several decades; specifically, until Myron turned 20. Another couple of drafts into this writing-as-therapy and I realized the need for a permanent ban. Natalie never questioned the writing. As in all things, she just wanted me to be honest. And it would take many drafts of the story before I was able to manage that. Many drafts, too, before I realized how seriously I'd corrupted our trust. Well, drafts and some marriage counselling. Lots of marriage counselling.

Quitting drinking at first was easy. And then it got hard. It got hard when I realized I should make this thing long term. I missed it. I missed the abandon. I missed the temporary alleviation of any responsibility whatsoever. How I missed the camaraderie of alcohol and drugs—of my once-mandatory place in the round-buying queue, and the easy nature of the acquaintance request, hey, want to go out for a beer?

Which did I miss more—the drinking or the drugs? It's got to be the drugs. I love drugs. But I missed the drinking almost as much. Quitting drugs is easy because quitting makes you just another member of society. Most people don't do drugs. Most people *do* drink. So quitting *that* makes you some kind of pariah.

I used to have a lot of friends. I used to go out a lot. There'd be some awkward conversation during the first hour. But inside that warm shower of shots and pints came the embraces and the declarations of love and we were boys together, boys who loved one another and voiced those feelings over pint glass rims. Now, the only conversation I had with guys was that first hour. It was all sober conversation, and man, that shit is *awkward*.

Most times I think it's positive—most times I bewail the umpteen hours I spent getting drunk and high and then recovering from it. But I do miss those altered states. Not having a hangover is kind of overrated. I kind of enjoyed the really kick-ass hangover. More importantly, I miss my friends.

And Christ, enough with the congratulations. Particularly the late-night ones, on those rare instances I've managed to stick it out in the bar. The hand on the arm and the lean in close and the between-you-and-me tone: "I really respect you, man." Or: "What you're doing is *so* great." Oh, fuck off. What's great about it? You know what? What would be *really* great is if

I didn't *have* to quit drinking. Every time someone congratulated me all I could think about was the way they were congratulating me on basically not being able to control myself. "Congratulations for fucking up," they might as well have said. Perhaps I should have been congratulating *them*—for their self-control. Thousands, millions, shit, *billions* of people on this globe called Earth are able to control their partying. And I'm not.

What appealed to me about crack was how hardcore it was. It seemed such an extreme thing to do. After one of those blind drunks where I ended up walking the streets 'til 5 a.m., smoking crack, I felt guilty, sure I felt guilty. But I also felt . . . exceptional. A certain kind of exceptional. A wildness. A defiance. Smoking crack was my outlaw proclamation: society had not yet domesticated me.

Abstinence, I've discovered, also is anti-social. It, too, is a statement that separates one from mainstream society. For a thirty-five-year-old, white dad who resides firmly in contemporary North America's middle class, not drinking is a gesture of defiance that is as alienating to his social circle, if not more alienating, than the illicit smoking of crack.

ALL I HAD TO DO, now, was run as hard as I could for 42.2 kilometres. We turned east onto the pitted pavement of Wellington, then south on Parliament and west on Lakeshore. Somewhere along this bit we passed the first kilometre flags. My stopwatch said 4:40. Almost a perfect pace. I had only to run the following forty-one kilometres at the same speed. The following couple ticked by and I was easily on pace. I swallowed my first Power Gel at the 5k marker. Shortly after that my earphones went silent. My iPod had fallen out of my pocket. I stopped, ran back about 15m, retrieved the iPod, reversed direction for the second time and tried to return to my previous speed. Suddenly my per kilometre pace was flagging—I hit a 4:45 when the iPod mishap happened, then a 4:50—12 seconds off the 4:38 I needed. The front runners passed going the opposite way along this dog-leg—one little skinny black guy, then another, then an all-black clutch followed by the first white runner. I tried to use them all as inspiration.

I saw my parents, then my friends Myles and Emma. One thing about the marathon: people mattered. Friends mattered. Supporters mattered. Even with an iPod on, even when the runner had James Hetfield hissing out "Seek and Destroy," as I did, the runner was alone with his pain and his doubts and his fears and the sight of someone he knew on the sidewalk, the sight of somebody cheering, was enough to pull him out of that little pain chamber and back into the world. "Gee," the thinking went. "They like me. They like me enough to shlep out of bed at 7 a.m. on a Sunday to cheer for me."

I slipped my sunglasses from the top of my head and put them on. They were splattered with my sweat. This was my first opportunity to realize how hard I was working. I wiped them off on my shirt, but that too was wet. So were my shorts. I held my sunglasses. I kept running. I passed my parents on the back side of the dog-leg and tossed them the sunglasses. My dad caught them. I felt good about that.

Then I saw Natalie. She was wearing her purple hoodie. It made her easy to see. She was holding Myron. Penny was behind them in the car-seat infant carrier.

"Myron!" I shouted.

He looked at me.

If this was a Hollywood movie he would have, like, high-fived me or something. Except, damn it, it wasn't, and I'm not sure he registered who I was, who had just shouted his name. "Hi Myron!" I shouted.

And I was past. What followed was a long straightaway. This was a road I'd run dozens of times. Full pace now. Another Power Gel. At the halfway point there was a scanning point for the running chips. I checked my time: About 1:38. My pacing was almost perfect. And I allowed myself to wonder: could I hold on?

Running fast for really long requires you to keep your mid-section pretty tight. Your arms swing more than they normally do, and same with your legs, and the abdominal muscles are what keeps everything together. Around the twenty-third kilo-metre, my abs twinged as though a bass player plucked the muscle fibre like a guitar string. I eased up. I ran a 4:50 kilome-tre. And another.

The Leslie Street Spit is a piece of the Toronto waterfront that has been created by dumptrucks dropping soil into Lake Ontario. Like the name suggests, it's a long, narrow promon-tory that juts into the lake. There aren't any spectators there. It's basically just a two-lane road with some fill on either side. Lots of potholes. The marathon route ran a 5k dogleg along the spit, out one lane, back along the other. Natalie and Myron stood just at the entrance. "Water, next time, K?" Nater nod-ded. And I was out on the spit. By this point I was holding my iPod in my hand. The music was getting to me. Metallica was too angry. I pressed pause. Suddenly the only sound was the steady slap of dozens of runners progressing toward a goal. I passed the twenty-seventh kilometre marker. The previous kilometre had taken me five minutes and thirty seconds—nearly a minute slower than my target race pace.

"Chris!"

My brother, running on the dogleg's opposite side. I waved. He waved, and we progressed along in our private agonies. I tried a trick that worked sometimes. I altered my gait. I got off a couple of strides and then—ping! My calf muscle. My left one. Like someone clutched the muscle in their grasp and wrung it out. I limped out another kilometre. There was the flag for the twenty-eighth kilometre. Even worse: 5:40.

The first person I saw coming off the spit was my dad. My dad, who years before had watched my first marathon; my dad, who set a standard for fatherhood I hoped to match. I tossed him my iPod. Maybe another hundred metres and I saw Natalie holding up a bottle of Gatorade and a bottle of water. She was like a mirage. "Water," I said, then noticed the wide mouth of the bottle. It would be tough to drink from it. "Gatorade!" It had one of those lids you twisted and sucked through. It was great.

Off the spit there was another long straightaway. I was flagging. With maybe half the Gatorade in me I threw away the bottle. I passed the 31k flag. Another egregious kilometre time: 5:40. Christ Christ Christ.

Boston wasn't a feasible outcome. Just like that. Should I back out? Should I just quit? I wasn't far from Natalie. I could just turn back. I envisioned the conversation that would follow with the other wives.

"What was Chris's time?"

"Oh," Natalie would have to say. "He didn't finish."

Up ahead was the 32k flag, then a bridge. Two hundred

metres after the 32k flag marked a spot where only 10k remained in the race. I made a deal with myself. I found a bush at the side of the road. I jogged off Lakeshore and peed behind the bush. I stretched my calf. I stretched my other calf. Down for a toe touch to unclench my hams, I could only manage to bend to about mid-shin.

Not running felt wonderful. But anyone could run 10k. This wasn't a marathon. It was only a 10k. I had only to endure for forty-five minutes and all this would be over. If I ran the remainder in five minute ks I could still eke out a personal best marathon time. I could still break 3:30.

How difficult it was now to track my progress. Was it thirty-six or thirty-seven? Natalie passed me in the car. I waved. With effort I pulled my face into a smile. I passed her a little farther on. She was stuck in a traffic jam. "See you at the finish!" she called.

I felt an intense and pure love for my wife.

I wanted it to be six hours ago. I wanted her warm against me in our bed.

For a stretch the course went under Toronto's Gardiner Expressway. Darkness. No spectators. The pavement had a volcanic grit to it. I could feel every stone under my runners. Every stone hurt. Everything hurt. My stopwatch said 3:20. I was three kilometres from the finish.

I wouldn't even beat 3:30.

There was an intense temptation to just stop. Even then. Even with just fifteen minutes between me and the finish. I just wanted this to be over.

Someone passed me. It was a guy in a blue singlet. He looked like he was in horrible pain. He looked like he was feeling worse than I was. I quickened my pace. I overtook him.

A spectator noticed my name on my bib. "Go Chris!" she said. "You're almost there!"

And I thought to myself: "Fuck you, spectator." I know. Uncharitable. Forgive me. My every thought was bile. I was in the best shape of my life and I was going to run one of my worst marathon times.

"I am going to beat you," I said to the marathon. "One of these days, I am going to beat you."

The Bay Street turn was at kilometre forty-one. The slight incline as we ran away from the lake—I felt that. In the distance I saw the first of what seemed a series of flags. One said, 500 metres left. I passed it. Even here I considered stopping. Probably I could find a ride. I couldn't see the finish. Bay Street turned just before the finish. I passed the 300 metre marker. Could I manage a kick? One final sprint? My limbs wouldn't let me. I was so locked into my stride there seemed the possibility, at the finish, I'd keep going, I wouldn't be able to *stop*. I envisioned myself continuing to run, forever, some accursed demon striding to the ends of the Earth.

With 200 metres left I passed a clutch of people. I could see a guy on the ground. Ambulance strobes flashed. Later my dad told me it was a guy who'd dislocated his knee. A paramedic popped the knee back in. The guy kept running.

I didn't see that. I was concerned only for myself. I was concerned only with keeping going until I didn't have to keep going anymore. When I strode over the mats that registered the finish, I felt nothing. I slowed to a walk. I checked my stopwatch's time: 3:33.45. Not my worst time, not my best. Someone slung a medal over my head.

And then I felt an emotion.

It wasn't disappointment. It wasn't frustration. About not

qualifying for the Boston, I felt no emotion at all. I had run as hard as I could. Apparently, I needed more than five months of training to qualify for the Boston. It wasn't something I could achieve in a summer. Perhaps it would take years.

The emotion I felt was relief.

It was over.

My brother materialized ahead of me. He looked like hell. "How'd you do?" he asked.

I shook my head.

"Not even close. Just couldn't. You break three hours?"

He shook his head. "I didn't qualify either."

"What was your time?"

He shrugged. "3:22."

I grinned. It seemed hilarious. My brother had blown up, too.

I felt dizzy. I sat on the curb and Mark scanned the approaching runners for Julie. Finally Julie materialized—ten minutes after her Boston time.

None of the Shulgan siblings qualified.

"That's why it's the marathon," I said to Mark.

THAT EVENING my friend Jeremy had a barbecue. (He ran the race, too. He also blew up.) As we were driving home, both kids were in the backseat. Both kids were asleep. Natalie and I held hands between our bucket seats in the front. It was stop and go along Dundas, but we weren't in any hurry. Outside it felt like fall. No radio, just the whispering of the heater on low. We were safe. We were a family.

"I've been trying to figure out why you ever wanted to have kids with me," I said.

We had been discussing photos—one Natalie found as she'd been cleaning out the basement, featuring her brother and sister and Natalie, the three of them wearing nice clothes. "We looked really cute," Natalie had said. "My mom dressed us really nicely."

"How old were you?"

"Nine? John was just little. We looked like a nice family, even then. We looked like we were fine . . ."

"Has your sister talked to her recently?"

"Nobody has . . . I hope she's okay."

Thinking about Natalie's mother's battles segued into thoughts of my own. How lucky I felt. Things could have been a lot worse. It was at that point I asked my question. "Why did I ever have kids with you?" Natalie repeated. "Maybe I was a little selfish. Maybe I didn't want to start over with someone else."

Natalie was playing with her wedding ring.

"Rain or shine," she said. She was referring to the words engraved on the inside of our wedding bands. "I really believe that. I'm committed to you. Plus, I had this crazy idea, that you'd be a really great father."

Outside seemed darker than any city nighttime should be. Perhaps the streetlights hadn't adjusted properly to autumn's encroaching evening. I thought about the way the defining narrative in Natalie's life was that of a parent who forsook her family for drugs. And in the silence, as we drove, I started to grasp how frightening my own drug consumption must have been for her.

How do I know I won't go back? At that point, I was well into the preliminary stages of what would become this book. Somewhere in the process I wondered about what drove me to write a book about these events. Was it an instinct similar to the one that led me to crack? Is this just one long, book-length proclamation: hey, I'm *different*! I'm hardcore! I used to smoke crack!

Look, maybe on the first draft, that was the motivation. But the book you have in your hands is my eighth or ninth pass through the story. I'd write it, and read it, and write it again. Each pass grew more real. Each pass exposed additional aspects of what happened. It took a long time for the words on the paper to approximate an honest chronicle. That bit about smoking crack while I was home alone with my baby? That didn't come out until the last draft. I wasn't ready to admit it to myself until then.

How do I know I won't go back? On some level, I don't. But this book stands as a reminder. This book is insurance against the lies. This book says: this is what you did. This is how fucked up you were, how close you got. Will you ever do it again? Christ, I hope not.

I told Natalie about the moment during the marathon, the sense that I had spent fifteen years distracted by going out, by drinking, by drugs. And how I felt I had returned.

"You remind me of the way you were when we first met," Natalie said. "Remember the way your baseball hat kept hitting my forehead?"

I couldn't. I recalled only the sense of possibility from that evening, the sense that something was beginning. And in the car, at the last light before home, I felt a similar sense.

THE FOLLOWING YEAR, I was in a burrito stand in Kensington Market with Myron and Penny. The three of us had just finished eating our burritos. Sated, I leaned back and watched my daughter slip off her chair to toddle into the unobstructed space by the entrance, where she squatted down and jumped up in time with the beat of the old-school hip hop pumping over the sound system. Both Myron and I giggled. There was something pure in Penny's enjoyment of the music; hers was dancing before she had any consciousness of the difference between good and bad dancing, or even what dancing was. She was exploring the pleasure of moving her body in time with music without realizing there was a name for the activity she conducted.

In the midst of this a couple of kids came in. They ordered, then selected the table next to us to wait for their take-out. Both males, both about twenty. The chunky glasses, the slim-fitting jeans, the plaid workshirt on one and the brimmed toque of his companion suggested they were skaters or art students. Perhaps prompted by the sight of my daughter, then fourteen months old, they discussed a friend who'd recently become a father. "The most immature guy I know," one of them said. "How's he think he's going to do it?"

"Totally not ready," the other agreed.

Sir Mix-a-lot came on. Myron asked for Penny's mango juice. I gave it to him. A few feet away my daughter spun and fell down and pushed herself up. She hopped and squatted, hopped and squatted.

"Which would you rather have," one of the students said as they both watched my daughter. "Glasses tattooed on your face, or a kid?"

The "glasses" component of this conundrum was a reference to a video making the online rounds the previous week, displaying the application of a tattooists' ink to a man's brow and temples. The marking went across the bridge of his nose and down around the ears, resulting in an illusion meant to suggest the man wore aviator sunglasses. It turned out the video was part of a viral campaign for Ray-Ban.

"Glasses tattoo," the one art student said. "With the tattoo, at least you can get it removed. The kid's always there."

And I thought: here were a couple of kids so mortified by fatherhood, so sold on the anti-parent myths of youth culture, that rather than subject themselves to the responsibility of child-rearing they'd prefer to get a tattoo so ridiculous it fueled an Internet meme. I was struck by the contrast in our reactions to my dancing daughter. How could anyone witness something so beautiful as Penny getting down to Sir Mix-a-lot and not ache to father something similar? That said, I recognized their attitudes. I shared them, before I became a father, and for some time after.

I considered schooling these young bucks about how wrong they were; how fatherhood is tough but the tough bits get evened out by the rewards. I wanted to tell them that fatherhood doesn't prevent a man from being a man. In fact, in my case, the rearing and education of Myron and, now, Penny, has prompted something like the consummation of my masculinity. Perhaps I'd be doing these boys a favour. Perhaps, I'd spare them the years of drinking and drugs that spanned my life since university. Then the counter guy called their number. They had to step around my daughter as they left. And the distaste on their faces suggested any effort on my part was likely to be futile. Nothing would sell these kids on the benefits of fatherhood. Nothing but their own children would have the power to do that. Perhaps it's only once you have kids that you realize what makes some guys ready for fatherhood is fatherhood itself—that for some, the presence of children inspires the coming of age required to care for them.

Minutes after, Myron and Penny and I made our own escape. Soon Myron's pleading forced a stop at a vendor selling sunglasses. Maybe $10 later Penny wore miniature pink Wayfarer knock-offs and Myron regarded the world from behind Spiderman wraparounds. Thusly protected we headed south through the market, past the cycling activists and the hackie-sack hippies, past the enviro-freaks and the anarchists. It seemed just bizarre to me that I'd once been too embarrassed by my recent fatherhood to take my newborn baby for walks in this neighbourhood. Now I swung my head around to check on the kids nestled in the wagon like the yin-yang symbol, each one's feet on a sibling's shoulders, and I felt only pride. Well, pride—and the intense desire to have another one.

IN LIEU OF THE USUAL DEDICATION...

If this book told a story about arts-granting organizations that genuinely want to help out writers then I'd dedicate it to the Ontario Arts Council and the Canada Council for the Arts, whose support is hereby gratefully acknowledged. If it was about a literary agency that hustles for its authors as well as the future vitality of the book, then I'd dedicate it to Anne McDermid, Martha Magor Webb, and Chris Bucci. If it was about an editor who gets what's so great about Han Solo then I'd dedicate it to Jane Warren at Key Porter. If it was about supportive friends willing to improve early drafts then I'd give the nod to people like Kaplan and Jeremy. Or siblings who also function as great sounding boards? Easy: my brother, Mark; my sister, Julie; and my sister-in-law, Jessica. Or parents who sometimes wonder what's with their oldest son, but love him anyway? My dad, Myron, and my mom, Nancy. About a pair of irrepressible kids who've graced their dad with a kind of reincarnation? Well, then Myron and Penny. Or a woman who figured her husband was worth sticking by, even when he questioned it himself? Then to Natalie. But it feels wrong to dedicate a book about my problems to the unadulterated benevolence that is my wife. And so I'll end things with an expression of my gratitude to all of the above, but mostly to Natalie. Always to Natalie. Forever to Natalie. Thank you.